T0270606

Shakespeare's Politic Comedy

Other Books of Interest from St. Augustine's Press

Shakespeare's Politic Comedy

WILL MORRISEY

ST. AUGUSTINE'S PRESS
South Bend, Indiana

Manufactured in the United States of America.

1 2 3 4 5 6   28 27 26 25 24 23

Library of Congress Control Number: 2022936501

Cloth ISBN: 978-1-58731-847-4
Ebook ISBN: 978-1-58731-848-1

∞ The paper used in this publication meets the minimum requirements of the American National Standard for Information Sciences – Permanence of Paper for Printed Materials, ANSI Z39.48-1984.

St. Augustine's Press
www.staugustine.net

Table of Contents

INTRODUCTORY NOTE:
THE 'POLITIC' CHARACTER OF SHAKESPEARE'S COMEDIES

Shakespeare's comedies have been described as "festive." And indeed they are, to some degree. Festivity suggests a relaxation of the laws—street closings, suspension of noise ordinances, Mardi Gras. Yet many observers also have noticed that his comedies look as if they might turn tragic at any moment, with their murderous plots and betrayals, their righteously or unrighteously enraged characters. Tragedy suggests not relaxation but violation of the laws.

Either way, whether laws are happily relaxed or painfully violated, 'the law is the law.' Law implies rule; ruling implies politics. In the comedies, the ruling characters avert tragedy by being 'politic' or prudent—by intervening with well-considered actions, plotted well in advance of the critical moment. Such wise practical judgment can be defeated, however, not only by some passion but by an idea, whether religious or philosophic. Sound politics thus requires the right coordination of ideas with actions, 'theory' with 'practice.'

This may be seen in two of Shakespeare's greatest comedies. *Measure for Measure* and *The Tempest* both invite audiences to think about rulers with 'theoretical' or philosophic inclinations who learn by hard experience that they must be politic. Duke Vincentio's Venice has suffered from his misrule because he concentrated his formidable powers of attention on himself, on the philosophic quest for self-knowledge. That is laudable in itself, but no ruler can rule well if he fails to know the citizens or subjects he rules, as well. As a result of the Duke's weak rule, Venice no longer has a *civil* society. Its inhabitants flock not to the assembly room or the town square but to the nunneries or the brothels. Neither celibacy nor adultery can produce citizens and soldiers; pious celibates may be above the law, whores and their clients beneath it, but neither respects the laws of the city, and neither can constitute the families upon which the city depends for its survival and flourishing. In ancient Rome, Pompey was a general; in modern Venice, he is a bawd. Put into Aristotelian terms, Venice suffers under two vicious ways of life, vicious because they are extreme in denying the nature of human beings as political animals. There is no 'mean' in Venice, no center between these extremes.

Seeing this, if belatedly, Duke Vincentio exiles himself while prudently leaving Venice under the rule of Angelo, an 'extremist' who would violently correct the immorality of Venetian whores, whoremongers, and clients. Unlike the nuns, his moral extremism does not shirk rule, although it exercises it tyrannically. It is in a way no wonder that Angelo, whose name suggests superhuman virtue, finds himself beguiled by Isabella, who is poised to take a nun's vows; he aspires to demi-godhood in politics, even as she aspires to it in rejection of politics. It takes an elaborate plot conceived and executed by the Duke to achieve justice, "measure for measure," to establish a new moral center between the Venetian extremes. Duke Vincentio becomes a man of prudential or 'politic' wisdom for the sake of re-founding a good regime in Venice, where he will now return to rule as the husband of virtuous Isabella.

In *The Tempest*, the Duke of Milan also finds himself in exile, but not by choice. He has been driven from his city for the same reason the Duke of Venice wisely absented himself from his: He preferred philosophy to ruling. He is forced to rule, not in Venice but on an island, where he exercises parental rule over his daughter and masterly rule over Caliban, who fits the description of what Aristotle calls a natural slave—one who cannot safely be allowed to share rule in any good regime. Here, the intention of the now-politic philosopher is not to regain rule over his city but to marry his daughter to a man who will make a fit husband, enable them to rule Milan, while he relinquishes his political power—now with the assurance that he has provided for good rule. That is, Prospero will be free to philosophize, to 'theorize,' in retirement but only after having become a political, indeed politic, philosopher, fulfilling his role as the duke by establishing a sound succession to his rule.

As these examples show, Shakespeare's comedies are not only funny and festive but serious and indeed politic. In what ways they are politic can be seen by considering a generous selection of them attentively.

In terms of Aristotle's well-known classification of political regimes into six types—kingship and tyranny or rule of the one, aristocracy and oligarchy or rule of the few, mixed regime and democracy or rule of the many—it is immediately obvious that Shakespeare concentrates his attention on the regimes prevalent in his own time, regimes of the one and of the few, without forgetting the possibility of regimes of the many. It is to plays depicting regimes of the one and of the few to which I turn initially, then to plays concerned with law and morality more generally, as they are inflected by such regimes. Finally, I consider plays concerned with politics as informed and deformed by religion, philosophy, and by pretended religion and philosophy, again as so inflected.

PART ONE

THREE REGIMES:
OLIGARCHY, ARISTOCRACY, MONARCHY

Aristotle classifies political communities into six principal 'species,' or regimes. The underlying feature of each regime is quantitative, as all such communities are ruled by one, a few, or many. The overarching feature of each regime is 'qualitative': the good monarchy is kingship, the bad tyranny; the good rule of the few is aristocracy, the bad oligarchy; the good rule of the many is the politeia *or* republic, *the bad democracy. The Merry Wives of* Windsor *portrays the regime of an English town—a small commercial republic within the larger monarchy.* Much Ado About Nothing *portrays Messina, a monarchy within the larger Kingdom of Sicily.* Two Gentlemen of Verona *is a play about aristocracy in commercial-republican Venice, and* A Midsummer Night's Dream *contrasts the human monarchy of Athens with the natural, fairy-ruled monarchy of the woods outside the city.*

CHAPTER ONE
SHAKESPEAREAN COMEDY:
TWO POINTS ON THE COMPASS

Shakespeare's only English comedy, *The Merry Wives of Windsor*, is also the purest of his comedies—the merriest, the most thoroughly funny, a bedroom farce in which almost no one gets into a bedroom. Set in continental Europe, *Much Ado About Nothing* threatens to veer into tragedy at any moment. The difference between the island nation of England and the nations of Europe inheres in the character of 'the few' who rule English civil society and 'the few' who rule Continental civil society.

At Windsor, the English knight, scion of warrior-aristocrats, has turned not merely to commerce but to the lowest commerce, swindling, the kind that has no respect for the property rights upon which commerce depends. Extended too far, the acquisitive spirit of commerce ruins the conditions of commerce, unwittingly contradicting itself. Trafficking in swindles more generally, Sir John Falstaff speculates on what is not legitimately his own, conniving schemes of adultery. The only other 'sir' in the play is another figure of fun, a Welsh parson living in a regime where foreigners are funny. In commercial England, the most serious characters are gentlemen and gentlewomen—the former a bit too serious, the latter witty and benevolent avengers.

Not so on the continent. There, peaceful commerce has yet to replace war. There, the aristocrats are lords and ladies, rulers of states. They make war as well as love, alliances as well as money. Foreigners could be marriageable friends or deadly enemies. *Much Ado About Nothing ultimately* isn't a tragedy. It's a comedy because it ends happily, but nearly does not.

Likely performed first at the Garter Feast on St. George's Day, in Greenwich, following the election of the new knights, preceding their installation at Windsor, *The Merry Wives of Windsor* has gentlewomen outsmarting one knight while teaching their husbands a lesson. As in so many Shakespearean comedies, the women are wittier than the men and act as the real rulers of society, but here their wit instructs the knights-elect in the audience, who are brought to witness the hazards of being laughable. The story goes that Queen Elizabeth, who had delighted in Sir John Falstaff as the most memorable comic figure in Shakespeare's English History Plays, wanted to see him in love. Since Falstaff is by nature incapable of being 'in love,' loving only food and drink, sex and money, Shakespeare entangles him in not one but two love triangles, which are really sex triangles as far as the rotund and covetous knight is concerned.

An English comedy might well turn on comic twists of the English language. This one does, throughout, with word-benders foreign and domestic hacking their way into the weeds of self-deception. At the outset, Justice of the Peace Robert Shallow complains of abuses of English law he's suffered at the hands of Sir John. His cousin, Slender, reverses the meanings of "successors" and "ancestors"—deranging time, that course upon which legitimacy in both law courts (with their respect for precedent), families and aristocracies (with their need for heirs) both run. Meanwhile, the Welsh parson, Hugh Evans, mixes up "luces," a species of fish (and symbol of the Christianity he professes) with "louses," a species of insect; the parson verbally deranges not time but nature, and perhaps spirituality along with it. As a churchman he stands ready to reconcile legalist Justice Shallow and lawless Sir John, but the judge would rather keep things out of the divine realm and take the case to the Star Chamber. Parson Evans then falls back on the attempt to deflect the men's attention toward a plot to marry Slender to Anne Page, a young lady of substantial dowry. If the churchman can't overcome Shallow's natural anger with divinely blessed peacemaking, he might do it with love, whether of woman or of money—the latter love held up as the root of all evil among the more pious men of the parson's calling.

They knock on the door of the father of Miss Page, but Falstaff is there, reviving Justice Shallow's animosity. "He hath wrong'd me, Master Page" (I.i.91). *He has beaten my men, killed my deer, and broken into my lodge. Indeed I have*, Falstaff replies in his own defense, *but the Council will laugh at your charges*. In the mind of Sir John, property claims in men, beasts, and buildings made by commoners will amount to very little in the judgment of his fellow aristocrats. Slender has his own charges against Falstaff's companion, Pistol, whom he alleges to have picked his pocket. Judging from his name, Sir John's confederate equally operates below the law, although it isn't certain that, like the knight, he supposes himself above the law while doing so. Slender draws a sober lesson from the experience: "I'll ne'er be drunk whilst I live again, but in honest, civil, godly company, for this trick. If I be drunk, I'll be drunk with those that have the fear of God, and not with drunken knaves" (I.i.162–66). In Slender, Pastor Evans has found a pious soul indeed, one hoping for companions who are Spirit-filled when next spirits-filled.

"The question is concerning your marriage," Pastor Evans declares (I.i.197–98), getting things back on (his) track. Imitating the court-language he would have picked up from his cousin on the legal concept of 'the reasonable man,' Slender allows that, "I will marry her upon any reasonable demands" (I.i.102–03)—specifically, the command of the justice of the peace, whom Slender purposes to obey as if he were his father. But the pastor wants dimwitted Slender to love, not to reason: "Let us command to know that of your mouth or of your lips; for divers philosophers hold that the lips is parcel of the mouth" (I.i204–07). For the first "mouth" he means "mind"; for the second "mouth," he is right literally—the lips can be considered part of the mouth—while contradicting his first assertion, which distinguishes merely verbal assurances from the true intent of the mind. In the Welshman's mangling of English, he continues to garble nature. He defines love agapically—"can you carry your goot will to the maid?" (I.i.207–08)—while Justice Shallow defines it more naturally, more mundanely—"can you love her?" (I.i.209). Slender remains the man of reason who cannot think for himself: "I hope, sir, I will do as it shall become one that would reason," a human being, a rational animal (I.i.210–11). At further prompting, Slender avers to his cousin with malaproprian determination, "I will marry her, sir, at your request; but if there be no great love at the beginning, yet may increase it upon better acquaintance" (I.i.220–22); of that "I am freely dissolved, and dissolutely" (I.i.225–26). "I think my cousin meant well," Justice Shallow construes (I.i.229).

The audience first sees Falstaff at The Garter Inn, his natural habitat, where he drinks in the presence of the inn's Host, along with Sir John's four sometime partners in crime. He plots the seduction of Mrs. Ford, the wife of a substantial Windsor citizen; "she gives the leer of invitation" to me

(I.iii.41)—a supposition his confederate Pistol takes to be wishful. "He hath studied her well, and translated her will out of honesty into English" (I.iii.45–46). In his own way truly English, Sir John's motive isn't so much erotic as economic; the lady "has all the rule of her husband's purse" (I.iii.49–50). As if to illustrate how dishonest English can be, Falstaff reads a love letter he will send both to Mrs. Ford and (spreading out his invest-ments) to the equally rich Mrs. Page, its language a parody of the English one reads in a medieval romance or a poem by Dante. In Falstaff, chivalry is dead, money's what counts and what one counts; aristocracy has reached its comic nadir.

Unfortunately for Sir John, there really is no honor among thieves. Pis-tol will tattle on him, doubtless angling for a material reward for himself.

The audience next meets the other rival suitors for the hand of Miss Page. They are Dr. Caius, a French physician, and Fenton, a young gentle-man. Dr. Caius mistakes Pastor Evans as a rival; the pastor has sent a mes-sage to the doctor's acquaintance, Mistress Quickly, asking her to intervene with Miss Page on behalf of Slender's suit, and the doctor assumes he must be angling for himself. For her part, mischievous Mistress Quickly sepa-rately assures both Caius and Fenton that Miss Page loves him and him alone, although she dismisses Fenton's chances: "I know Anne's mind as well as another does" (I.iv.147–48).

Falstaff's identical letters meet with the indignation of both respectable married ladies. They plot revenge upon him. But in one respect their cir-cumstances differ. Mrs. Page's husband is not a jealous man; Mrs. Ford's husband is, and his disposition is not improved when Falstaff's false pals inform him of Sir John's intentions toward his wife and her alleged attrac-tion to him. Therefore, the wives' counterplot against Falstaff's scheming must not only punish Falstaff but correct Ford. Eventually, they will need to run three counterplots, one after the other, as Sir John persists in his lechery and avarice, and Ford remains adamant in his jealousy. Putting the situation in Aristotelian terms, Falstaff the adulterer and Ford the jealous husband are the extremes, Page the virtuous 'mean' between them.

Letters being composed of words, which are composed of letters, all are capable of being rearranged for comic effect, usually by provoking anger, whether the indignation is righteous, foolish, or both at the same time. When Falstaff describes Mr. Ford as a peasant, cuckold, and knave to Ford disguised as another man, Ford sputters with fury at the imagined infidelity of his wife and the verbal affronts to his honor. [1] When the French doctor challenges the Welsh parson to a duel over Anne Page, Justice Shallow asks, mockingly, "What the sword and the word! Do you study them both, Master Parson?" (III.i.40–41). The Host arrives at the dueling site and (in the tradition of the English pub-keeper) plays the real peacemaker: "Disarm them, and let them question; let them keep their limbs whole and hack our English" (III.70–71). Let there be peace between "soul-curer and body-curer" (III.i.89). "Am I politic? Am I subtle? Am I a Machiavel? Shall I lose my doctor? No; he gives me the potions and the motions. Shall I lose my parson, my priest, my Sir Hugh? No; he gives me the pro-verbs and the no-verbs," the 'dos' and the 'don'ts' (III.i.91–95). Since verbs are words of action and actions speak louder than words, Gentlemen, do nothing injurious to one another. The Host gets at the essence of comedy, if not the Word of God—the human comedy, not the divine one. In merry England, the Host is a more effective peacemaker than the keeper of the Heavenly Host.

In the first of the ladies' counterplots against Falstaff, they lure him to Ford's house. He woos Mrs. Ford but she proves the more adroit manipulator of words: "Well, heaven knows how I love you," she accurately replies to his suit; "and you shall one day find it," she rightly predicts (III.iii.69–70). "Keep in that mind; I'll deserve it," Falstaff returns, condemning himself unknowingly in the act of avowing his prowess (III.iii.71). When on cue Mrs. Page approaches, announcing the imminent arrival of Mr. Ford, they hide Falstaff in a laundry basket and have him carted away, instructing the servants to dump him in the Thames. This recalls the scene in Aristophanes' *The Clouds* in which Socrates is hoisted up toward the heavens in a basket; Falstaff at the mercy of the merry wives is Socrates as Aristophanes portrays him, a ridiculously false claimant to wisdom. His baptism in good English waters won't cleanse his soul, any more than Socrates' elevation heavenward turns him into a god.

For his second go at Mrs. Ford (urged upon him by the duplicitous Mistress Quickly), Falstaff again shows up at the Ford house. He falls for the same routine, as Mrs. Page arrives to warn of Mr. Ford's approach. This time they disguise Sir John as a woman, for, as Mrs. Page tells her friend, "We cannot misuse him enough. / We'll leave a proof, by that which we do, / Wives may be merry and yet honest too" (IV.ii.88–91). That is, the proof of wit and honor, the argument of their action, won't be in ever-elusive, ever-manipulable words, the things to which Mr. Ford gives too much credence, but in irrefutable deeds. When the self-beleaguered Ford does arrive, he's told that the disguised Falstaff is his wife's maid's aunt, a witch, a fortune-teller, a spell-caster—that is, an abuser of words who exploits the witless. Outwitted and gulled once again by words (words that nonetheless truthfully point to Sir John's inner nature), Ford beats 'her' out of his house, thus expediting the escape of the man he expected to capture *in flagrante.*

Finally told of his own folly, Ford reforms, acknowledging his wife's honor and chastising himself with such vigor that Mr. Page intervenes to tell him to "be not as extreme in submission as in offense" (IV.iv.11). But bruised, humiliated Falstaff still won't give up. As water and blows haven't dissuaded him, the ladies turn to spiritual terror and a suggestion of hellfire. Mrs. Page recounts a legend of Windsor Forest, an old wives' tale about Herne the Hunter, the late gamekeeper, whose spirit returns every winter, decked with "great ragg'd horns," changing the cows' milk to blood and frightening all those who see him (IV.iv.30). She proposes that they tell Falstaff to rendezvous with them in the forest, disguised as Herne. They will arrange for local children disguised as urchins, elves, and fairies to encircle him, dance, pinch him and burn him with candles. After "the unclean knight" has been so tormented, "we'll all present ourselves; dis-horn the spirit, / And mock him home to Windsor" (IV.iv.54–56). Pastor Evans pronounces this a set of "fery honest knaveries" (IV.iv.79–80)—a noble lie in action, worded as a Welsh-accented pun on "fairy."

Meanwhile, Sir John conceals his most recent humiliation, defending his remaining illusions of aristocratic honor with an ignoble lie. The Host of the Garter Inn hears that a fat old woman has gone up to Falstaff's room. Falstaff claims that yes, there was a woman, but she is gone now, after having "taught me more wit than ever I learned before in my life, and I paid nothing for it neither, but was paid for my learning" (IV.v.54–56). In defending himself against the suspicion that he has employed a prostitute, Falstaff offers another parody of an incident in the life of Socrates, who tells the tale of Diotima, his teacher in the philosophy of love. Socratic eros begins with the love of beautiful bodies, ascends to love of beautiful souls, and culminates in the love of "beauty as a whole," of *philo-sophia,* the love of wisdom. Falstaff indeed would do do well to begin his ascent on this ladder of love, but he will need a hard-earned lesson in modest practical wisdom before he can aspire to the heights.

He isn't the only erotic schemer in Windsor. All of Anne Page's suitors know she will participate in the Falstaff-tormenting fairy dance. Each plans to spirit her away. Mr. Page tells Slender that his daughter will appear in white; Mrs. Page tells Dr. Caius that she'll be dressed in green. Anne has feigned to consent to both parents, but she's written to her favorite, Fenton, saying that others will be dressed in those costumes and that she will elope with him.

All goes according to the lovers' plan, as inscribed within Anne's parents' plan. Slender makes off with the figure in white, Caius with the figure in green, Anne and Fenton with one another to a waiting vicar. Falstaff receives his just reward, after Anne, as the Fairy Queen, intones, "Evil be to him that evil thinks" (V.v.67). Parson Evans earlier had distinguished what is said from what is thought, condemning hypocrisy; it is Anne Page, in the guise of a native English spirit-ruler, who enforces the Christian command to put thought before action, true conviction before law. At last the right words fit the right deeds, as the children, singing "Lust is but a bloody fire," singe the old bounder with candles. Duly mocked, Falstaff admits to having been an ass, while Ford vows never to distrust his wife again. When Pastor Evans mocks Falstaff in his heavy Welsh accent, Falstaff exclaims, "Have I liv'd to stand at the taunt of one that makes fritters of English?" (V.v.136–37). He has, indeed, and as Anne Page as the Fairy Queen has suggested, it's the thought that makes language and action good or bad. Mr. Page promises him forgiveness at the price of further ridicule at dinner.

But what of the deceived suitors? Slender reports first, complaining that the fairy he ran off with was "a great lubberly boy" and, compounding the indignity, the son of a postmaster (V.v.176). Slender resolutely attempts to grasp a shred of dignity by averring, "If I had been married to him, for all he was in woman's apparel, I would not have had him" (V.v.182–83). Deceived by words and apparel, he can at least uphold the natural standard. Dr. Caius wasn't so lucky. The French physician didn't identify the nature of his 'bride' until the ceremony was finished. "I'll raise all Windsor," he declaims, a move that may not improve his professional reputation in the town (V.v.197).

As Mr. Ford understates it, "This is strange" (V.v.200). "Who hath the right Anne?" (V.v.200). The young lady herself stops by, husband by her side, asking her parents' pardon for her disobedience. Fenton offers the apologia for love according to the principles of nature that fake-Socratic Falstaff could never learn from his fake Diotima—that is, from himself. "You would have married her most shamefully, / Where there was no proportion held in love" (V.v.208–09). In love, reciprocity is the natural way as indeed the merrily indignant wives and the jealous husband had understood, when thinking of themselves and the rogue knight. Not only nature but God is on the true lovers' side: "Th'offense is holy that she hath committed; / And this deceit loses the name of craft, / Of disobedience, or unduteous title, / Since therein she doth evitate and shun / A thousand irreligious cursed hours, / Which forced marriage would have brought upon her" (V.v.212–17). Even Falstaff sees this, saying to the Pages, "I am glad, though you have ta'en a special stand to strike at me, that your arrow hath glanc'd" (V.v.221–22). Both Fenton and Falstaff have spoken in better English than any Slender or Caius could have offered, and the Pages, defeated at their own game of wit against each other and against their daughter's good, concede defeat with grace and good humor. Mr. Ford is satisfied that he will sleep tonight with Mrs. Ford.

Shakespeare's English comedy defends the right use of the English language, the right use of convention in the service of just love, love in proportion, the reciprocal love that animates the reciprocal rule of a husband and a wife over their household. The Falstaff of the comedy differs from the Falstaff of the history plays; he is 'lower,' less clever, because in the histories he operates in the presence of warring kings, whom he cannot underestimate, while here he finds himself in the presence of mere gentrymen and women, whom he can and does underestimate. Commercial, no longer aristocratic, English civil society lends itself to comedy in its denizens' readiness to make sharp deals by hawking falsely advertised merchandise. In this kind of society, where there are no lions but plenty of foxes, nature as seen in love must live by the wits of true lovers. They can triumph, achieve comedy's peaceful and happy ending, but only if their prudence in plotting counter-deceptions equals their ardor.

The Continental regimes enjoy no peace. In *Much Ado About Nothing*, they are always warring or preparing for war. The aristocrats are noble or, in one instance, evil, but not figures of fun. The witticisms have sharper points. Love and marriage unite ruling families, not merely prosperous ones, and a failed courtship might ruin an international alliance, incite another war. This play is a comedy without merriment. It ends happily, but only just. The fathers here are rulers, not merchants, and there are no mothers; the women are witty and good (more precisely, one is more witty than good, the other more good than witty), but they are daughters and nieces, and do not rule the action.

Leonato is the governor of Messina in the Kingdom of Sicily. Don Pedro is a prince of Aragon, under which kingdom Sicily has thrived as a subordinate but largely self-governing regime. Aragon itself had merged with Castile in 1479, forming the nucleus of modern Spain, Tudor England's great rival. The Spanish Armada had sailed only ten years before Shakespeare wrote the play.

Don Pedro has arrived triumphantly in Messina, having won a battle comically, happily, as it were, his troops having suffered few casualties. "A victory is twice itself when the achiever brings home full numbers" (I.i.7–8), Leonato tells his daughter, Hero, and his niece, Beatrice—eligible young ladies who themselves might well be 'doubled' or married to eligible suitors. They hear from the messenger who has brought this good news that a young Florentine named Claudio has acquitted himself well in the fight, "doing, in the figure of a lamb, the feats of a lion" (I.i.12). He will prove a fitting hero for Hero. As for Beatrice, she inquires after a "Signor Mountanto," by whom she means Signor Benedick of Padua, a man she denigrates as a trencherman and lover-boy (his name suggests as much), leaving the audience wondering why a lady of her stature would inquire after such a nullity. But he is no nullity, Don Pedro's messenger insists; he is a man of virtue, a brave soldier. Ah, but "You must not, sir, mistake, my niece," Leonato replies; "there is a kind of merry war betwixt Signor Benedick and her; they never meet but there's a skirmish of wit between them" (I.i.53–54). Beatrice immediately claims near-total victory in their last war of words, after which "four of his wits went halting off, and now is the whole man governed with one," leaving him at best human, all-too-human, "a reasonable creature" but little more (I.i.58–59, 62–63). Serves him right, too, as he "wears his faith but as the fashion of his hat; it ever changes with the next block" (I.i.66–67).

The victors enter. Claudio loves Hero, openly. Benedick exchanges verbal arrows with Beatrice, concluding, "I will live a bachelor" (I.i.213). Don Pedro wisely doubts it. But Claudio has no inclination to camouflage his feelings: Having looked upon Hero "with a soldier's eye" before the war, having "had a rougher task in hand / Than to drive liking to the name of love," upon returning, with "war-thoughts… left in their places vacant, in their rooms / Come thronging soft and delicate desires, / All prompting me how fair young Hero is, / Saying I lik'd her ere I went to wars" (I.i.261–67). Don Pedro promises to intervene with Leonato and Hero on his friend's behalf.

But Don Pedro's bastard brother, Don John, resents his brother's patronage. "I had rather be a canker in a hedge than a rose in his grace" (I.ii.22)—a sentiment anticipating Milton's Satan, who would rather rule in Hell than serve in Heaven. And like Satan, Don John knows himself: "It must not be denied that I am a plain-dealing villain" (I.ii.25–26), who, "if I had my liberty, I would do my liking" (I.ii.28–29). Don John has an aristocratic lineage but no aristocratic standing; he is illegitimate in the strict sense, unlawful. He therefore defines liberty like a democratic, as doing whatever he wants, not as freely doing what is lawful. Upon hearing that his brother has negotiated the beginning of a courtship between Claudio and Hero, he vows, "If I can cross him any way, I bless myself every way" (I.ii.58); evil will be his 'good,' his *summum bonum*. He has no interest in the lovers whose happiness he would ruin, wanting only to injure his gracious brother, resenting the superiority grace implies. To Don John, the lovers are mere collateral damage. Unlike Falstaff, his vice is unnatural; he is not so much a bad man as an evil one who would ruin both brotherly love and chaste erotic love.

For her part, Beatrice echoes Benedick's anti-marital vow. "Not till God make men of some other metal than earth" shall she take one as her husband (II.i.51–52). More wittily, "Adam's sons are my brethren; and truly, I hold it a sin to match my kindred" (II.i.55–56)—and there is indeed a touch of brotherly-sisterly raillery in the repartee of the obviously well-matched pair.

Don John's first plot against his brother has him lying to Claudio, telling him that Don Pedro really woos Hero for himself. When Claudio confides his anger to Benedick the scheme quickly dissolves, as Benedick tells Don Pedro, who announces the real result of his suit, confirmed by Leonato: "Count, take of me my daughter, and with her my fortunes; his Grace hath made the match, and all grace say Amen to it!" (II.i.271–72). So the romance seems to conclude with joy. Don Pedro next intends to exercise his matchmaking skills on the harder challenge posed by Benedick and Beatrice, enlisting Claudio and Hero as his allies.

But Don John won't surrender. I will "cross this marriage" (II.ii.7), thanks to a plan thought up by his follower, Borachio. Borachio's lover is Margaret, one of Hero's gentlelady attendants. If Don John can arrange to have Don Pedro and Claudio near her chamber window at night, Borachio will address her as Hero, letting them 'discover' Hero's infidelity. This scheme has the advantage over Don John's abortive one, as it arranges for its victims to see and hear for themselves.

At the same time, Don Pedro plots his own much more benevolent deception of Benedick, letting it drop that Beatrice is secretly in love with her verbal fencing partner—also while arranging for the unknowing lover to listen in. Don Pedro deplores the lady's unwisdom in this, but Leonato, who's in on the scheme, excuses his niece, saying, "O my lord, wisdom and blood combating in so tender a body, we have ten proofs to one that blood hath the victory" (II.iii.150–51). Claudio chimes in with the claim that Hero has told him that poor Beatrice will surely die if Benedick continues to spurn her. Don Pedro adds, "I love Benedick well; and I could wish he would modestly examine himself, to see how much he is unworthy of so good a lady" (II.iii.189–90). The staged conversation appeals first to Benedick's real if unrealized love for Beatrice, while removing his hitherto-reasonable doubt that the lady regards him with favor. The conspirators also appeal to Benedick's Christian humility combined with his aristocratic pride (sure to make him want to prove that he is indeed worthy of so good a lady). Their conversation has its intended effect on the young nobleman, who then converses with himself, saying, "If I do not take pity of her, I am a villain"—not the good man, the aristocrat, I know myself to be (II.iii.239). "If I do not love her, I am a Jew" (II.iii.240)—not the Christian I know myself to be. To confirm this self-knowledge, "I will go get her picture," that is, go see her and fall more fully in love (II.iii.240–41).

And Hero goes to work on Beatrice, with the identical strategy: a conversation with her other attendant, Ursula, fashioned for the ears of her 'eavesdropping' friend, whom she describes as too prideful and self-absorbed to respond to Benedick's love, which she duly reported. "Nature never fram'd a woman's heart / Of prouder stuff than that of Beatrice. / Disdain and scorn ride sparkling in her eyes, / All matter else seems weak." (III.i.50–54). After they leave, Beatrice steps forward, ashamed of herself and ready to requite Benedick's love. Later, Hero will see Beatrice come down to natural equality with others of their sex, "look[ing] with your eyes as other women do" when they are in love (III.iv.81–82).

At this point, Benedick and Beatrice, the seemingly 'hard case,' are well on the way to a comedic finale, but Claudio and Hero have been charted firmly toward as tragic an end as Romeo and Juliet, by as malignant a villain. Enter, however, a band of English-like clowns who will blunder themselves into saving the day. Constable Dogberry (both his title and his name are English) selects a night-watch, charging them to guard Leonato's door, "for the wedding being there tomorrow," there must be no disturbance tonight (III.iii.84). From this post, the watchmen hear Borachio tell another of Don John's followers how well his scheme worked, how Don Pedro and Claudio heard him courting Margaret-as-Hero, with Claudio swearing that he would go to the wedding ceremony and expose her betrayal to all the guests. The watchmen determine to report to the Constable this, "the most dangerous piece of lechery"—they mean treachery, but what's in a word?—that "ever was known in the commonwealth." Initially, however, when Dogberry attempts to tell Leonato of the plot, he is too buffoonish to get to the point, and the governor can only tell him to go back and complete his investigation.

At the church, Claudio accuses Hero ("She's but the sign and semblance of her honor"); Don Pedro testifies against her ("upon my honor"); Don John condemns her vices as being beyond the "chastity" of language to be uttered in polite company; her father wishes she were dead or, better, never born (IV.i.32,87,96). Under the weight of these sudden, false accusations, Hero collapses. Among the nobles, only Benedick doubts the charge; only Beatrice defends her.

But unlike the notoriously foolish, corrupt, ineffectual clergymen elsewhere in Shakespeare's plays, the Friar who was to have performed the marriage ceremony shows perception ("I have marked / A thousand blushing apparitions / To start into her face"), prefers not to exclaim or declaim, and speaks with the authority of both religion and experience without expecting any to defer to him on account of them, or of his own status (IV.i.158–60). He insists that "there is some strange misprision in the princes" (IV.i.185). This gives Benedick an opening to express suspicion of "John the Bastard, / Whose spirits toil in frame of villainies" (IV.i.189). This in turn makes Leonato doubt his daughter's accusers: "If they wrong her honor, / The proudest of them shall well hear of it" (IV.i.191–92). That is, he will chastise even a prince of the kingdom that rules, albeit lightly, over the kingdom in which he governs one region. The same honor that inspires aristocrats to defend their countries and their allies stands in defense of their families, and if family honor is impugned, civic honor will be shaken. It is Don John's bastardy, his illegitimacy, that puts him at odds with all aristocratic and monarchic regimes, makes him suspect in the mind of Benedick and to those he reminds of that suspect character. At the same time, it is the Friar's equal and opposite condition as an 'outsider' to the regime, *in* but not *of* it, that enables him to raise the initial question, a question based not on special knowledge derived from the Church confessional, from hearsay, but from natural observation.

Harmless as a dove, but prudent as a serpent, only Friar Francis sees the way to satisfy the requirements of honor and to defend civic peace, a way that exists because human nature is what it is, a way that the Friar sees because he understands human nature and also knows how it may be brought to follow justice. "Pause awhile, / And let my counsel sway you in this case" (IVi.200–01). Hero has fainted and her accusers have walked out; let them believe her to be dead. This alone will change "slander to remorse" (IV.i.211). Hero will be "lamented, pitied, and excus'd, / Of every hearer; for it so falls out / That we have we prize not the worth / Whiles we enjoy it, but being lack'd and lost, / Why, then we rack the value, then we find / The virtue that possession would not show us / Whiles it was ours. So it will fare with Claudio." (IV.i.216–22). (Does it so fare with heroes generally? That they are admired more in death, or in seeming death, than in life? And that poets perpetuate their memory, keeping them alive in the minds of audiences, including playgoers and readers? More radically, is that what God knows about human beings—that they will honor him more if He comes to live among them and then seems to die? A wise friar is one who might think along these lines.)

Benedick puts his own honor on the line, telling Leonato that he will find a way to vindicate his daughter, Hero. But first he must deal with his enraged fiancée, Leonato's niece, spirited Beatrice, who demands that he kill slandering Claudio. This is her love test, set for the man she'd accused of waywardness at the beginning of the play. In her ferocity, she wishes she were a man so that she could "eat his heart in the marketplace" (IV.i.304)— a use of the marketplace that would not occur to the English at Windsor. An oligarch, even a gentlewoman, conceives of a marketplace as a public place primarily for private transactions; an aristocrat conceives of a marketplace as a public place simply, in this instance a place in which to exercise bloody, even cannibalistic vengeance, supposed to be just. Although Benedick tries to calm her, she extracts a vow to challenge the calumniator. Again, tragedy threatens.

Fortunately, the forces of English common law, remarkably at play in Messina, are still on the case. Constable Dogberry calls his officers to order, inquiring, "Is our whole dissembly appear'd?" (IV.ii.2) Dissembling schemers Borachio and his accomplice, Conrade, are indeed present, and the interrogation of the accused and their accusers wends its way eccentrically toward establishing the facts of the case. They report back to the governor's house in time to interrupt Benedick, who has duly challenged Claudio, then departed. Borachio confesses. But Leonato continues his own plot, telling Claudio that although innocent Hero is dead, he has a niece who looks just like her, who stands to inherit not only his own estate but the estate of his brother, Antonio. Claudio happily accepts the substitute wife (it *is* a comedy, after all), and the wedding is set for the morrow.

As for Benedick, he must return to a conversation with a lady who expects him to return with his shield or on it. He returns with it, his shield being his wit. After telling her that he has indeed challenged Claudio, who will either answer the challenge or be deemed a coward, he distracts her from her anger by reinitiating their badinage, asking her to say "for which of my bad parts didst thou first fall in love with me?" (V.ii.52–53). Tellingly, this new sally turns the satire on himself, away from his beloved; he has indeed learned humility. Why, "for all of them together; which maintain'd so politic a state of evil that they will not admit any good part to intermingle with them" (V.ii.54–56)—a suggestion of Aristotle's 'mixed regime' and an anticipation of the kind of arguments Publius will unfold in *Federalist* 51.

This will be a politic *and* loving marriage of separate and balanced powers, better together than they are alone.

"Thou and I are too wise to woo peaceably," Benedick remarks (V.ii.63). Hardly so on your side, the maid replies, since the wise man rarely praises himself by calling himself wise. "An old, an old instance, Beatrice, that liv'd in the time of good neighbors; if a man do not erect in this time his own tomb ere he dies, he shall live no longer in monument than the bell rings and the widow weeps" (V.ii.66–69). Benedick is an aristocrat who understands the modern world, where humility no longer wins honor because neighbors no longer know or love you. For once, Beatrice can bring no ready counter-witticism to mind. When Ursula interrupts with the news that Hero was falsely accused, that Don Pedro and Claudio were abused, and that Don John has fled the country, they hurry to the governor's house. (As for Shakespeare, he busies himself in erecting his own tomb, one with many mansions, an *imitatio Christi*, perhaps. His Continental admirer, Chateaubriand, later took the hint, writing his memoir *"d'outre tombe."*)

At the governor's house, Hero unmasks herself as Leonato explains, "she died…but whiles her slander lived" (V.iii.66); her slander now dead, her honor vindicated thanks to the Friar's wise ruse, she has risen. She will marry Claudio. And after a bit more verbal sparring, which they begin by telling one another that they love one another "no more than reason" (V.iii.75,78), Benedick and Beatrice are kindly exposed by the newlyweds, who produce letters from each confessing love for the other. "A miracle!" Benedick pronounces it. "Here's our own hands against our hearts" (V.iii.91)—really his own telling actions against their words. He silences any more less-than-beatific chatter by kissing his bride-to-be; the man Beatrice had derided as Signor Mountanto delivers a sermon from the mount in loving action, winning their war of words as surely as he had won the war which preceded the play's beginning. That makes two miracles, uniting two couples; *Much Ado About Nothing* is as close to a divine comedy as Shakespeare would ever write.

When Leonato tries to delay the celebratory dance, Benedick makes bold to countermand his order, telling him to get a wife, as "there is no staff more reverend than the one tipp'd with horn," a merry joke about cuckoldry in the wake of one wedding and in prospect of his own (V.iii.117–19). A messenger then brings word that Don John has been captured and will return to Messina tomorrow, under armed guard. It isn't Governor Leonato but Benedick who concludes, "Think not on him till tomorrow. I'll devise thee brave punishments for him. Strike up, pipers" (V.iii.121–23).

And why not? He and Beatrice were the first among the aristocrats to suspect Don John's perfidy, Hero's innocence, and the others' error. Although decent Claudio and Hero are the heirs to the fortune of the Governor and his brother, Benedick and Beatrice will be the real rulers of the city as the wittiest and wisest aristocrats in town. Friar Francis, attuned to human nature as his saintly namesake was to the animals, may offer counsel as needed. A victory is twice itself when the victor brings home full number, Leonato had intoned. He has just been shown how his aphorism might be enacted.

In his English comedy, Shakespeare shows how a decadent aristocracy in a peaceful, commercial society can be well supplanted by the wit of the gentry class or upper 'bourgeoisie'—crucially, the wit of women, wives whose virtues can now rule because commerce has supplanted war. But on the continent, wars will continue. In Shakespeare's continental comedy, the witty woman needs to find her match in an equally witty, or even wittier, man who retains the warlike virtues of aristocracy, virtues the aristocratic female can respect. And even they will need the assistance of a wise, politic clergyman who knows how to moderate the tempers of still-indispensable warrior-aristocrats while awaiting the ascendance of the better angels of their nature. In commercial England, a tavern host serves as peacemaker, the parson as a good-natured foreign language-bender.

In England, English words prove unreliable in dealings commercial and marital; actions speak louder. On the Continent, words might prove unreliable, dishonest, but also whetstones of wit; actions bespeak love (a kiss to silence a too-contentious mouth) and harmony (a betrothal dance). In England, love requires the wit of deception to defend itself against the low, farcical eroticism commerce encourages. On the Continent, love requires the wit of perception to defend itself against malignant scheming and excessive aristocratic spiritedness. In England, wit and prudence defend love against base assaults and surmises; on the Continent, they defend love by detecting evil plots and contriving 'miracles' or deceptions to counteract them.

The English know how to muddle through, in England. The common law is nothing less, and sometimes nothing more, than high-level muddling through. On the Continent, its representatives also muddle through, but never come close to ruling because the Continent knows no rule of law, only the rule of aristocrats, secular and divine, who prefer loving and fighting to litigating. Since the Continent is big and England small, the English in Shakespeare's audiences need to understand the aristocrats who rule the Continent, if only to protect themselves. How do aristocrats rule? What is the nature of the gentlemanliness they embody? To answer this question, he takes us to Milan, where two Veronese gentlemen have arrived, looking for brides.

Note

1. In a partial parallel, *The Merchant of Venice*'s Shylock rages laughably over the loss of his daughter and his ducats. Both merchants bluster over the loss of property but the English mercantile class retains a quasi-aristocratic esteem for honor instead of money.

CHAPTER TWO
GENTLEMEN AND GENTLEMANLINESS

What is a gentleman? Are these two Veronese gentlemen true gentlemen? Why Veronese gentlemen, and not gentlemen from some other city? Why bring them to Milan?

And while we're at it, Shakespeare concludes *Two Gentlemen of Verona* with a reconciliation that we now find utterly implausible, even for a comedy. What was he thinking? Is the fault in the stars, in the brilliant Shakespearean constellation, or in ourselves?

In the 1590s, when Shakespeare wrote the play, Verona was ruled by commercial-republican Venice. It may have been known as a city of romance; Shakespeare set *Romeo and Juliet* there, and it has surely been known as such ever since. So, gentlemen of Verona may be expected to be looking for love, for girls happily to wed. For gentlemen, marriage matters politically; aristocratic households not only possess wealth, they rule. Good marriages perpetuate aristocratic regimes, bad marriages ruin them. All regimes concern themselves with the problem of continuity, with the transfer of authority from one generation to the next. Monarchies see dynastic struggles and fear imbecilic heirs on the throne; in the American republic, young Lincoln lectured schoolboys on "the perpetuation of our political institutions," as the founding generation passed from the scene.

Milan has another regime, under another imperial ruler. Conquered by the Romans in the third century BC, it served as capital of the Western Roman Empire, beginning in the third century AD. There the Emperor Constantine issued the Edict of Milan in 313, granting religious toleration throughout the empire and thereby enabling Christianity to spread unimpeded by persecutors. The Roman aristocracy would need to adjust to the new religion now, just as the modern European aristocracy would need to adjust to commerce and democracy, centuries later.

In modern times, the Christian ruler of Milan, Ludovico il Moro, committed a notorious mistake. Needing an ally against rival, ever-squabbling Italian city-states in the 1490s, when other enterprising Italians were sailing for the New World, he called the king of France, Charles VII, into Italy. In 1500 Charles returned, this time to stay and rule—an example of misguided policy by a Christian Italian prince Machiavelli would later deplore. In 1525, Hapsburg Spain took over, and in Shakespeare's time Milan was part of the Holy Roman Empire.

As a reading of Titus Livy will confirm, for centuries, Roman gentlemen knew exactly who they were, and what a gentleman was. But if the Empire becomes holy, at least in name, possibly in aspiration and even a bit in fact, what is a gentleman then, and who is one? 'We democrats' of later modernity miss the point of the play if we do not see that it's about these questions, about aristocracy, the regime that claims to be the rule of the few who are best, men and women who claim the right to rule on the basis of their excellence—whether of virtue (as in Aristotle), 'birth' (social rank), wealth, or some combination thereof. In modernity, aristocracy often founds its claim to rule on knowledge or expertise, calling itself 'meritocracy'; traditionally, another sort of learning, learning in the liberal arts, enhanced a young man's eligibility for holding positions of authority. Christians are numbered among 'the elect'—a new sort of aristocracy, chosen not on the basis of virtues natural or conventional but by God, gratuitously.

Given these cross-cutting, sometimes contradictory claims to rule by self-styled aristocrats, what is a young gentleman of Verona to do, and to think? Proteus, named for the classical world's legendary changeling, who wrestled with Odysseus, intends to stay in his native city, close to his honorable beloved. Valentine, whose name means "as one containing valor," has no beloved. [1] He prepares instead for an odyssey, intending to leave Verona, "To see the world abroad" (I.i.6). Valentine criticizes love as a dubious investment of sentiment ("If haply won, perhaps a hapless gain") and intellect ("a folly bought with wit, / Or else a wit by folly vanquished") (I.i.32–35). If Valentine is an Odysseus and Proteus a Proteus, they will square off someday (and Homer's readers won't bet on Proteus). Now, however, they part as friends, agreeing to correspond. Proteus thinks Valentine seeks not so much the wonders of the world as honor, traditionally the aristocrat's delight par excellence, the ruling passion of the noblest minds, as

Publius would call it, nearly two centuries later. For the moment, Proteus' mind is closed to wonder, his love for Julia having "metamorphos'd" him (he soliloquizes, recalling his Ovid), causing him to "neglect my studies, lose my time, / War with good counsel, set the world at nought," making his "wit with musing weak," his "heart sick with thought" (I.i.63–69). He experiences erotic love the way a devout Christian experiences the love of God; his love turns him away from 'the world.' His immediate worry is Julia's failure to answer his most recent missive.

Julia asks her lady-in-waiting, Lucetta ("light") if she would "counsel me to fall in love" and, if so, with which of the suitors she should do so. Lucetta recommends Proteus but has "no reasons" for her recommendation "but a woman's reason; I think him so because I think him so" (I.ii.23–24). This unilluminating counsel fails to impress Julia; Proteus "never moved me" because in "little speaking [he] shows his love but small" (I.ii.29). Lucetta then produces the letter, which Julia pretends to scorn but delights in, tears up, then attempts to reassemble. Lucetta isn't fooled, knowing that her mistress has made up her mind. But Julia's initial concern will prove just.

Proteus' father, Antonio, also receives advice from a servant, or rather from his brother, a priest, who conveys it through his servant. Why does his lordship allow Proteus to stay at home, "While other men, of slender reputation, / Put forth their sons to seek preferment out," whether to war, to voyages of discovery, or to "the studious universities" (I.iii.5–10). Antonio confesses to having thought the same thing. His son "cannot be a perfect man," a man with a just claim to rule, without "being tried and tutor'd in the world: / Experience is by industry achiev'd, / And perfected by the swift course of time," which his son is now wasting in Verona, Venice's subordinate, while his friend Valentine is off (as servant Panthino reminds him) to the Holy Roman Emperor's court in Milan (I.iii.20–23). When Proteus enters, reading Julia's return letter, he lies to his father about its sender, telling him it's from Valentine. This only confirms Antonio's intention to send Proteus to the imperial city; after all, he will be reuniting the young man with his friend. In lying, Proteus tells himself, "I shunn'd the fire for fear of burning" only to drench himself "in the sea, where I am drown'd" (I.ii.78–79). This hard lesson will not prevent him from lying many more times, however. This Proteus is a verbal shape-shifter, protean in mind not body. The crucial question is whether an 'Ovidian' metamorphosis effected by love will be merely 'Protean' or will it instead bring out the nature of the lover, a nature that can remain faithful, unchanging?

At the Duke's palace in Milan, Valentine's servant, Speed, baits his master, who has reversed his opinion of love, having fallen for the Duke's daughter, Silvia. Valentine has been so profoundly "metamorphos'd" by love that "I can hardly think you my master" (II.i.26–27). For his own sport, Speed takes up Valentine's former critique: "If you love her, you cannot see her" because "Love is blind" (II.i.61–63). With both Lucetta and Speed, the servant attempts to moderate a young boss. Valentine differs from Julia, however, because he makes no attempt to deceive his master respecting his correspondence with Silvia; he chaffs Speed right back. Having no need of maidenly modesty, he has no need of maidenly secrecy.

Being a maid, Silvia does have need of a ruse. Valentine has been gazing at her at table, and no woman in the world who isn't blind as Love would fail to notice such behavior. She has charged him with writing a letter to her (supposed) beloved, and she's come to tell him that "I would have had them writ more movingly" (II.i.117). She will permit him to revise and re-submit. "O excellent device!" Speed exclaims (II.i.128); the lady flirts well, having "taught her love himself to write unto her lover," whom he now sees to be Valentine (II.i.156)—as he explains to his uncomprehending, disbe-lieving, love-tortured master. Is his servant in earnest but wrong, in earnest and right, or deliberately wrong and still baiting him, as his wont? Love is a chameleon, as Speed now and Valentine soon will remark, living on air (as chameleons were said to do)—that is to say, on hope—and changing colors in its blushes, its excitation, its jealous rages. The skin, the surface, of love is Protean.

Changeling Proteus implausibly pledges his constancy to Julia and then heads to Milan, where Valentine lauds his character to the Duke when told of his impending arrival. Proteus, Valentine avers, is a man of ripe judgment and "all good grace to grace a gentleman" (II.iv.70). So trusting, he does not hesitate to tell Proteus of his beloved, to extol her beauty and saintliness, and to introduce her to him. Between now and the flirtation over the letter, Speed has been proven correct; the couple are betrothed, and they plan their elopement. Proteus now has other plans, having instantly conceived a passion for Silvia. His love, "like a waxen image 'gainst a fire / Bears no impression of the thing it was. / Methinks my zeal to Valentine is cold, / And that I love him not as I was wont. / O! but I love this lady too much… " (II.iv.197–201). As for Julia, he has "quite forgotten her" (II.iv.191)—a Proteus of love, indeed. "If I can check my erring love, I will; / If not, to compass her I'll use my skill" (II.iv.209–10). It doesn't take him long to logic-chop his way to the latter course. He even concludes his 'reasoning' with a prayer, a prayer to Love: "Love, lend me wings to make my purpose swift, / As thou has sent me with to plot this drift" (II.vi.42–43). Back in Verona, meanwhile, Julia tells Lucetta that Proteus' "words are bonds, his oaths are oracles, / His love sincere, his thoughts immaculate," and so on (II.vii.75–76). She plans to disguise herself as a man and run off to Milan to be with him. Sensible Lucetta doubts her mistress's faith in Proteus to be well-placed but, loyal herself, will not betray her plan.

Proteus easily thwarts the elopement by disclosing Valentine's plot to the Duke, who banishes the plotter. The Duke would marry his daughter to the wealthy Thurio, a Thor in name only—vain, cowardly, and blustering, a Thor of big thunder and small hammer, despised by prudent Silvia. For his part, Proteus offers 'friend' Valentine mock-moderate advice: "Cease to lament for that thou canst not keep" (III.i.241); trust to time. Write to Silvia and send your letters through me, as I shall deliver them faithfully. As it happens, Proteus' servant, Launce, has formed a better estimate of Proteus than Valentine has done; "I am but a fool, look you, and yet I have the wit to think my master is a kind of a knave" (III.i.261–62). He suspects his master of being willing to launce, a lot. In this comedy, then, it is usually the case that the servants are smarter than their masters and mistresses. Even Launce's dog, subordinate of a subordinate, routinely outwits his master, puts him to shame, induces his master to serve *him*. [2] This is 'foolish' Christianity ill-conceived, an otherworldly Christianity in comical abdication of political responsibility, mock-Christian misrule. Who, then, are the true aristocrats? How will the aristocrats-by-convention improve themselves, become worthy of the authority they claim?

The Duke isn't doing so well, in that regard. His purpose as an aristocratic father with an eligible daughter is to choose a worthy suitor and so to continue his line, assuring that his family will continue to rule in the next generation. He too trusts Proteus, asking him for advice on how to make Silvia forget Valentine and love Thurio. Proteus is more than happy to meet him exactly halfway on that request, and to use what there is of the Duke's prudence for his own advantage, against the Duke's intention. Slander Valentine, the would-be Machiavel thoughtfully advises, "with falsehood, cowardice, and poor descent— / Three things that women highly hold in hate" (III.ii.32–33). Yes, but I cannot deliver such a message, the duke calculates; it must come from the one "she esteemeth as his friend" (II.ii.37). Needless to say, Proteus promises to undertake the task, adding that he shall praise Thurio in the bargain, as Thurio himself is the first to suggest. The Duke and Thurio can trust Proteus, the Duke explains, because Proteus is "already Love's firm votary / And cannot soon revolt and change [his] mind" concerning his lovely Julia (III.ii.58–59). That Proteus has already revolted and changed his mind, that his quick betrayal of Valentine proves him capable of doing just that, does not occur to the Duke or to Thurio. Milan's rulers are misfits, aristocrats in name only. As for Proteus, he puts his faith in the power of poetry to persuade Silvia, and again the Duke concurs: "Much is the force of heaven-bred poesy" (III.ii.72). Proteus knows that not all poesy need be heaven-bred, but he does trust in its power; he trusts in what he knows to be human artifice, not in nature and not in God. Shakespeare also knows that not all poesy is heaven-sent and wants his hearers to know it. He also knows the power of some poetry but prefers to use it to illuminate and not to deceive. Hilariously, he has the dolt Thurio choose to write the sonnet.

A natural aristocrat will find his way to rule in nature itself. So we see when Valentine, self-exiled from Verona and banished from Milan, meets a gang of outlaws in a forest on the frontiers of Mantua. To win their esteem, along with his own and his servant's safety, he tells them a prudent if not noble lie—that he was banished for killing a man, although "without false vantage or base treachery," there being honor among killers as well as thieves (IV..i.29). Suitably impressed, upon learning that Valentine also possesses a useful knowledge (foreign languages) as well as the requisite *virtù*, they will have him for their king. "Some of us are gentlemen," one of their number explains, outlaws only because they committed murder and "such-like petty crimes" in "the fury of ungovern'd youth" (IV.i.44–45). It should be remarked that aristocratic regimes which fail to govern their youth, whether in love or in anger, cannot last long. Valentine agrees "to make a virtue of necessity" (as one outlaw puts it, in a sort of *précis* of

Machiavellian thought). In return, they will "do thee homage, and be rul'd by thee, / Love thee as our commander and our king," albeit upon pain of death if he demurs (IV.i. 62,66–67)—a serviceable example of how to make a virtue of necessity, to say nothing of how to make a Hobbesian social contract. Judging that these new outlaw-allies may be more honest than some of those he has known in civil society, Valentine consents, "Provided that you do no outrages / On silly women or poor passengers" (IV.i.71–72). Of course not. Being gentlemen *manqué*, "We detest such vile base practices" (IV.i.73).

As Proteus' servant serves, doglike, a dog, so (Proteus admits), "spaniel-like," the more Silvia "spurns my love / The more it grows and fawneth on her still" (IV.ii.14–15). With sonnet in hand and musicians in his train, Thurio arrives beneath Silvia's room, where the Duke has confined her. Julia is there, too, disguised as a boy, listening to the preposterous serenade. Proteus' betrayal stands exposed after Thurio gives up and Proteus has another go at winning Silvia. More lies follow: Julia is dead, he says, so he's free to court another; Valentine is, too, so Silvia is equally free. After her scornful rejection, he begs for her picture as consolation, which she promises to send in the morning, "loath" though she is "to be your idol" (IV,ii.124).

Rid of him, she spins a counterplot with her friend Eglamour, whose name Shakespeare has borrowed from a hero of a medieval romance. Sir Eglamour of Artois is a Christian Hercules, performing heroic deeds in a story of courtly love that, counter to the conventions of courtly romance, leads to marriage and family. A good name, indeed, and Silvia knows him as "a gentleman"—valiant, wise, remorseful [i.e., compassionate], well accomplished" (IV.iii.11–13). Like Julia, she would escape her father's injustice and seek her beloved. She will need no protective disguise, as Julia did, because Eglamour consents to accompany her, although this will put him at odds with the Duke. His compassion or pity, consonant with both nature and Christianity, brings him to agree to guard her. Apart from Valentine, he is the only real gentleman in the play, although, being human and no demi-god, he will defend her in a less-than-Herculean way.

Disguised Julia calls herself "Sebastian," recalling the saint martyred after attempting to persuade the Roman Emperor Diocletian from persecuting Christians. "Sebastian" means "be ashamed," and Proteus, who doesn't recognize her in disguise, shows no more shame at his betrayals than the

Emperor did at killing saints. Having judged his own dog-serving servant unreliable, he asks 'Sebastian' to deliver a ring to Silvia, which of course is the same ring Julia had given him at the time they pledged mutual fidelity. Unlike Proteus, who uses deception to betray his friend, Julia will faithfully offer the ring to Silvia. "I am my master's true confirmed love, / But cannot be true servant to my master / Unless I prove false traitor to myself. / Yet will I woo for him but yet so coldly / As, heaven it knows, I would not have him speed" (IV.iv.98–102). Silvia unwittingly proves more faithful to Julia than Proteus, plotting, saying, "Tell him from me, / One Julia, that his changing," Protean, "thoughts forget, / Would better fit his chamber than this shadow"—the picture of herself that he wants her to exchange for the ring. Silvia rejects the ring because even her finger "would not do his Julia so much wrong" (IV.iv133). 'Sebastian' reveals herself not as Julia but as Julia's servant, whom Silvia accordingly rewards with a token of respect for her loyalty. Having proved herself good and faithful, Julia also proves vulnerable to a touch of jealousy; left with the picture of Silvia, she supposes herself no less lovely than her rival, concluding that Love is indeed "a blinded god" (IV.iv.193). In judging, justice is blind to persons; in pursuing, love is blind to judgment. To found a just regime, men and women will need to learn to love prudently and to judge justly, forming families aristocratic in the natural sense of the word, the rule of those best by nature, as guided by God. Before leaving in search of Valentine, Silvia goes to confession. Although her name suggests the natural, the 'sylvan,' and she will indeed venture into the woods, she will do so only under Christian auspices.

Before Thurio left Silvia, Proteus told him to meet him the next morning at St. Gregory's well. It is an unwittingly ironical choice, as St Gregory was the man who sent Christian missionaries to England, where they led the Anglo-Saxons to conversion. Proteus intends no such holy purpose, but his mission will soon come to an end. By the next day, the Duke has discovered Silvia's escape, correctly guessing that she's left in search of Valentine. All parties will soon converge in the forest, in nature, outside the city and its conventions, where a re-founding of the Milanese regime may occur rightly, by the light of natural justice.

An outlaw intercepts Silvia; Eglamour's disappearance will remain unexplained, and he will not return. Howsoever things may have gone, the outlaw faithfully brings the lady to his captain, even assuring her: "Fear not, he bears an honorable mind, / And will not use a woman lawlessly" (V.iii.12–14). His fidelity to his promise not to harm women will serve him well in the end. Valentine already knows that his men "love me well; yet I have much to do / To keep them from uncivil outrages" (V.iv.21). But now he hides, seeing intruders in the forest.

They are not strangers. Proteus and Julia/Sebastian are with Silvia, whom Proteus has seized from the outlaws. Hoping to put her in his debt, he insists that they "would have forc'd your honor and your love" (V.iv.21). "How like a dream is this I see and hear!" Valentine thinks; like Proteus, he prays to Love, not for swiftness in the execution of a plot, as Proteus had done, but for exactly the opposite, for the "patience to forbear awhile" (V.iv.26–27). Although he prays to a pagan goddess, Valentine's love is Christian not erotic: "*Agape* suffereth long and is kind; *agape* envieth not, *agape* vaunteth not itself" (I Corinthians 13:4). Christian love is patient, not protean, faithful not wavering. Christian love enables not only the innocence of doves but the prudence of serpents. In terms of the names in the play, "Speed" is the servant of Valentine, a person under his rule; Proteus imagines speed a virtue, and his servant is "Launce."

Fortified with this loving patience, Valentine listens as Silvia laments her misery in having been rescued by "false Proteus," exactly the sort of man to whom she would never want to be obliged (V.iv.35). He listens as she adds, "O, heaven be judge how I love Valentine, / Whose life's as tender to me as my soul!" (V.iv.36–37). And he hears his beloved lover reveal not only her faithful heart but her clear mind. When Proteus complains of "the curse of love" (Love's final answer to his evil, impatient prayer), that "women cannot love where they're beloved," she rejoins with crushing logic that "Proteus cannot love where he's beloved!"—in Verona by Julia (V.iv.43–45). The Protean soul contradicts itself by rending its faith "into a thousand oaths," by committing perjury, by saying two opposite things at once (V.iv.48). "Thou has no faith left now, unless thou'st two, / And that's far worse than one," because it makes him a "counterfeit," a false double, "to thy true friend!" (V.iv.50–53). This reduces Proteus first to appealing to convention masquerading as nature ("In love, / Who respects friend?"); when Silvia refutes this ("All men but Proteus"), he threatens to "love [her] 'gainst the nature of love—force ye"—the very act he had begun by praising himself for saving her from (V.iv.5–54). Unblessed or even cursed by nature, or by the goddess Love, he would treat her as Machiavelli urges the prince to treat the protean, faithless Lady Fortuna, to master her by force. "I'll force thee to yield to my desire" (V.iv.59). The source of Proteus' proteanism is the disorder of his soul, which he has turned in precise contradiction to its natural order. His reason serves his desires, and when reasoning (or rather logic-chopping) fails to get him what his desires want, he resorts to spiritedness, to angry threats of force. Since (as Socrates observes in the *Republic*) our appetites are foolish and inconstant counselors, he constantly bends himself out of shape.

Valentine, whose soul is so ordered that his reason contains his valor, now puts that virtue to use, commanding Proteus to "let go that rude uncivil touch" (V.iv.60). In the wild, natural forest, outside civil society, his mind and heart command civility, speech over touch. Machiavelli teaches that one learns best not through hearing, or faith, not through seeing, or reason, but through the sense of touch—touch, which caresses or annihilates, mastering Fortuna. Valentine doesn't need force to defeat the astonished Proteus; he need only address him as "Thou common friend, that's without faith or love" (V.iv.63). Common: that is to say, here 'in' nature, outside the city, he reveals Proteus as a commoner by nature. By the standard of nature, Proteus is no real gentleman, and therefore is unworthy of ruling anyone because incapable of ruling himself as a human being would do, if fully human, truly natural. "Proteus, / I am sorry I must never trust thee more, / But count the world a stranger for thy sake. / The private wound is deepest" (V.iv.68–71). Valentine's own status as a ruler crumbles if civil or even personal friendship disintegrates. Aristocracy requires the virtues of courage, moderation, justice, prudence, fidelity in friendship and in love. For an aristocrat to be a counterfeit, aristocratic in title or appearance only, ruins aristocracy, makes the world itself a stranger, which is to say a foreigner, not merely an illegal but a natural alien. Machiavellianism alienates nature, and in doing so destroys not only conventional aristocracy, the political balance-wheel between 'the one,' the prince, and 'the many,' the commoners, but destroys the real, natural aristocracy upon which every conventional aristocracy must finally rely.

Here is where 'we democrats' misunderstand the ending of the play. Proteus, for all his faults, retains an element of aristocracy in his soul. He has attempted to play the leonine and vulpine Machiavellian prince, but he retains a core of virtue that his would-be *virtù* cannot quite smother. He can still feel shame, the reverse side of the honor that is the ruling passion of the true aristocrat's mind. Confronted by the outraged friend he has betrayed, he admits that "My shame and guilt confounds me" (V.iv.74). Instead of offering battle—which would show him a hardened villain and make the play a tragedy—he asks for forgiveness. Only in a soul formed and informed by natural right and Christian or agapic love can this response make sense. The same is true of Valentine's response:

Then I am paid;
And once again I do receive thee honest.
Who by repentance is not satisfied
Is not of heaven nor earth, for these are pleas'd;
By penitence th' Eternal's wrath's appeas'd.
And, that my love may appear plain and free,

All that was mine in Silvia I give thee (V.iv.78–83). If God forgives penitent sinners, and if nature does, too, why should humans not forgive them? Is Proteus' sudden show of shame and guilt, along with his repentance and humble request for forgiveness, only another shape-shift, soon to be forgotten by him? Is Valentine's immediate reversal of his distrust, his natural (that is, rational) and Christian forgiveness, implausible, or even a ruse, a deeper Machiavellianism? Unlikely: This is a comedy, and Shakespeare does not intend to appeal to the supposed realism of Machiavellians or democrats but to the realities of natural right and Christian grace, which Tocqueville identified as the democratizing gift of aristocratic society. The resulting democratic society yet stands in need of aristocratic guidance, Tocqueville added.

But what of Julia, still disguised as Sebastian? Overwhelmed by all of this, she covers and reveals herself by stepping out of the shadow of her disguise, as Valentine had stepped out of the shadows of the forest. She too rebukes Proteus, invoking his shame at his own commonness, baseness, vulgarity. Behold the woman:

Behold her that gave aim to all thy oaths,
And entertain'd 'em deeply in her heart.

How oft has thou with perjury cleft the root!
O Proteus, let this habit make thee blush!
Be thou asham'd that I have took upon me
Such an immodest raiment—if shame live
In a disguise of love.
It is the lesser blot, modesty finds,
Women to change their shapes than men their minds. (V.iv.101–10)

The root of nature, the heart, will be cleft by the many-minded, self-contradictory man. The relation of heart to mind, of morality to reason, deranged, ought to shame not only an aristocrat but a man as such.

And so it does. Proteus admits "'tis true:"(V.iv.110). Inconstancy is the
original sin, the "one error that fills [man] with faults," making him "run
through all th' sins"(V.iv.111–12). To run: to be impatient, to hasten, to
change senselessly, to be ruled by the desires. "What is in Silvia's face but I
may spy / More fresh in Julia's with a constant eye?" (V.iv.114–15). That
is, constancy of heart is the indispensable condition of clarity of mind, of
the reasoning mind whose exercise shows men human and makes aristocrats
just. At this, Valentine again intervenes. With right relations restored, he
proposes reconciliation of both the friends and the lovers. Proteus and, crucially, Julia agree to the covenant. What Christian aristocrats of the Tudors'
English regime once understood and accepted as plausible, at least in an
instructive stage comedy, we modern democrats, petty Machiavels, do not.
Were they the deluded ones, or are we?

As for Valentine and Silvia, there remains the matter of her father, the
Duke, who now blunders in, accompanied by thundering arch-blunderer
Thurio. Upon seeing Silvia, Thurio claims her as his own, but Valentine
proves the more valorous of the two (no hard thing), threatening to thrash
him if he touches her, and the false Thor instantly decides that only a fool
"will endanger / His body for a girl that loves him not" (V.iv.133–34). The
Duke has prudence enough to recognize the obvious: "the more degenerate
and base art thou / To make such means for her as thou hast done / And
leave her on such slight conditions" (V.iv.136–38). No true aristocrat, Thurio. Therefore "by the honour of my ancestry"—in the name of his aristocratic lineage—"I do applaud thy spirit, Valentine, / And think thee worthy
of an empress' love" (V.iv.139–41). Valor is the spirit of the true aristocrat,

and the Duke now sees that he needs to re-found his regime by ending Valentine's banishment and, more, to "Plead a new state in thy unrivall'd merit" (V.iv.144). This new state, this new regime, founded both literally and in principle in nature, will find support in the man he now addresses as *Sir* Valentine. "Thou art a gentleman, and well-derived; / Take thou thy Silvia, for thou has deserv'd her" (V.iv.146–47). The Duke of Milan has clearly stated what a gentleman really is, and it is on this true perception, made possible by a reformed because dis-illusioned heart, that the renewed and more truly aristocratic regime will rest.

Valentine's first act as co-ruler of that regime is to reincorporate its remaining unrepentant scapegraces, the outlaws who preceded him in banishment. They are, he tells the Duke, "men endu'd with worthy qualities," deserving now of forgiveness, having become "reformed, civil, full of good, / And fit for great employment, worthy lord" (V.iv.154–57). The Duke immediately pardons them along with Valentine, telling his future son-in-law to "Dispose of them as thou know'st their deserts" (V.iv.158–59). Clearsighted because virtuous, Valentine knows them because he is clear-sighted, and will then be able to exercise the virtue of justice wisely—justice and wisdom being the virtues of the ruler par excellence, the virtues most needed in political life. Having found right in nature, rulers present and future can return to the political order, the regime, corrected. The Duke then proposes an extraordinarily "royal progress" back to Milan—extraordinary because they shall proceed "with triumphs, mirth, and rare solemnity" (V.iv.161). The circumstance makes celebration of victory understandable enough, but how can mirth and solemnity combine? Only in comedy: The high seriousness of tragedy has no mirth, but comedy treats "high" or noble things with a happy ending, an ending whereby all the elements that might make for tragedy harmonize, as a graceful spirit and the rule of reason over hearts corrected by grace take hold over the rulers. Comedy is aristocracy gone right, tragedy aristocracy gone wrong. Too much democracy will form souls that blink uncomprehendingly at both.

There is even a hint of philosophy to come. Valentine introduces the Duke to Julia, still in boy-disguise. "I think the boy hath grace in him; he blushes," the Duke observes, happily noting an aristocratic sense of shame in the supposed lad (V.iv.165). Valentine warrants 'him' "more grace than boy," and when the Duke asks what that could mean he promises to tell the story in the triumphant, mirthful, and solemn return trip (V.iv.166), promising in addition that the Duke will "wonder" at the tale (V.iv169). Before embarking on his odyssey into nature, Valentine had said he intended to see the wonders of the world abroad; Proteus had supposed Valentine's motive to be the quest for honor. Valentine has seen the wonders and found honor, as well. As for Proteus, it will be, Valentine remarks in his final act of justice, Proteus' act of penance to hear "the story of your loves discovered" (V.iv.171).

After that, Valentine promises, the regime will be re-founded on the two marriages, re-founded on "One feast, one house, one mutual happiness!" (V.iv.174). Love and friendship, sundered by the chaotic soul of Proteus, and a sundered aristocratic regime, nearly ruined by the overbearing and imprudent father-Duke, will both achieve reunion on the only stable foundation for private and public good, fidelity. Henceforth the private fidelity of marriage and the public fidelity of justice will reinforce one another, securing the truly human purpose, happiness.

Notes

1. Shakespeare's Valentine is named for the third-century Roman saint. Although Valentine initially exemplified Christian, agapic love (in his *caritas*, he cured a girl of blindness and ministered to persecuted Christians), in the Middle Ages he became associated with the tradition of courtly love, a tradition carried on today, albeit in much attenuated forms.
2. See II.iii.1–29 and IV.i.1–36.

CHAPTER THREE
ROYAL DREAMING

In *A Midsummer Night's Dream,* Shakespeare turns from regimes of 'the few' to monarchy, the regime of 'the one.' There can be at least two such regimes. In a good monarchy the ruler will govern himself first of all, often accepting the constraints of law, as in a 'constitutional monarchy.' In a bad monarchy the ruler will govern others without moral or legal restraint of any kind, as in a 'tyranny.'

Whether good or bad, monarchies often make regime continuity depend upon one family, its perpetuation in rule. Royal marriages aim at regime perpetuation. Duke Theseus of Athens has won his betrothed not with consent but with force, the only appeal that could have impressed her—the Amazon warrior-queen, Hippolyta. According to the ancient Greek story, Hippolyta was the daughter of the war god, Ares, who gave her a magical belt which was supposed to protect her in battle. Theseus captured her anyway, and she became the only Amazon ever to marry. Four days before their nuptials, the Duke addresses her: "I woo'd thee with my sword," Theseus says, "And won thy love doing thee injuries; / But I will wed thee in another key, / With pomp, with triumph, and with reveling" (I.i.16–19). If love is akin to war, marriage provides the foundation of political rule. Love strains against conventions, often against the rule of parents; marriage, which often makes parents out of lovers, requires the re-entrance of the lovers into civil society. Ares himself may have seen this. Though a god, and the warrior god at that, he couldn't or at least wouldn't defend his daughter from the love-suit of the Athenian statesman, evidently knowing that war's purpose is the re-establishment of civil peace.

Civil peace brings disputes under the law. Egeus arrives before the duke with his daughter, Hermia, and her two suitors, Lysander and Demetrius. Egeus, whose name means 'shield,' 'protection,' wants to shield his daughter from Lysander, whose name means 'free man,' 'liberator.' Hermia, whose name is the feminine form of Hermes, the messenger-god, has been giving her father a message he doesn't want to hear, namely, that she loves Lysander, wants him to be the one who liberates her from her father's edicts by joining her in marriage. Egeus prefers Demetrius, whose name means 'devoted to Demeter,' the goddess of agriculture and harvest, Demeter 'Law-Giver,' bringer of civilization. Egeus would rather marry his daughter to a man devoted to the household instead of a man devoted to civil liberty, citizenship. But in fact he depends upon the city to enforce his parental authority. Invoking "the ancient privilege of Athens" (I.i.41), whereby the city can require his daughter to marry the suitor the father chooses, upon pain of death "according to our law" (I.i.44), Egeus would overrule the love his daughter feels for Lysander. While there is a glance here at the 'Old Law' of the Bible as distinguished from the 'New Law' of love enunciated by Jesus as the sum and substance of the old, the primary distinction is the one between family and city, both liable to disruption by nature in the form of love. Egeus, the 'old man' of the law, and Demetrius, the young man of immature and flighty love, turn out be allies in an attempt at subverting the natural love that is the right foundation of families that form the right foundations of cities.

In the ancient monarchic regimes, the king's principal role was not as an 'executive' but as a judge; hence the term, 'the royal court.' "What say you, Hermia?" Duke Theseus asks (I.i.46). Your father "should be as a god" to you, being "one to whom you are but as a form of wax, / By him imprinted, and within his power / To leave the figure or disfigure it" (I.i.50–52). Hermia admits that Demetrius is a worthy gentleman, but Lysander is no less so; she wishes her father "look'd but with my eyes" (I.i.57). Theseus sides with her father: "Rather your eyes with his judgment must look" (I.i.57); as Athens' ruler, he will enforce the ancient law, finding her guilty of having neglected her father's mature judgment as well as his patriarchal authority. At this, spirited Hermia wants to know the penalty for disobedience; Theseus cites the death penalty her father had mentioned, adding that the alternative is a life of virginity in service at the temple of Diana, the virgin goddess of the pale moon. Since "my soul consents not to give sovereignty" to either her father or her father's choice of her husband, she chooses the temple over the household (I.i.82). Temporizing, the duke gives her four days to deliberate—to "examine well your blood," your nature as both woman and daughter (I.i.68)—ending on the day of his own nuptials, when Diana's new moon will appear.

Demetrius appeals to Hermia to relent and implores Lysander to yield "thy crazed title"—love—"to my certain right"—paternal authority, as recognized by the law of the city in which Lysander is a free man, a citizen (I.i.92). Lysander jibes, "You have her father's love, Demetrius; / Let me have Hermia's; do you marry him" (I.i.94). Egeus intervenes to grant that yes, Demetrius does have his love, "and what is mine my love shall render him"; since Hermia "is mine," I lovingly give my daughter to him, not to you (I.i.96–97). Against this, Lysander charges that his rival previously had courted another lady, Helena, "and won her soul"; even now she "dotes in idolatry, / Upon this spotted and inconstant man" (I.109–10). The nature of the man to whom you give your daughter is defective, whatever his social condition may be. It might be said that Demetrius lacks the very settled, civilized character of the goddess to whom his name implies devotion.

Duke Theseus halts the dispute. Conceding that before this he had been "over-full of self-affairs" to speak with Demetrius about this matter (I.i.113)—concerned more with the foreign war to win his bride and establish his family than to attend to his monarchic duty to regulate his subjects' conduct—he summons Egeus and Demetrius for "some private schooling" (I.i.116). But whatever this private conference may entail, he doesn't change his ruling. "For you, fair Hermia, look you arm yourself / To fit your fancies to your father's will, / Or else the law of Athens yields you up" (I.i.117–19). It appears that he intends to reprimand the father and intended son-in-law 'in chambers,' as a modern judge would say, without openly breaking the law of the city which, as judge, he must uphold. His betrothed is a foreign queen whose father, being the god of war, evidently had no objection to the winning of his daughter in a display of military prowess. But Hermia is a child of peace, of civil society, and unless some equitable out-of-court settlement can be reached, not the law of love but the rule of law must prevail.

Or must it? Only if the lovers remain in the city. In the city as ruled by the Duke, Hermia faces two unnatural choices: marriage to a man she does not love or a life of virgin austerity in service of a goddess. After the others depart, Lysander and Hermia remain to formulate a plot. Since "the course of true love never did run smooth" (I.i.134)—nature faces conventional roadblocks laid down by men—and since it is "hell to choose love by another's eyes," as Hermia says (I.i.140), let us flee the city, Lysander the liberator proposes, go to the home of his "widow aunt" who has no natural children and so regards him as her own; there "may I marry thee; / And to that place the sharp Athenian law / Cannot pursue us" (I.i.156–63). Hermia consents to the plan, which requires them to leave the city and plunge into the woods surrounding it, into the nature their love bespeaks, away from the city that denies nature. The free man, the citizen, faced with laws and rulers that are *contra natura*, has no choice but to retreat to the pre-political life of the bridegroom's family, outside the city.

Helena arrives, in search of Demetrius. Hermia's friend from childhood understands that Hermia has in no way encouraged his suit except by being beautiful, that is, by her nature ("would that fault were mine!") (I.i.201). That fault will no longer be on display to Demetrius, Hermia explains, telling her of her impending self-exile with Lysander and trusting that their lifelong friendship will ensure that Helena will respect the confidence. This proves a false expectation. When the lovers leave to their separate homes, Helena stays, telling herself and the audience that she will inform Demetrius of their plot. She explains that, like fickle Cupid himself, a mere child, a frivolous game-player, Demetrius first vowed "that he was only mine" and then ran off in pursuit of her more beautiful friend (I.i.243). She predicts that Demetrius will pursue the lovers into the woods, but her pain at his departure out of her sight, she hopes, will be recompensed by his gratitude upon returning to the city with the deserving informant who will follow him, still hoping to convince him to repent of his unfaithful love. This seems a desperate plot because Helena cannot know what will happen in the woods, what will result from Demetrius' pursuit. But it's the only one she can think of—betraying her friendship to regain her love.

Still another plot must coincide with these: preparations for the duke's nuptials. Some local tradesmen intend to perform a play to entertain the Court on the wedding day. A weaver, Nick Bottom, joins a carpenter, a joiner, a bellows-maker, a tinker, and a tailor to discuss a play with a self-contradictory title, "The most Lamentable Comedy and Most Cruel Death of Pyramus and Thisbe." Ovid tells the story of Pyramus and Thisbe in the *Metamorphoses*. As scholars have noticed, those two lovers resemble Romeo and Juliet more than Lysander and Hermia, as the barrier to their marriage is the hatred of their two rival families; they do share with the Athenian couple a plan to elope, which ends tragically when Pyramus commits suicide after mistakenly thinking Thisbe has been killed by a lion. Ovid's story is thus lamentable without being comic, but it's sure to become so in the hands of these players. It transpires that Bottom's theatrical ambitions know no bounds and want none, as he insists on playing several parts—a changeling, a metamorphosis-man, indeed. Shakespeare will leave him, and his colleagues, to their own devices until the third act of his own comedy, which few have lamented.

Other than beasts of prey, what else lives in the woods outside Athens? Fairies do. One of them, who "wander[s] every where" in the service of the Fairy Queen (II.i.6), derides Puck as the lout among the spirits, a "shrewd and knavish sprite" also known under the deceptive name of Robin Goodfellow, a trickster-spirit who delights in petty annoyance of rustic households—curdling cream, chipping dishes (II.i.33–34). Puck serves not the queen of the fairies but their king, which makes him no good fellow at all in the opinion of the queen's attendant. The royal couple are estranged. Queen Titania has angered King Oberon by taking into her entourage "a lovely boy, stolen from an Indian king" (II.i.22), whom he covets for himself. This makes the queen's attendant doubly dubious of the spirit who plays court jester to Oberon and does his bidding.

Oberon and Titania enter and quarrel, each jealous of the other's lover, real or imagined. Titania accuses Oberon of having caused climate change; the seasons themselves are mixed up, as Midsummer's Eve (the late-June night when fairy tricksters roam freely, tormenting honest human households) is coming in May, the month of lovers. She denies any love for the Indian boy, who is the orphan of a mortal friend of hers and now under her protection. In revenge, jealous and unbelieving Oberon plots with Puck to use an herbal potion which will cause Titania to fall in love with the first creature she sees upon awakening from her next sleep. The fairies live outside the city, in all the woods of the world, but they delight in pranking households in city and countryside; they also exercise some control over the nature in which they reside, a control that depends not on magic so much as knowledge of nature and a consequent ability to rule the minds of humans and fairies alike.

When the fairies depart, the humans wander in. Demetrius searches for Hermia and Lysander but can't shake Helena. "I love thee not, therefore pursue me not," he tells her, rather in contradiction of his own conduct toward Hermia (II.i.188). "Where is Lysander and fair Hermia? / The one I'll slay, the other slayeth me" (II.i.189–90). Helena is no less self-contradictory, in her own way, telling him her heart is "true as steel" (II.i.197), but then averring, "I am your spaniel," and "the more you beat me, I will fawn on you" (II.i.203–04)—completing the mixture of images by comparing herself to a deer pursuing a tiger and a dove pursuing a griffin. Demetrius' infidelity has caused this couple to be the one unnatural being in nature.

Oberon intends to fix that. He's listened in on their quarrel and decides to treat Demetrius with the same nature-cure he has in mind for Titania. He tells Puck to apply the herbal potion to Demetrius' eyes, even as he, Oberon, will apply it to hers. Since Puck has never seen Demetrius and Oberon doesn't know that there are any other Athenians in the woods, Oberon commands him to dose the next sleeping man he sees who wears "Athenian garments" (II.i.264). Puck mistakenly treats sleeping Lysander, who wakens, sees Helena, falls in love with her, and now determines to kill Demetrius, who had betrayed and insulted his new beloved. Completing the delusion, he announces that "the will of man is by his reason sway'd; / And reason says you," Helena, "are the worthier maid" (II.ii.115–16). When I was young, he continues, I was "ripe not to reason," but now "reason becomes marshal to my will" (II.ii.119–20). Lysander's bizarre change, and his even more bizarre explanation of it, makes sense to Helena only as mockery, an unjust attempt "to flout my insufficiency" (II.ii.128). She runs off; when Hermia awakens, she cries out, "What dream was here! / Lysander, look how I do quake with fear. / Methought a serpent eat my heart away, / And you sat smiling at his cruel prey" (II.ii.147–50). But Lysander has already left, chasing after Helena.

The would-be players have also entered the woods, probably to keep their wedding-ceremony performance a secret, as it would be too much to credit them with a prudent effort to spare civilization from their rehearsing. This enables Puck to transform Bottom's head into an ass's head (thus revealing Bottom's true nature), and to ensure that he will be the one Titania first sees in the morning. When she declares her love for him, the ass nonetheless speaks truer of reason than Lysander had done: "Methinks, mistress, you should have little reason for that. And yet, to say the truth, reason and love keep little company together now-a-days" (III.i.131–32). "Thou art as wise as thou art beautiful," Titania sighs, truly enough (III.i.135). Like many a mortal woman, she would take the one she loves and transform him into what she wants, promising to "purge thy mortal grossness" and to turn him into a spirit (III.i.146).

Oberon has accomplished his mission, with Puck's help, but Puck's mistake now comes to his master's attention: "Of thy misprision must perforce ensue / Some true love turned, and not a false turn'd true" (III.i.90–91). A trickster even when he doesn't intend to be, Puck can only appeal to the underlying rule of fate. No fatalist, Oberon acts to right matters, quickly, ordering Puck to find Helena and bring her here, then to apply the potion—compacted of a flower of "purple die," the royal color—to sleeping Demetrius (III.ii.102). Puck reconnoiters and returns, announcing the lady's imminent arrival, pursued by Lysander. He proposes more fairy sport: "Shall we their fond pageant see? / Lord, what fools these mortals be!" (II.ii.114–15). Oberon evidently doesn't mind toying with the mortal fools a bit, allowing the mad show to proceed. It will be a comedy of errors, with the fairies behaving like merry wives of Windsor.

Demetrius awakens at the noise, falls in love with Helena, who once again assumes that she's being mocked by both, who have conspired against her. "If you were civil and knew courtesy, / You would not do me thus much injury.... You both are rivals, and love Hermia; / And now both rivals, to mock Helena." (III.ii.147–48, 155–56). When Hermia catches up with them and Lysander rejects her for Helena, Helena simply assumes that even her former friend is in on "this confederacy" (III.ii.192), much to Hermia's bewilderment. But it is precisely the impossibility of civility in this woods that renders Helena's indignation vain. The moonlit woods are nature's darker side. At night, the woods are ruled by the fairies, who include trickster Puck, a trickster even when he faithfully follows the benevolent if imprecise commands of the Fairy King. Misdirected, the natural love potion brings out the worst nature of the human lover—Helena's timid and suspicious side, Demetrius' fickleness, Lysander's sharp temper, and Hermia's equally sharp temper, coupled with insecurity. (When Helena calls her a puppet, she takes it as a jibe at her shortness of stature, despite her acknowledged beauty). All these bring the two men to the edge of violence against each other, urged on by the women. Whether ginned up by herbal medicine or not, the passion of love itself matters less than who or what it's aimed at. [1]

Unlike his court jester, Puck, Lord Oberon has a fundamentally just nature, and now moves to intervene, Theseus-like, lest the comedy turn tragic. [2] "This is thy negligence," he tells Puck, unless you arranged this out of willful knavery (III.ii.345). Puck truthfully protests that he was only following a too-vague command, while admitting he's enjoyed the results. *Very well, then, what I can see clearly,* Oberon replies, *is the brewing fight, and you shall put a stop to it by calling for a black fog,* which "will lead these testy rivals so astray / As one come not within another's way" (III.ii.358–59). You will then dose Lysander with the herb, the "virtuous property" of which will remove from his eyes "all error" and "make his eyeballs roll with wonted sight" for his real love, Hermia (III.ii.367–69). "When they next awake, all this derision / Shall seem a dream and fruitless vision; / And back to Athens shall the lovers wend / With league whose date till death shall never end" (III.ii.370–73). Their natural loves restored, the lovers will be fit to re-enter civil society and marry. As for already-married Lord Oberon, "I'll to my queen, and beg her Indian boy; / And then I will her charmed eye release / From the monster's view, and all things shall be peace" (III.ii.375–77). Knowing better than to disobey his lord's command, and now knowing the man who is its object, Puck applies the juice to the eyes of sleeping Lysander, incanting a precept of natural right, "the country proverb known": "That every man should take his own, / In your waking shall be shown: / Jack shall have Jill; / Nought shall go ill" (III.ii.458–62). At his lord's direction, the trickster does the right thing, bridling his preference for misrule.

As the ruler of the night in nature, Oberon tempers his justice with mercy—very much in contrast to Duke Theseus, the ruler of the day in the city. Considering his Fairy Queen as she sleeps, he "begin[s] to pity" her "dotage" on the human ass (IV.i.44). Having already confronted her with the act of infidelity he had caused her to commit, then having exacted from her the Indian boy with whom he suspected of having committed real infidelity, and now with the boy transported to his own "bower in fairy land," he will release her from the delusive spell (IV.i.58). He chants: "Be as thou wast wont to be; / See as thou wast wont to see. / Dian's bud o'er Cupid's flower / Hath such force and blessed power" (IV.i.68–71). Invoking the chastity of moon-goddess Diana (which to follow would have given Hermia an unnatural life), Oberon restores the married queen of Fairy Land to her rightful place at the side of its king. He does so by restoring her natural sight, so that she will again recognize a human ass for a human ass. In symbolic terms, he restores her capacity for *noēsis*, for intellectual insight and, with it, the capacity for the right classification of natural beings. Upon awakening, Titania believes that the reality she experienced under the spell was only a vexatious dream, but Oberon immediately points to the sleeping Bottom. She wonders, questions—the beginning of wisdom, as a philosopher might say. Oberon, the one who can answer her question, has won the battle Theseus has already won over the Amazon queen, establishing his authority. He intends to "dance in Duke Theseus' house triumphantly" tomorrow night, "and bless it with all prosperity," as it will now see the weddings of "faithful lovers," lovers brought together then divided by Cupid, corrected by reason not law, and now prepared for a lifetime of Diana-like chastity under the bond of marriage, the bond of faithful and lawful love, the love that's right for civil society.

Daybreak impends. The night-rule of the fairies evanesces; the day-rule of Theseus returns. Theseus, Hippolyta, and Egeus have pursued the lovers into the woods, and now discover them. The youths have some explaining to do, and Lysander honestly relates what he and Hermia intended to do— much to the outrage of Egeus, who demands capital punishment under the ancient law. But Demetrius comes to his friend's defense. Oberon's royal potion has corrected his passion, restoring it to fidelity. By "some power" he does not know, "my love to Hermia, / Melted as the snow": "All the faith, the virtue of my heart, / The object and pleasure of mine eye, / Is only Helena. To her, my lord, / Was I betroth'd ere I saw Hermia. / But, like a sickness, did I loathe this food; / But, as in health, come to my natural taste" (IV.i.162–71). Oberon's herbal potion, his nature-cure, acted as a poison when Puck dosed the wrong person with it, but acted as a restorative, an agent returning the young man to his true nature, when applied to the right person, according to the reason of the just monarch-physician.

This is enough for Theseus. "Egeus, I will overbear your will," return to Athens, and bring the two couples, with himself and Hippolyta, to wed, exactly as Oberon had foreseen (IV.i.176). "Our purpos'd hunting," an act of what had seemed a just war, "shall be set aside" (IV.i.180).

On what grounds? Does Egeus not still have Athenian law on his side, the law that enforces fatherly authority over daughters?

Yes, but the duke had won his own beloved by overcoming the power of the Amazon queen's father's chastity belt. A wise and just ruler will enforce the laws of the city; but the initial sin, the one that deranged the civil order, was Demetrius' betrayal of his vow of betrothal. Egeus is attempting to enforce a law that does not justly apply to the circumstance, inasmuch as a violation of the suitor's legal oath invalidates the betrothal the father would impose. Theseus' ruling parallels that of Oberon. Just as Oberon corrected Puck's misapplication of the nature-cure, which works rightly only when given according to the circumstance, so Theseus applies his law-cure rightly by adjusting it to the circumstances at hand. Both natural and civil law require the reasoned, prudential rule of the statesman-judge who is there to see things for himself.

All are now awake, poor Bottom the last. "I have seen a rare vision," he tells himself. "I have had a dream, past the wit of man to say what dream it was. Methought I was—there is no man can tell what. Methought I was, and methought I had, but man is a patch'd fool, if he will offer to say what methought I had" (IV.203–08). His friend and fellow-player Peter Quince will write "a ballad of this dream. It shall be call'd 'Bottom's Dream,' because it hath no bottom" (IV.i.212–13). Wrong on all counts, Ass Bottom. The vision was no dream; the wit of man can explain it quite readily; the 'dream' has a bottom, and it is himself, his nature as a fool. He intends to sing the ballad over the dead body of Thisbe, at the end of his play at the wedding. In that one thing he's right, in his own goofy way, inasmuch as the song is a fitting coda for a lamentable comedy. He returns to Athens and to his worried friends, back in his right place, in his right role.

The next day, at the palace, Theseus and Hippolyta discuss the lovers' story. Theseus dismisses it. "I never may believe / These antique fables, nor these fairy toys. / Lovers and madmen have such seething brains, / Such shaping fantasies, that apprehend / More than cool reason ever comprehends" (V.3–7). "Lunatics, lovers, and poets are of imagination compact," making 'somethings' that are really 'nothings' out of nothing but their joys and fears (V.i.8). For her part, Hippolyta isn't so sure that the lovers' tale must be some midsummer night's dream. She considers the unanimity of the testimony, the unlikelihood that "all their minds transfigur'd so

together" (V.i.24). Reason, thought governed by the principle of non-contradiction, lends support to their story, however implausible its perceptual
premises may be. Less dogmatically 'rationalistic' than Theseus, she attends
to the preponderance of the evidence, and in terms of the play she is right.
After all, has the play's audience not witnessed the players? Have the onlookers not been transfigured together?

The governing irony, of course, is that this is Theseus conversing with
an Amazon queen—both figures in an antique fable, lately translated to a
London stage by a poet. Theseus, the mythological Athenian statesman,
here echoes Socrates' critique of poetry in the *Ion*. But he is no Socrates.
Acting together as the ruling couple of Athens, Hippolyta's socially-oriented
practical wisdom will supplement the political practice of Theseus, skeptical
of ancient tales and of ancient laws, inclined toward hasty generalization.
Theseus draws his practical wisdom from observation of human types; Hippolyta draws her practical wisdom from attending to opinion. Both kinds
are needed to rule well, and it is the playgoing audience that sees the whole
truth, with Shakespeare—the whole truth being indispensable in a law
court.

As Oberon answers Puck, so Theseus answers Hippolyta, by directing
attention away from the dubious and towards what's in front of their eyes—
in this case, the righted lovers, "full of joy and mirth" (V.i.28), after the
marriage ceremony. The wedding revelers have three hours until bedtime,
and in reviewing the several entertainments proffered, Theseus chooses
what's described as, "A tedious brief scene of young Pyramus / And his love
Thisby; very tragical mirth" (V.i.56–57). Rationalist as he is, he expects di-
version from such a self-contradictory show. When he learns that men who
have "never labor'd in their minds till now" will be the players (V.i.73), this
confirms him in his choice—not however because he wants to laugh at the
men who work with their hands, but because "never anything can be amiss
/ When simpleness and duty tender it" (V.i.83–84). He may not be a man
of theoretical wisdom, but he has a statesman's practical wisdom, earned
by observing men. "The kinder we, to give them thanks for nothing. / Our
sport shall be to take what they mistake; / And what poor duty they cannot
do, noble respect / Takes it in might, not merit"—that is, the intention of
the deed (V.i.89–92). This magnanimity is the opposite of Helena's and
Hermia's small-souled mindset, which had made mortal insults out of

trifles. Sure enough, in the prologue to the play-within-the play, Quince announces, "If we offend, it is with our good will" (V.i.108).

The workers' play parodies the regime of the woods, with the players as fairies without power. Lamentably comic Pyramus and Thisbe duly dispatch themselves, completing the laughable tragedy wherein no fairies rule the night by (in the end) wisely exerting the powers of nature. With kind irony, Theseus excuses Bottom from speaking an epilogue ("for your play needs no excuse") and thanks the players for their "notably discharged" effort (V.i.345, 350). He then bids the members of the wedding party to retire to their marriage beds—the end of comedy, even as graves are the end of tragedy. Without knowing it, the players have reminded the lovers of the bad turn their once-disordered love might have taken.

Theseus doesn't have the last word, however. That is left to the rulers of the night, who re-emerge when the married couples retire. Oberon and Titania chant blessings on them—"ever true in loving be" (V.i.397), their families' nature perfected. Puck speaks the epilogue/apologia Bottom did not need to offer, asking the audience's pardon for any offense "we shadows" may have give (V.i.412), and reminding them of the greater pardon all Christians enjoy; our "unearned luck / Now to scape the serpent's tongue," the same serpent that had threatened Hermia in her dream about Lysander's infidelity (V.i.421–22), but more immediately the hissing disapproval of an audience at the end of a bad play. As human beings depend on God's grace, so do the ruled depend upon the grace of the rulers, whether they are subjects of monarchs or players in front of playgoers who sit in judgment.

Although routinely regarded as a well-wrought farce, *A Midsummer Night's Dream* is as politic a comedy as Shakespeare ever wrote. A charming play about charms, it also shows how the loves of young lovers can and should be directed away from the impassioned fickleness of Demetrius while protected from the soul-deadening legalism of Egeus. That young love needs sound direction is easy to show, although not so easy to show to the young, who are the ones who need it, and sometimes difficult to show to the old, who try. This can be done by Shakespeare, whose comedies are love-potions applied to sleeping eyes, which he opens and directs to love the right kind of persons.

Notes

1. C. L. Barber isn't quite right in calling love in this play an "impersonal force beyond the persons concerned" (Barber: *Shakespeare's Festive Comedies*, Princeton: Princeton University Press, 1959, 130). The young are likely subject to it, but the mature (Theseus, Hippolyta, Oberon, Titania) can direct it rightly, even if one of them (Egeus) would misdirect it.

2. Barber cites Shakespeare's Puritan contemporary, Philip Stubbes, who regards Oberon as a Satan figure (Barber, op. cit., 119). As a Puritan, Stubbes inclines to regard all spirit-beings other than angels as devilish; in our time, many Christians in the Puritan tradition similarly frown over the antics of J.K. Rowling's Harry Potter, although C.S. Lewis and J.R.R. Tolkien usually get a pass. Shakespeare's woods, even in the moonlight, are still nature, not Hell. Oberon keeps Puck in check there.

PART TWO

THE RULE OF LAW

With the exception of some tyrannies, all regimes rule in part through the device of law, written or unwritten. Shakespeare's England famously did so. Shakespeare wrote two comedies first performed at the Inns of Court in London: The Comedy of Errors *and* Twelfth Night. *Law, judges, and lawyers serve as conduits between rulers and citizens or subjects, reinforcing regime principles in civil society. The intention is serious, although the results can often be funny.*

CHAPTER FOUR

COMIC ERRORS, LEGAL SLAPSTICK

Solinus, Duke of Ephesus, has handed down a judgment on Aegeon, a merchant from Syracuse. Ephesus and Syracuse are engaged in a trade war, very much with a vengeance. The Duke of Syracuse has been holding Ephesian merchants for ransom and executing the unredeemed. As "our well-meaning countrymen" (I.i.7) are being treated so cruelly, Duke Solinus has "excluded all pity" from his judgment of Aegeon (I.i.10): pay a heavy ransom by sundown or you will be put to death. It's nothing personal, but "By law thou art condemn'd to die" (I.i.25). As his name suggests, Solinus is a man alone—judge, jury, and executioner.

Why, Aegeon, did you come here in the first place? Perhaps hoping for some shred of mercy, and knowing that the law is against him, Aegeon readily explains himself, "that the world may witness that my end / Was wrought by nature, not by vile offense" (I.i.33–34). His wife, Aemilia, had given birth to identical twin sons—they "could not be distinguish'd but by names," by convention (I.i.53)—and he purchased twin boys from an indigent woman to serve as their slaves as both sets of twins grew up. Soon after, the family was sundered by a shipwreck in a storm; the wife, one son, and one slave were picked up by Corinthian fishermen; [1] Aegeon and the other two boys were picked up by a ship from Epidamnum. Before the family could be reunited, the Epidamnian rescuers were themselves shipwrecked on a rock. "In this unjust divorce of us, / Fortune had left to both of us alike / What to delight in, what to sorrow for" (I.i.105–07). By the time he and the boys were rescued a second time, he had no way to know where his wife and the other boys had been taken. [2]

When he reached the age of eighteen, his son "became inquisitive / After his brother" (I.i.126–27), begging Aegeon to allow him to search for him and for the brother of his slave. Aegeon agreed, though "hazard[ing]

the loss of whom I lov'd" (I.i.132). His son and his son's slave never returned, so Aegeon himself undertook a separate mission, which has now
extended to "five summers" in "farthest Greece" and Asia Minor (I.i.133).
He came to Ephesus in desperation, "loath to leave unsought…any place
that harbors men" (I.i/136–37). Aegeon has traversed the Aegean and beyond in search of his lost wife, sons, and slaves. His argument in self-de-
fense, then, is indeed that his "end" or purpose in coming to Ephesus was
natural (I.i.159): a husband and father's quest for the lost members of his
household. He evidently hopes that his appeal to nature will override the
appeal to law, to convention, in the mind of his judge.

Duke Solinus sympathizes but holds firm. He blames Aegeon's plight
on "the fates," not on Aegeon. If it were "not against our laws, / Against
my crown, my oath, my dignity, / Which princes, would they, may not dis-
annul, / My soul should sue as advocate for thee" (I.i.143–46). A "passed
sentence may not be recall'd / But to our honor's great disparagement"
(I.i.149), but I will do what I can, allowing you to seek ransom within the
limits of the city—a lesser, shorter, landlocked voyage, and one that "hope-
less and helpless" Aegeon will undertake "to procrastinate," as the convicted
man says of himself, "his lifeless end" (I.i.158–59). Friendless and unknown
in Ephesus, he has no way to raise the money.

In this scene, playgoers find neither comedy nor errors. They do find
the themes of *The Comedy of Errors*: the necessities of ruling a city—laws,
crown, oath of office, dignity and honor of the ruler—in conflict with the
family, with fatherly and brotherly love. The family is more natural than
the city (Aegeon's cross-border quest emphasizes this point), but the city
has its own real necessities, including the defense of fair commerce across
its borders and the need of rulers to uphold the law in order to be considered 'legitimate' in the eyes of those they rule. These are the themes of
tragedy, as seen in the *Antigone*. But Aegeon is no royal princess. As a merchant, he has no claim to consideration as a member of some monarchic
or aristocratic line, nor does he arouse suspicions as a rival for the throne.
As with Shakespeare's more famous merchant, the merchant of Venice, he
is 'low,' or at least lower than any ruler, a fit character for comedy.

The play was first performed for the Honourable Society of Gray's Inn,
one of the four Inns of Court in London. These were professional associa-
tions of barristers and judges; they also served as law schools. In

Shakespeare's time, Gray's Inn was the most prestigious of them, enjoying the patronage of Queen Elizabeth. At Christmastime, when *The Comedy of Errors* premiered, the students were allowed to rule the Inn for a day, electing a Lord of Misrule (an office for which any number might have been well-qualified). A comedy about law, its relation to nature and especially the problem of understanding evidence—ultimately the question of how we can know—would have been a timely means of inviting lawyers and judges to think about what they do, and to invite their students to think about what they will be doing.

Although Shakespeare's characters can never entirely rule the fates, Shakespeare as playwright does so rule, determining that the other searchers, Antipholus and Dromio of Syracuse, are also in Ephesus. Antipholus sends Dromio back to the Centaur, the inn where they are staying, with the money an Ephesian merchant had been holding for him, and now has returned. Syracusan Antipholus tells Dromio that he intends to "view the manners of the town, / Peruse the traders, gaze upon the building" (I.ii.12–13)—learn a thing or two about the Ephesian regime by studying its way of life. The kindly merchant advises him to tell people he's from Epidaurus, given the ban on Syracusans and the news that another Syracusan merchant has already been apprehended, tried, and condemned. When the merchant departs to attend to business, Antipholus soliloquizes, "I to the world am like a drop of water / That the ocean seeks another drop, / Who, falling there to find his fellow forth, / Unseen, inquisitive, confounds himself," "los[ing] myself" in his search for "a mother and a brother" (I.i.35–40). 'Pholus' means 'den' or 'lair' in Greek, 'leaf' or 'lightweight thing,' 'inconsequential thing' in Latin. *Anti*-pholus of Syracuse has no home, wishes he were not a mere drop of water in the ocean of the world.

When Dromio comes up to him, Antipholus takes him to be his slave, Syracusan Dromio, but in fact it's Dromio of Ephesus. Why have you returned so soon? Equally nonplussed, Ephesian Dromio tells him that he's late for noontime dinner; the mistress of the household is "hot" because "the meat is cold" (I.ii.47). Antipholus assumes that his ever-joking attendant is playing with him, but "I am not in a sportive humor now" (I.ii.58). "These jests are out of season" (I.ii.68). What did you do with my money? For continuing his presumptive charade by insisting that Antipholus is married and living at the Phoenix, not the Centaur, Esphesian Dromio earns a beating. Antipholus describes Ephesus as "a town full of cozenage," suspecting that some sleight-of-hand artist, or one of the local sorcerers "that change the mind," or one of the "soul-killing witches that deform the body," or one of the other "disguised cheaters, prating mountebanks" of the city has been at work (I.ii.97–101). He will return to the Centaur. "I greatly fear my money is not safe" (I.ii.106).

The man-beast, the centaur, was part wise man or prudent adviser to rulers, part warrior-cavalryman; the centaur symbolizes the man of the ancient world, the man of *logos* and *thumos*. The Phoenix, the bird that arises from its own ashes, symbolizes rebirth, the sun that rises after setting, and in Christendom the Son, the Man who rose from the tomb. In another play, Shakespeare uses it to symbolize the princess and future queen, Elizabeth, a sort of Christian goddess named after the mother of John the Baptist. Syracusan Antipholus is an 'ancient'; possibly Ephesian Antipholus will prove a Christian.

In Ephesian Antipholus' house, his wife Adriana and her sister Luciana await the return of husband and slave. Attempting to moderate Adriana's impatience, Luciana observes that "A man is master of his liberty" and time is the master of men (II.i.7). "Why should their liberty than ours be more?" Adriana indignantly demands (II.i.10). "Because their business still lies out o' doors" (I.i.11). This is true not only in a rural village but even in a trading city. Adriana is having none of that: When Luciana calls Antipholus "the bridle of your will," she riposte, "There's none but asses will be bridled so" (II.i.13–14). Luciana points to nature: beasts, fishes, and fowls of the wild all exhibit rule of males over females. "Man, more divine, the master of all these" creatures, "Lord of the wide world and wild wat'ry seas, / Indu'd with intellectual sense and souls, / Or more pre-eminence than fish and fowls / Are masters of their females, and their lords" (II.i.20–24). Therefore, "let your will attend their accords" (II.i.25). Like Aegeon, Luciana appeals to nature against the harshness of her sister's judgment of Antipholus.

Nothing doing, Adriana says in her rebuttal: *You, Luciana, are unwed, and the reason you stay that way is that you know the score; you don't want to be subjected to a man's rule. No, sister,* Luciana innocently replies; *rather, I take as my principle,* "Ere I learn to love, I'll practice to obey" (II.i.29). *Nonsense,* says Adriana: *If you do have a husband someday, your "fool-begg'd patience" will evaporate* (II.i.41).

Ephesian Dromio returns home, complaining that his master has boxed his ears and denied that he has a wife. "Too unruly deer," Adriana hastily concludes; "he breaks the pale, / And feeds from home" (II.i.100–101). Calling her a victim of "self-harming jealousy" (II.i.102), Luciana tells her that she has no real proof of her husband's infidelity, merely hearsay evidence. Only "unfeeling fools" think so, Adriana shoots back; "I know his eye doth homage otherwhere" (I.i.104). *On the contrary, you are the fool,* Luciana retorts; *you are maddened by jealousy.* 'Luciana' means 'light'; her reasonable patience has served her well, if not in the eyes of her sister, an Adriana in need of an Ariadne's thread. Her name means 'dark.' As both accuser and judge, Adriana commits the error of jumping to a false conclusion based on insufficient evidence.

Back in the marketplace, Syracusan Antipholus runs into 'his' Dromio, of whom he demands an explanation of his antic behavior—having pretended, as Antipholus assumes, not to know that he has received gold to be deposited at the Centaur, and claiming that his master is married. *I, Antipholus, have been entirely too indulgent of your jesting; this permitted familiarity has bred contempt in you.* ("Your sauciness will jest upon my love" [II.ii.280]). So he beats him.

Loyal Syracusan Dromio protests, "Was there any man thus beaten out of season, / When in the why and wherefore is neither rhyme or reason?" (II.ii.47–48) he asks, rhyming and reasoning in his rhetorical question. Well, then, servant, "learn to jest in good time; there's a time for all things" (II.ii.63–64). To rhyme, to harmonize with the mood of the audience, jokes must be rightly timed, well-reasoned in their placement.

Hearing the word 'time' in this statement of comedic principle, Dromio finds the thread to follow that will lead his master out of his mood. Father Time is bald. Hair is "a blessing that [Time] bestows on beasts, and what he hath scanted men in hair he hath given them in wit"—the source of all their rhyming and their reasoning (II.ii.79–80). "I knew t'would be a bald conclusion," Antipholus sighs, concluding the repartee with his fool. Like Adriana, Syracusan Antipholus judges hastily, but unlike her, he relents in good humor.

Another error-in-the-making arises with the entrance of Adriana and Luciana, looking for Ephesian Antipholus and finding his Syracusan twin. Adriana rebukes her putatively unfaithful husband. "If we two be one, and thou play false, / I do digest the poison of thy flesh, / Being strumpeted by the contagion" (II.ii.141–43). That is, reasoning from the Christian doctrine that the husband and wife are "one flesh," she must be a strumpet if he is a philanderer. Both sets of twins are of one flesh, but by nature rather than divinely instituted matrimony. Adriana's error consists of mistaking the nature of her husband and compounding the error by her consequent misapplication of true, rightly understood religious doctrine. [3] Indeed, even her theology is misappropriated, since adultery would make her a cuckold, not a strumpet; such a charge does fuel her indignation, however, and that seems to be what a thumotic soul is inclined to do. Her anger makes her 'mad,' irrational even as she tries to reason.

All of this lands Antipholus in an epistemological crisis. "What, was I married to her in my dream? / Or sleep I now, and think I hear all this? / What error drives our eyes and ears amiss? / Until I know this sure uncertainty / I'll entertain the offer'd fallacy" (II.ii.181–85). When the only certain thing is uncertainty, the reasonable person will test the claim made immediately in front of him; in this, Syracusan Antipholus resembles Luciana. Less rational, more superstitious, slavish Dromio can only exclaim and fear: "This is fairy land…. We walk with goblins, owls, and sprites, / If we obey them not, this will ensue: They'll suck our breath, or punch us black and blue" (II.ii.188–91). Both men question their self-knowledge, their identities, knowing themselves somehow transformed, but not knowing how. As they don't know who they are, they equally know not where they are: "Am I in earth, in heaven, or in hell?" (II.ii.211) Antipholus asks. He remains 'all at sea,' even when on land. For her part, raging Adriana simply assumes that they mock her.

Act One began with the harsh but necessary consequences of rule. These appeared tragic, and they might yet become so. Act Two introduces a new and comic path. 'Dromio' or the Latin *dromus* means 'path'; comedy takes the 'low' or slavish path. That path will have its twists, but they might be understood either in reason or in fear, either in the way of the master or the way of the slave. Comedy is philosophic, looking to correct the error or confusion caused in the human soul by appearances that convention, nature, or chance places in front of it. Philosophy thus takes the slavish path—which is why 'aristocratic' Nietzsche demanded that it be made tragic.

Ephesian Antipholus arrives in front of his house with Angelo, a gold-smith, and Balthazar, a merchant. Antipholus asks Angelo to make excuses for him with his wife, to tell her that Antipholus' delay in coming home was caused by lingering in the goldsmith's shop as Angelo put the finishing touches on a gold necklace for her. Dromio catches up with his master. He is still smarting from the beating he received from Syracusan Antipholus, an act his master denies having done, taking his slave to have been drunk and delusional. Dromio can only say, "I know what I know" (III.i.11). When it comes to knowledge, his physical experience, his sense-perceptions, cannot give way to his master's authority; *in extremis*, brute nature must prevail, at least in the 'low' mind of the slave.

The minds of both master and slave then confront a more immediate problem, a problem of ruling authority. When Dromio seeks to enter the house, Syracusan Dromio denies entry to him, then to his indignant master. "O villain," Ephesian Dromio sputters, "thou hast stol'n both my office and my name" (III.i.44). Hearing the commotion, Adriana comes and also denies entry to these fellows, whom she cannot see from behind the door. Perhaps suspecting that his wife entertains another man—we know he is not wrong!—Antipholus would like to break that door down. Balthazar prevails upon him to be patient, citing his wife's "sober virtue, years, and modesty" (III.i.90); otherwise, Antipholus will injure his own reputation by 'making a scene.' *Let us withdraw and dine at The Tiger*, and not insist on dining with (what Balthazar does not suspect is) the tigress within. A hungry man is a cranky one, so let him eat elsewhere, then return in the evening alone, "To know the reason of this strange restraint" (III.i.97). Balt-hazar has learned the lesson of his biblical namesake: Prudent caution may prevent anyone from writing ominous handwriting on the wall.

Antipholus prefers to dine at The Porpentine and to give the necklace to the hostess there, a genial courtesan who evidently treats him better than his wife does. "I shall do this, be it for nothing to spite my wife" (III.i.118), who has "sometimes upbraided me" in the past (III.i.113). This raises the question of exactly what did delay Antipholus' return home for noontime dinner. Legend has it that if you get too close to a porpentine it will shoot its quills at you. Antipholus risks a sticking.

They leave; next, Luciana reproves and advises the man she mistakes for her sister's husband, whose denial of his marriage vow has made her assume his infidelity. If you married my sister for her wealth, then "for her wealth use her with more kindness" (III.ii.6); if you "like elsewhere," then at least disguise yourself by being "secret-false" (III.ii.15). The sin of infidelity is bad enough; do not compound it with brazenness. Having no idea of what she's going on about, but having fallen in love with her, Syracusan Antipholus protests, "Your weeping sister is no wife of mine" (III.ii.42). Calling her a siren, he willingly succumbs to the sound of her voice, proposing marriage on the spot. Luciana can only say, "What, are you mad, that you do reason so?" (III.ii.43). Reasoning based on a true premise can only seem irrational to one who reasons from a false premise.

Syracusan Dromio comes out of the house, fleeing a kitchen-wench who has mistaken him for Ephesian Dromio and claimed him as her beloved. The wench is dirty, ugly, fat, and sweaty, the slave reports, his slavishness not having impeded his sense of esthetics. Like his brother, Syracusan Dromio knows by means of his sense impressions. Worse, Nell makes her own claim to sense-knowledge, as she knows all his birthmarks. What can Dromio make of this? Only an explanation that reaches beyond his senses: "I, amaz'd, ran from her as if a witch" (III.ii.142).

That does it. At this point, Antipholus the Syracusan just wants to get out of town. He too now believes the stories about Ephesus. "There's none but witches do inhabit here, / And therefore 'tis high time that I were hence, / She that doth call me husband, even my soul / Doth for a wife abhor," but her sister's "sovereign gentle grace" and "enchanting presence and discourse, / Hath almost made me a traitor to myself" (III.ii.178–79). Odysseus-like, "I'll stop my ears against the mermaid's song" (III.ii.161).

To top off his confusion, Angelo now appears, necklace in hand, mistaking him for Ephesian Antipholus, who had told him to bring it by his house. Syracusan Antipholus chooses to grasp the reality he sees, taking the necklace on the grounds that "there's no man so vain"—so empty of common sense—"that would refuse so fair an offer'd chain" (III.ii.178–79). Like his slave, his sense of esthetics (in this case his love of beauty rather than his repulsion from ugliness) rules him. That gold chain will turn into an iron chain, soon enough.

The comedy of the central, third act of the play amplifies the problem of knowledge. What counts as true evidence, and how can one reason from it? I know what I know when I'm driven to that knowledge by sheer physical evidence. Ephesian Dromio is right in knowing what he knows, that way. But the knowledge needed to rule well, including the knowledge needed to judge, is trickier. Appearances are deceptive, often confused by the need to know motives, which are not sensually perceivable, and by the ruler's need to keep up appearances, for authority's sake. To achieve knowledge, a rule needs more indirect ways of approaching than a box on the ears. Love, and especially married love, faces the same problem. What is the real nature of my beloved? Does the jealousy engendered by a suspicion of my beloved's violation of marital vows, according to the laws of the city, not preclude me from knowing, or at least interfere with it?

Act IV begins in "a public place," where merchant Angelo and an officer of the law discuss how to obtain payment for the gold chain Angelo gave to Syracusan Antipholus, under the erroneous assumption that he was his Ephesian twin. Angelo needs the money now, as he owes money to another merchant, who is about to leave for Persia on business. Angelo proposes that they go to Antipholus' house to collect the payment.

But no need: Ephesian Antipholus and his Dromio happen by, having dined with the courtesan at The Porpentine. Antipholus sends Dromio to buy a rope, with which he intends to whip "my wife and her confederates" as punishment for locking him out (IV.i.18). Antipholus complains to Angelo that he hasn't received the chain. Judging him a cheat, Angelo has him arrested: "I shall have law in Ephesus" (IV.i.84)—law being indispensable to any commercial society, the defender of property rights. When Syracusan Dromio comes along and reports that the ship is about to depart from Ephesus, Ephesian Antipholus has no idea what he's talking about, but orders him to go to Adriana to get bail money. The slave can only sigh, "Thither I must, although against my will, / For servants must their masters' minds fulfill" (IV.i.113–14). There, Luciana has been telling her of Syracusan Antipholus' love-suit, confirming Adriana's suspicions concerning her husband's character. Dromio arrives and gets the bail money, along with a command from the enraged wife to bring her husband home, where she plans some punishment of her own devising.

Syracusan Antipholus has been walking through the market, marveling at the warm reception he has received from people he's never seen before. "There's not a man I meet but doth salute me / As if I were their well-acquainted friend" (IV.iii.1–2). 'Knowing' that Ephesian men are crooks, even as he now 'sees' that the women are witches and sorceresses, he decides that these must be "imaginary wiles," possibly sorcerers' lures (IV.iii.10–11). Syracusan Dromio now offers him the bail money, which Ephesian Antipholus had told him to bring. Antipholus assumes that his slave has gone mad. He's not the only one: "The fellow is distract, and so am I; / And here we wander in illusions / Some blessed power deliver us from hence!" (IV.iii.37–38). Evil spirits have deranged their minds and senses. With no natural explanation at hand, he can only pray for divine salvation.

So, when the courtesan comes up to him and asks him for the necklace he'd promised her, Antipholus takes her for the Devil, or maybe a sorceress. At dinner, his twin had accepted her ring as a token of amity; since Antipholus won't give her the necklace, she demands that he give it back. "I hope you do not mean to cheat me so" (IV.iii.73), the injured, innocent courtesan remarks. At this, the men flee in horror. The courtesan deems him mad—"else would he never so demean himself" (IV.iii.78). She will go to his house and report his misbehavior to his wife.

Thus Syracusan Antipholus and Dromio explain the inexplicable spiritually and seek spiritual assistance to escape the city, in pre-Christian anticipation of the yearning to escape the wicked City of Man for the safety of the City of God. For her part, the courtesan explains the inexplicable in terms of nature and seeks material satisfaction from the wife who might well suspect a courtesan of being her rival.

The officer of the law is leading Ephesian Antipholus away when Ephesian Dromio returns with the rope, instead of the bail money his master now needs a lot more. Another beating, along with more comic whining, ensue. Adriana, Luciana, and the courtesan find them; they've brought with them Pinch the Schoolmaster, who pronounces master and slave alike to be mad, and proposes to exorcize Satan from their bodies. When Antipholus complains of having been locked out of his own house, this only confirms the diagnosis. For his part, Antipholus calls his wife a "dissembling harlot," guilty of entertaining another man while leaving her husband outside (IV.iv.48). The real courtesan, along with his wife and sister-in-law, have him bound, along with his slave, but the officer of the law objects: "The debt he owes will be required of me," the bailiff. As might be expected, Adriana remains inflexible and orders her supposed husband to be carted home. When the officer tells her that Antipholus owes money to the goldsmith, she stops, saying, *bring me to him.* "I long to know the truth hereof at large" (IV.iv.140).

The Syracusans arrive, swords drawn. In the *Odyssey*, Hermes teaches Odysseus how to counter Circe's spell over his men, whom she has changed into swine. Hermes digs up the root of the moly plant and shows him its nature—the first known mention of the word 'nature' in Western literature. A concoction of moly will reverse the effects of the witch's potion; that is, nature will 're-nature' the men who have been de-natured, metamorphosed into animals. The god also tells him that sorcerers and sorceresses must be routed with swords. Confirming the truth of the Syracusans' error, the women and Pinch flee; indeed, they must be so many witches, the Syracusans imagine. "I see these witches are afraid of swords," Antipholus tells Dromio (IV.iv.145), reprising the experience of his distinguished predecessor in questing on the wine-dark sea.

The fifth act begins with Angelo and the merchant in front of a priory. Perhaps taking his words from their surroundings, Angelo assures his creditor that Antipholus enjoys "a most reverend reputation" in Ephesus—his "credit infinite," the man himself "highly beloved" (V.i.6). A saint among merchants. When the Syracusans walk by, Angelo's faith is put to a test more severe than he can bear; there is the chain around Antipholus' neck, the very chain "he foreswore most monstrously to have" (V.i.11). Accused by both men, Antipholus indignantly protests, "Thou art a villain to impeach me thus"; he challenges the merchant to a duel (V.i.29).

Before the men can do any injury to one another in this contest of mercantile honor, the women arrive. The priory evidently affects Adriana's language, too: "Hold, hurt him not, for God's sake! He is mad." (V.i.33). She orders husband and slave to be bound again and returned to the house. They run into the priory to request sanctuary. The Abbess soon emerges. Hearing Adriana's lament, initially she reproves her for being insufficiently severe in chiding her husband for his supposed adultery, then reverses herself and criticizes her for being too severe: "The venom clamors of a jealous woman / Poisons more deadly than a mad dog's tooth" (V.i.69–70). Against Adriana's claim of demonic possession, the Abbess offers a naturalistic explanation: unquiet meals lead to indigestion, and fire in the stomach causes madness. ("What's a fever but a fit of madness?") (V.i.76). In addition, sexual deprivation causes melancholy, that "kinsman to grim and comfortless despair," which, in consort with the wife's deprivation of her husband's "life-preserving rest," causes "a huge infectious troop of pale distemperatures and foes to life" (V.i.80–82). Convinced that she can care for Antipholus better than Adriana can, she refuses to release him. She will "bring him to his wits again" (V.i.91), in keeping with "a charitable duty of my order" (V.i.107). Given her diagnosis of madness as an illness caused by bad food, sexual deprivation, and nagging, one might be forgiven for suspecting that her interest in the gentleman is less a matter of *caritas* than of *eros*–even if, as it will be seen, she's old enough to be his mother. Adriana has lost her husband to another woman, after all—not a courtesan but a nun, and an abbess, at that.

As comic fortunes would have it, along come the Duke of Ephesus and his doomed prisoner, Aegeon, heading for the gallows. Not one to let a crisis go to waste, Adriana interrupts the solemn procession, demanding justice against the Abbess. The Duke agrees to investigate, and a quasi-judicial inquiry begins. A messenger then arrives with the news that Antipholus has broken free from the house, not before delivering some humiliating punishments to meddlesome Pinch. But no, Adriana insists, he just went into the priory. When her real husband and his real slave do arrive, the vexed lady can only shout, switching now from spiritual to legal language, "Ay me, it is my husband! Witness you / That he is borne about invisible / Even now we hous'd him in the abbey here, / And now he's there, past thought of human reason" (V.i.186–89).

For his part, Ephesian Antipholus also demands justice—against his termagant of a wife. Citing his faithful wartime service to the Duke as evidence of his character, he charges that the woman "whom thou gav'st to me to be my wife" has "abused and dishonored me" with her false charges (V.i.198–99). He delivers a detailed explanation of the affair of the necklace and the payment, followed by his illegal house arrest. After further witness testimony, the Duke delivers his verdict: "I think you all have drunk of Circe's cup" (V.i.270), that "you are all mated"—that is, bewildered—"or stark mad" (V.i.281). An equal-opportunity explainer, the Duke is quite willing to entertain spiritual or natural causes for their behavior; for all he can see, they might be bewitched, bothered, and/or bewildered. And indeed they all are mated—not only bewildered but related to one another by blood or marriage, and by error.

Aegeon mistakes his Ephesian son and slave for the Syracusan son and slave he saw five years ago. The Antipholus in front of him says, "I never saw my father in my life" (V.i.318), and the Duke, who knows Antipholus has been in Ephesus for many years, takes the old man to be senile. When the Abbess comes out of the priory with the Syracusans, Adriana reacts with, "I see two husbands, or my eyes deceive me" (V.i.330). But she only sees one husband, and it is her mind that deceives her, not her eyes. The Duke has recourse to the spiritual realm, taking "one of these men" to be "genius to the other" (V.i.331). "But which is the natural man, / And which the spirit? Who deciphers them?" (V.i.332–33). If Pinch were there, he would claim such a power of discernment, but he evidently remains indisposed, back at the house.

The Syracusans recognize their father immediately. Having questioned them, the Abbess reveals herself as Aemilia, Aegeon's wife. 'Aemilia' means 'rival,' and she did indeed become the rival of her unbeknownst daughter-in-law over possession of her son, now restored to both women in his rightful stature in name (to his mother) and in law (to his wife). Aemilia had been separated from her children, first from the twin raised by her husband in Syracuse but also from the twin she had saved, who had been ripped away from his mother by some "rude fishermen of Corinth," who boarded the Epidamnumian ship which had rescued mother, son, and slave (V.i.348). Fishers of men, indeed. "Thereupon these errors are arose," Syracusan Antipholus now sees (V.i.387).

The Duke tells Ephesian Antipholus he will pardon his father. Before, he was steadfast in enforcing the rule of law. What has changed?

Although he now has much more convincing evidence that Aegeon's story is true, that need not be dispositive. The law is still the law; Ephesus remains in a trade war with Syracuse, which as far as he knows continues to abuse Ephesian merchants. But now he knows that Aegeon's son is not only the merchant respected and even loved throughout the city, but a man to whom he owes a debt of gratitude for his military service to that city. The debts that Antipholus has asked him to repay by prosecuting Adriana (who has suffered and, presumably, been chastened enough) will now be discharged by pardoning the father.

"Thirty-three years have I but gone in travail / Of you, my sons," Aemilia tells them (V.i.399–400). "And till this present hour / My heavy burden ne'er deliver'd" (V.i.400–01). Thirty-three years, Christ's lifespan, has indeed brought them to being born again, in their parents' eyes. They retire to the priory. Syracusan Antipholus reminds Luciana of his suit, now known to be legitimate. Beleaguered Ephesian Antipholus and his much-agitated wife might reconcile. The two Dromios, however, leave the audience in doubt. After a short discussion of who should precede the other on the basis of prior birth, Ephesian Dromio settles the matter on the basis of natural equality: "We came into this world like brother and brother, / And now let's go hand in hand, not one before the other" (V.i.423–24).

In this Christmastime play for lawyers, judges, and law students, Shakespeare gives his audience the laughs they want, in a sort of Three-Stooges-meet-Rumpole-of-the-Bailey slapstick farce. He nonetheless gives them something to think about—assuming they can recall what they've witnessed after their revelries are over.

Law, Shakespeare reminds them, contrasts with both nature and mercy, the criterion of the 'ancients' and the criterion of the Christians. To apply the law rightly, the judge needs to take account of fortune, producer of the circumstances which, as the saying goes, alter cases. Law may override fortune in the sense that it can correct the 'errors' or injustices fortune metes out, compensating bilked creditor, punishing scammers, all in defense of the commerce and property the city was founded to protect. The judge (or, in the case of a married couple, both spouses) must coordinate the exigencies of law, the reason that understands nature, and the divine example of mercy, without disregarding the political necessity of maintaining respect for law, for the judges who decide cases under them, and the regime of the city which enacts the laws. Judges, political and familial, must also recognize that commerce in the city and 'commerce' in the household requires fidelity and trust, always at hazard if either is misplaced and a violation of civil or marital law occurs.

How, then, is a judge to judge rightly? What counts as evidence? What is knowledge? "Know the reason," Balthazar advises, but that proves easier said than done. Presented with baffling, contradictory evidence, logic not fallacy is the first prerequisite, Adriana's jealous passion precludes logic. And even if the reasoning is sound, one still needs to establish right premises for one's syllogisms.

For that, Shakespeare builds on the fact that English lawyers had won the separation of the common law from canon law, centuries earlier. But the boundary needs to be guarded by its inheritors, his audience, as human beings tend to violate it. Do not, then, assume that witches and demons are the cause of apparently irrational behavior, as indeed Puritans did and would continue to do, during and after Shakespeare's lifetime. Dreaming and madness may be regarded as spiritually or naturally caused, but they too may not be causes of the events at issue in the courtroom. Drunkenness and passion may or may not be the cause of the behavior you are considering. The passion of jealousy, in particular—a deformation of the love of one's own—ruins good judgment, whether confined to the family or in the city at large. Even sense-perception, the most nearly self-evident form of knowledge, can mislead, as it needs to be interpreted correctly.

Judgment can mean life or death, as the play's first act establishes. It can mean the continuance of a marriage or its dissolution, with the right rule or the ruin of a family at hazard. It can mean the protection or loss of property which, along with family, determines the prosperity or destruction of a city. There being no such thing as being 'non-judgmental' when it comes to human choices, and especially rulers' choices, there can be no evading these matters.

The Comedy of Errors has Shakespeare's judges of family and city saved from their own hasty judgments based upon false premises. They learn the true premise the Socratic way, by testing the various stories they hear against one another, by finding the rationally coherent overall story that accounts for each piece of each person's narrative—the comprehensive argument that encompasses all the others in a non-contradictory way.

Shakespeare also invites his audience at Gray's Inn to reflect on what the law they apply to cases protects. Fundamentally, the common law reflects the natural human love of one's own. That love can be rightly or wrongly directed. In the family, the husband and wife have property in one another; a degree of jealousy properly registers that right, but extreme jealousy violates and undermines it. Parents and children rightly love one another, but incest (hinted at, comically, when the Abbess temporarily appropriates a man who turns out to be her son from his wife) perverts that love. In civil society, property sustains life, liberty, and happiness; we are right to love it. But loving it too much is covetousness and greed, leading to theft and cheating. One's country deserves just love, patriotism, seen most simply in the human longing for a homeland. It also can be abused, sometimes provoking trade wars. Attorneys, judges, and law students should stay alert for the manifestations of all these sentiments and passions.

This being a comedy, the story ends happily. The parents who were divorced by fortune operating on nature's most 'fortuitous' element, the often-chaotic sea, renew their marriage. Syracusan Antipholus, who begins as a self-described drop of water in that sea, a person of no consequence with no family and no real homeland, an Odysseus with neither an Ithaca nor a Penelope to come home to, finds a likely wife in a city where his new-found brother already enjoys credit and standing. Ephesian Antipholus, a husband with a shrewish wife who understandably distrusts him but lets her jealousy run wild, giving neither herself nor her husband a proper home, defends himself at the bar of both wife and fellow-citizens; he may yet find stability in a household in which the Christian-Ephesian precepts of wifely submission and husbandly love complement one another. Luciana, an eligible young lady with no suitor, a respectable woman and too much so, over-committed to upholding appearances (to the extent of having instructed her future husband on how to conduct an extramarital affair—an error indeed), now has the prospect of a marriage in which the reality will need no such hypocrisy.

As for the slaves, Shakespeare gives the last word to Ephesian Dromio, his master's partner in advancing toward Phoenix-like rebirth. He is the one who coordinates the natural relation of brotherliness with the spiritual relation of equality before God, before entering God's kingdom insofar as it lives on earth, in the priory where Aemilia found refuge from the chaos of the sea.

Notes

1. Corinth and Epidamnum: Corinth evokes the Apostle Paul's letter to the Corinthians, with its teaching on Christian love and salvation; Epidamnus looks like a pun on 'damnation,' the judgment Christian love and salvation prevent.
2. It is unlikely to be a coincidence that the Apostle Paul states this doctrine in his letter to the church in this city, Ephesus. Writing of the Church, he explains, "We are members of [Christ's] body, of his flesh, and of his bones. For this cause shall a man leave his father and mother, and shall be joined unto

his wife and they two shall be one flesh.... Let every one of you in particular so love his wife even as himself; and the wife see that she reverence her husband." (Ephesians V.30–33).

3.   The story of Circe's cup, the potion which transformed Odysseus' crew into pigs, had accumulated at least two traditions before Shakespeare's time that he has appropriated. It was said to be a cautionary tale against drunkenness, a condition often associated with sailors; recall that drunkenness had been one of the explanations offered for bizarre behavior here. Circe had also become a traditional figure of female jealousy. Ovid tells the story of Glaucus, enamored of the nymph, Scylla, who asks the sorceress for a love potion. When Circe falls in love with him and he refuses her advances, in her jealous rage she turns him into a monster.

CHAPTER FIVE
WHAT WILL YOU?

Like *The Comedy of Errors*, *Twelfth Night* was first performed for lawyers, judges, and law students at the Inns of Court—this time at the Honourable Society of the Middle Temple, formerly the home of the Knights Templar. And again the performance occurred during Christmastide; Twelfth Night is the final night of the Christmas season, Epiphany Eve. Following the star never seen before, three Wise Men visited Jesus in the manger at Bethlehem, knelt, and prayed, bearing witness for the first time to the manifestation of God incarnate to the Gentiles.

Subtitled "What You Will," the play suggests a departure from lawful sobriety, and its heroine describes Feste the Clown as a man who aims to please his audience. Aiming to please, as Shakespeare too must, requires a certain kind of prudence, a knowledge of one's audience and of 'how far to go' with all the elements of a performance, especially if legal restrictions have been relaxed, no longer providing discernible guidance. Not the least of these elements will be what you intend to tell them. A principal character in the play is called "Malvolio," which means 'bad will.' This raises the question of whether "what you will" is good or bad. That goes for the audience, the playwright, and the playwright's characters alike. Unmoored from the law, who or what will rule them? Will they become "Lords of Misrule"?

Shakespeare sets his comedy in Illyria and the seacoast "near it." As almost always in the comedies, he infuses his place and the people in it with certain English and Christian characteristics. His comedies are not 'history plays.' Fact and fancy mingle in them—another departure from restriction.

Orsino, Duke of Illyria commands his musicians, "If music is the food of love, play on, / Give me the excess of it, that, surfeiting, / The appetite may sicken and so die" (I.i.1–3). Twelfth Night, to be followed by Lent, similarly invites over-feasting as a physical and psychic preparation for the starvation to come. The Duke claims to want a cure for love, but, then,

70

love cures itself, he says, like a river flowing into the sea, its velocity moderated as its waters drown in the larger body. He loves Olivia, a wealthy countess, who considers his suit coldly; better, then, to stop loving her. This play for lawyers initially has little directly to do with the law, but it begins with a suit—not a lawsuit but a love-suit. Trials and tests or temptations will follow. Unlike a lawsuit, a love-suit between adults (indeed rulers) has no third-party judge. Unlike court musicians and attendants, and unlike parties in front of a judge, the one who is beloved may not obey her lover's command.

This becomes evident when the Duke's attendant, Curio, asks "Will you go hunt, my lord?"—specifically, "the hart" (I.i.16,18). Yes, the Duke replies, picking up on the pun. He hunts "the noblest" heart he knows, the heart of the Countess Olivia (I.i.19). But the hart-hunt is coercive, ending in the death of the deer, whereas the successful heart-hunt must preserve the life—more, win the consent of the beloved, win her heart the hunter chases. "What you will" for a lover wooing his beloved, and for a playwright wooing his audience, is a phrase that poses a more difficult challenge than it does for a ruler in firm command of his regime or a hunter in search of his prey.

What is Olivia's will? A courtier named Valentine enters to report that Olivia mourns her dead brother and will not leave her house for seven years. This only makes the Duke the more in love with her, admiring such loyalty, such steadfast love of her brother. How much more intensely, then, will she love "when the rich golden shaft / Hath kill'd the flock of all affections else / That live in her" (I.i.35–37). The Duke wants no Lent in his loving, after all. And insofar as he does (mis)conceive of his quest as a hunt, hoping to seize his beloved's heart, he verges on tyranny, without intending to.

The next scene shifts to the Illyrian seacoast, where a woman, a sea captain, and some sailors have survived a shipwreck. Viola's brother, Sebastian, was on board, now unaccounted for. A man of "courage and hope," in his sister's estimation (I.ii.13), like Arion on the dolphin's back he bound himself to a mast, and so may have survived. The bard Arion jumped off a ship to escape sailors who wanted to murder him, then so enchanted a school of dolphins with his music that they carried him to safety. Does Sebastian too have enemies? And whom will he enchant? With what music?

Viola exhibits an aristocrat's political awareness, wanting to know not only what country this is but "who governs here" (I.ii.24); an Illyrian by birth, the captain knows the story of Olivia, too—how her father and brother both died in the past year, and how the "virtuous maid" is beloved of Duke Orsini. ("What great ones do the less will prattle of" [i.ii.33], he rightly remarks.) Unlike Viola, who doesn't know what the status of her own "estate" is, given the question of her brother's survival, Olivia already knows of her brother's death. Ostensibly on account of it, she has "abjur'd the company / And sight of men" (I.ii.40–41). Both women are still 'at sea' respecting their future estates, albeit in different ways. Observing that "nature with a beauteous wall / Doth oft close in pollution, yet of thee," Captain, "I will believe thou hast a mind that suits / With this thy fair and outward character" (I.ii.48–51). Viola will confide in him and request his assistance. She would like to become Olivia's servant until her own circumstances "mellow" (I.ii.43)—that is, come to fruition, ripen. In the meantime, she asks that the Captain present her to the Duke. She will disguise herself as a eunuch, neither a threat nor (as she expects) a temptation to anyone. She can sing, she says, "speak to him in many sorts of music" (I.ii.58), in keeping with her musical name. Unknowingly, then, she will be able to feed his appetite for love.

At Olivia's house, her uncle, Sir Toby Belch, and Maria, her waiting woman, quarrel over his conduct, and Olivia's. Sir Toby criticizes the Countess's extended period of mourning, being "sure care's an enemy of life" (I.ii.2). Maria says that she and Olivia disapprove of the late hours he keeps: "You must confine yourself within the modest limits of order" (I.ii.7–8). What is more, Sir Toby's choice for Olivia's suitor, one Sir Andrew Aguecheek, is a fool and a prodigal, to which charge the knight replies that he has "all the good gifts of nature" (I.iii.25).

Two conceptions of nature: the good nature Viola sees in the Captain, which the Captain sees in the Duke and the Countess; the 'capable' nature of Sir Andrew, whom Sir Toby praises for knowing languages and playing musical instruments, for being tall, and for his future wealth. Maria is unimpressed with Sir Andrew's prospects; being a fool, quarrelsome, and also a coward (which, "allow[s] the gust he hath in quarreling") (I.iii.29), he will soon be parted from the money he inherits. When the controversial Sir Andrew arrives, he estimates his chances of winning Olivia to be poor, despite (or perhaps because) "I have no more with than a Christian or an ordinary man has" (I.iii.79–80). More, since she refuses the Duke's suit, why would she notice me at all? Because, Sir Toby explains, she's told me "she'll not match above her degree, neither in estate, years, nor wit" (I.iii.103). *You, Sir Andrew, are suitably beneath her. And you know how to dance; show that off, and you might win her.* There is considerable truth in this absurdity. "What I like about you is, you really know how to dance" was an entirely plausible pop-song lyric in the United States, decades ago. Olivia may well attend to a more refined music than that; if so, she's unlikely to be impressed by Sir Andrew's tallness, linguistic fluency, musical talent, and ability to gyrate. But there are those who would be, and how can her real nature be known if untested? As it happens, however, Sir Toby only encourages Sir Andrew's suit because he's amused by the man's folly, and because in his prodigality Sir Andrew supplies Sir Toby with a ready flow of money.

Back at the palace, the Duke's gentleman-attendant Valentine converses with Viola in the guise of Cesario, an assumed name that suggests one who, having come and seen, will conquer. Valentine assures Cesario that the Duke is not "inconstant in his favors" (I.iv.6). The Duke comes in and commands Cesario to go to Olivia's house and insist upon an audience. "Be clamorous and leap all civil bounds" (I.iv.20), even as Sir Toby does, in his drunken carousing. When admitted, "unfold the passion of my love" (I.iv.13); if you convince her to reverse her intention, "thou shalt live as freely as the lord" (I.iv.38). The Duke's command, and his promise (which Cesario now hears he is likely to keep) appeals to the Belchian aspect of human nature, the desire for freedom defined as living as you want, free of civil bounds. Although the Duke assumes that this appeal will motivate his new attendant, the opposite is true. Viola has fallen in love with him; that is her motive for obeying the ruler's will. "Myself would be his wife"; in her self-chosen role of Cesario she will be "wooing" a potential rival (I.iv.40–41).

At Olivia's house Maria is scolding the Clown, who has been absent from the household without leave, and therefore deserves hanging, she judges. The Clown, more sober and more witty than Sir Toby, the other butt of her ire, rejoins, "Many a good hanging prevents a bad marriage" (I.v.18). Olivia enters, with her steward, Malvolio. She orders the fool's departure and he concurs, saying, *Go away, Countess.* A woman of equanimity, she engages: *Prove me a fool, fool. You are a fool, Countess, because if your brother is in Heaven, why mourn*? Malvolio is not amused. "I marvel your ladyship takes delight in such a barren rascal" (I.v.79). But Olivia is quite amused, rebuking her steward. "O, you are sick of self-love, Malvolio, and taste with a distemper'd appetite. To be generous, guiltless, and of free disposition, is to take these things for bird-bolts that you deem cannon bullets." (I.v.85–87). She defines freedom quite differently than either Sir Toby or even the Duke define it. Olivia's freedom is both non-egocentric and thoughtful, not impassioned either for someone else (as is the Duke's love) or for herself (like Malvolio's self-love). Her freedom never magnifies the small, refrains from quarreling over a straw because she sees her honor isn't really at stake. After all, isn't the Clown right? How foolish is he, in Christian terms? But is her mourning the result of melancholy passion, now moderated by his jibe, or a device of prudence—a delaying tactic, a wise use of time?

And if she won't love the Duke, possibly because she won't marry 'above herself,' whom will she love? We don't wait any longer for the answer. The Countess admits Cesario when Malvolio tells her that 'he' is only an adolescent—no danger to a woman. When Cesario prefaces her speech by calling it 'poetical,' Olivia immediately stands on the authority of her wit: It is "the more likely to be feigned," in that case; "I pray you keep it in" (II.v.183). What is more, "I heard that you were saucy at my gates, and allowed you approach rather to wonder at you than to hear you" (I.v.184–85); she not only esteems the Clown's wit but likes to wonder. "If you be not mad, be gone; if you have reason, be brief; 'tis not that time of moon with me to make one in so skipping a dialogue" (I.v.186–89). She can distinguish between madness and the sane inanity of youth; rejecting both, she admits rational discourse, if her interlocutor is capable of it, while stipulating that stem-winding rhetoric will not be countenanced. Only Socratic brevity will do. Nonetheless, she commits an error, suspecting the truth of Cesario's speech without suspecting the truth of 'his' identity. In a Shakespeare play as much as in a Platonic dialogue, one must always both follow the arguments and understand the persons making them.

Cesario requests a private audience, a secret speech by one whose identity is secret. Olivia permits this esotericism. There is good reason for Cesario to want no onlookers. 'He' praises Olivia's natural beauty, her physical excellence. But like the Clown, 'he' is unimpressed with her soul. "I see what you are: you are too proud; / But, if you were the devil, you are fair, / My lord and master loves you" (I.v.234–36). Olivia replies that it isn't her body, her looks, that the Duke should be considering. "Your lord does not know my mind; I cannot love him," although "I suppose him virtuous, know him noble, / Of great estate, of fresh and stainless youth; / Invoices well divulg'd, free, learn'd and valiant, / And in dimension and the shape of nature / A gracious person" (I.v.241–46). This only increases Viola's love for him, and she wonders why Olivia cannot love such a man. If I were her suitor, 'he' tells her, I would camp out at your gate in a cabin made of willow, symbol of unrequited love. I would write you love poems to sing at night, make your name echo in the hills, give you no rest until you pitied me. In their privacy, Olivia drops her hint: *You* "might do much," young Cesario (I.v.260). She invites 'him' back, and Cesario departs, saying, "Farewell, fair cruelty" (I.v.272).

Love has begun to humble Olivia by teaching her fear. For the first time, she is dependent upon the approval of another, unfree. "I do not know what, and fear to find / Mine eye too great a flatterer for my mind," she confides to Malvolio (I.v.292–93). She can only appeal to Fate to "show thy force" in the matter (I.v.294). Knowing herself in love, she no longer believes that she rules the course of events.

Act One presents the theme of the play: rulers in love. The Duke and the Countess are both good rulers. They are honorable, prudent, just, even magnanimous—rulers by nature. But human nature also loves, and in loving challenges even good rule and good rulers. It makes good rulers dependent upon the good graces of another person. Insofar as it does, it denatures rulers as rulers, compromises their self-command, puts in question their habitual authority over others. Nature as love makes slavery not rulers. The Duke responds by redoubling his efforts to win his beloved; the Countess responds by appealing to a higher power and resigning herself to its verdict, while hoping to arrange circumstances in such a way as to give a favorable outcome a chance to occur.

Viola's brother, Sebastian, has survived the shipwreck, rescued by a sea-captain, as she was. Like Olivia, he feels buffeted by Fate, believing his sister drowned. She was called beautiful, he tells the captain; being her twin, he modestly abstains from affirming it. But "she bore a mind that envy could not but call fair" (II.i.26–27). Although he asks his new friend, the sea-captain, to leave him—"It were a bad recompense for your love to lay any of [my evils] on you" (II.i.1]—Antonio demurs. And when Sebastian tells him he intends to head for Duke Orsini's court, Antonio insists on accompanying him, despite the fact that "I have many enemies in Orsini's court" (II.i.40). Twinship is one natural pairing; love aims at another; friendship is a third. Rescuer Antonio may not have been enchanted by Sebastian, who exhibits no Arionic musicianship, but love and friendship can prove as powerful as enchantment, and more lasting.

In a street in the city, Malvolio catches up to Cesario, saying he returns a ring 'he' gave to the Countess. When 'he' refuses it, Malvolio throws it on the ground and walks away, not caring if Cesario picks it up. Viola is bewildered, having left no ring, but she understands that "my outside" has "charm'd" the lady (II.ii.16). "She loves me, sure" (II.ii.20). "I am the man," she avers, with the double irony of saying so while posing as a woman and echoing the acknowledgement of Jesus by His disciples. She now sees that "disguise," what she had supposed a clever ruse, "art a wickedness / Wherein the pregnant enemy"—Satan, always 'big' with mischief—"does much" (II.ii.25–26). "Fortune" has caught her in a love triangle drawn by her own wit. "O Time, thou must untangle this, not I; / It is too hard a knot for me t'untie!" (II.ii.38–39). She has run out of plots, out of schemes to outmatch Fortune. Like her rival/beloved, Olivia, she can only appeal to a higher power—not Fate or Fortune, which has conned her, but Time, which many ignore but no one can think himself clever enough to rule.

That night, at Olivia's house, Sir Toby, Sir Andrew, and the Clown are in a celebratory mood, as usual. They agree that life consists of eating and drinking, and fools though they may be, they too know Time has no master. It is as the Clown sings: "What is love? 'Tis not hereafter, / Present mirth hath present laughter / What to come is still unsure. / In delay there lies no plenty, / Then come and kiss me, sweet and twenty; / Youth's a stuff will not endure" (II.iii.46–51). They are celebrating Twelfth Night. Maria warns them that Malvolio will throw them out and, sure enough—demanding, rhetorically, "Is there no regard, of place, personage, or time in you?"—he steps in, telling them to shape up or ship out (II.iii.89). To which Sir Toby replies, "Dost thou think because thou art virtuous, there shall be no more cakes and ale?" (II.iii.108–09). To Malvolio's austere conventionalism (including his conventional notion of time), Sir Toby opposes nature, low nature though it is. If Malvolio ruled, there would be no Christmastides, and all of life would be Lenten.

Giving him up, Malvolio turns to Maria, complaining of "this uncivil rule" (II.iii.115) and threatening to report it to the Countess. Although she herself has reprimanded Sir Toby for his unbounded misbehavior, Maria can't stand Malvolio at all. She conceives of her own plot, her own scheme to manipulate Fortune, in order to "make him a common recreation" (II.iii.127). "Sometimes he is a kind of Puritan," but not a real one (II.iii.131); in reality he is nothing "constantly but a time-pleaser," so intensely self-loving that he imagines all others share in his love (II.iii.137–38). Viola hopes that Time may somehow bring a solution for her dilemma, while knowing it will go as it goes, Malvolio is Time's sycophant, vainly hoping to please it. Malvolio's self-love and lack of self-knowledge make him a sort of unintentional hypocrite, a Puritan without purity who preens himself in his self-conceit. "On that vice in him will my revenge find notable cause to work" (II.iii.142–43). She will forge a letter from the Countess confessing her love for him, dropping it where he will find it. This will be "sport royal" (II.iii.161), a prank hatched by a servant but fit for a queen. The trickster-servant will rule the scheming steward.

At the palace, the Duke once more calls for music. The previous evening he'd heard an "old antique song" (II.iv.3). "Methought it did relieve my passion much, / More than light airs and recollected [i.e., studied] terms / Of these most brisk and giddy-faced times" (II.iv.4–6). The simplicity and sobriety of old music calms the passions, whereas modern, Renaissance music anticipates the clever, over-sophisticated tunes Cole Porter would invent, centuries later. The Duke tells Cesario that a woman should marry men older than herself in order to be "level in her husband's heart" (II.iv.30). His purpose is identical to Olivia's: equality in marriage. But he recommends the opposite means to that end. That is because men's "fancies are more giddy and infirm" than those of women—"More longing, wavering, sooner lost and won, / Than women's are" (II.iv.31–33). Men's love attaches to women's beauty; women's beauty fades like roses; ergo, men's love evanesces quickly. This opinion recalls the *carpe diem* sentiments expressed in the Clown's song to Sir Toby and Sir Andrew. But the old antique song he esteems strikes an entirely different tone. It gives voice to one who dies of unrequited love: "I am slain by a fair cruel maid" (II.iv.53). No one mourns the lover. Does the Duke's liking of the song bespeak the moderation and sobriety of antiquity or merely his own self-pity?

As in the opening scene of the play, the Duke changes his mind almost immediately, now telling Cesario what is obvious, that his love for Olivia is constant, that he loves her for her nature, and that Cesario must now return to her house to tell that to her "sovereign cruelty" (II.iv.80). He cares nothing for her lands, for "the parts that Fortune hath bestow'd upon her" (II.iv.82); like all things Fortune bestows, they are as easily taken away. It is the "gem" of nature's gifts in her that "attracts my soul" (II.iv.85). And if she "cannot love you, sir?" Cesario asks (II.iv.86). Impossible, in the end, the Duke insists, for "there is no woman's sides / Can bide the beating of so strong a passion / As love doth give my heart" (II.iv.92–94). A woman's love is delicate but superficial, a matter of "the palate," whereas a man's love is deep, a "motion of the liver" (II.iv.97–98). His love is "all as hungry as the sea, / And can digest as much" (II.iv.99–100). From claiming that men's love is giddy and infirm he has gone to calling it steady and deep, although he uses exclusively physical terms to describe it.

Cesario, who knows the power of the sea to devour ships, also knows that a woman's love can equal a man's in its depth and power. "In faith, they are as true of heart as we," 'he' tells him (II.iv.106). 'His' own father had a daughter who loved so, who "pin'd in thought" for her undisclosed beloved, sitting "like Patience on a monument, smiling at grief" (II.iv.113–14). And, diagnosing the Duke's love for Olivia, "We men may say more, swear more, but indeed / Our shows are more than will; for still we prove / Much in our vows, and little in our love" (II.iv.115–17). As if to confirm her suggestion, the Duke sends her off again to Olivia with a jewel symbolizing his lover's natural gifts, saying, "My love can give no place, bide no delay" (II.ii.123–24). He would besiege the Countess, as if she were a fortress to be conquered. It is hard to separate his desire for the fortress from his love of the challenge. In this, the central scene of the play, Cesario/Viola tries to teach the Duke the nature of women, which is not so far from the nature of men, not so unequal to them as he imagines.

As we've seen, the rulers aren't the only plotters, in Illyria. In Olivia's garden, away from the ears of authority, Sir Toby, Sir Andrew, Maria, and Fabian (a servant of Olivia's) further Maria's plan against Malvolio, whom Fabian detests because he reported Fabian's bear-baiting to disapproving

Olivia—another of the steward's attempts to restrict the recreations of the people, and not only the people. King Henry VIII and Queen Elizabeth I were also fans. Puritans attempted to ban bear-baiting, especially when held on the Sabbath, so Malvolio acted true to his type.

Maria has kept the letter just mysterious enough to engage Malvolio's curiosity, engage him in thought; it "will make a contemplative idiot of him" (II.v.17–18), lure him like a trout to the fly-concealed hook. And it has exactly that effect. Reading the letter, which encourages him to "cast thy humble slough and appear fresh" (he doesn't notice that he's being compared to a snake), he muses to himself that it can only be from Olivia. If he marries her, he will become a count. ("Look how imagination blows him," Fabian whispers—*blows him like the wind that wrecks ships*) (II.v.39–41). Malvolio soliloquizes on how he will command his future subordinate, Fabian. "Some are born great, some achieve greatness, and some have greatness thrust upon them" (II.v.132–34). His "Fates have opened their hands"; he needs only to embrace them (V.vi.134–35). As count, "I will be proud. I will read politic authors. I will battle Sir Toby" (II.v.143). This is no power fantasy whipped up by ambition and self-love, he tells himself, "for every reason excites to this, that my lady loves me" (II.v.146). He walks off, entranced. In this garden, it is the serpent who is tempted, not to eat an apple (no food for snakes) but to shed his skin, his humbleness, which on Malvolio is indeed but skin-deep, an implausible disguise.

Maria comes by, a comic Eve triumphantly taking vengeance on her enemy, to the delighted applause of her confederates. "I would marry this wench for this device," Sir Toby exults (II.v.162). She is not done. She will advise Malvolio to approach the Countess wearing yellow, cross-gartered stockings, which she loathes, and to smile at her constantly, crossing "her disposition" as well as his stockings (II.v.181). She is sure to regard him with "a notable contempt" (II.v.182). If Maria will not exactly bruise the serpent's heel, she'll make a laughingstock of his calves.

Twinship, love, and friendship are natural and noble; eating, drinking, and laughing are natural and low, but not to be despised. All of these are life-giving and life-enhancing, yet curtailed by the curse pronounced in the Garden of Eden, a curse brought on by the Serpent's temptation of Eve. Death puts a limit to natural life, even as it is now part of nature. Death makes human 'timing' more urgent, human beings more in need of wit.

Fortune or the Fats can serve to derange these natural bonds and pleasures. A certain kind of religiosity and a certain narrow or conventional civility can also derange them. The ineluctable fact of ruling in human societies complicates love, bringing to it questions of equality and dependence, as well as the danger of mixing love with ambition—as seen in a serious way in the Duke's willful wooing, comically in Malvolio's illusive desire for superiority.

Prudent plotting can sometimes cure Fortune's derangements, but this can go wrong (as with Viola's disguise) or right (as with Maria's letter). Time is a more reliable remedy, as Fortune balances out her gifts over time, allowing nature to emerge during the long voyage.

Act III begins and ends in Olivia's garden, and persons will continue to be led into temptation there. The 'low' characters have now departed, Cesario and the Clown have come in. Unlike the Duke in his palace, Cesario wants to hear no music, seeks no love-cure. 'He' exchanges not tunes but words with the witty Clown, who offers a lesson on the ambiguity of words. Telling 'him' he lives by a church, he draws from her the question, "Art thou a churchman?" (III.i.i4). No, his house is by the church, ergo, he lives by the church. "A sentence is but a chev'ril glove to a good wit. How quickly the wrong side may be turned outward" (III.i.10–12). If a sentence is a kid glove, it may do more than cover a wolf in sheep's clothing, be more than a humble skin covering an ambitious snake; a sentence or a word might *itself* be turned inside-out, revealing not the nature of the thing it covers but its own duplicity, its own opposite or self-contradicting nature. This, the Clown continues, puts into question the use of reason itself, which depends upon the principle of non-contradiction. I am not "the Lady Olivia's fool," as Cesario supposes, "but her corrupter of words," the serpent in the garden of her thought (III.i.34).

This Eve isn't fooled. After the Clown leaves to tell Olivia's household that Cesario has arrived, Viola considers him carefully. "This fellow is wise enough to play the fool; / And to do that well craves a kind of wit" (III.i.57–58). A costumed play-actor herself, Viola/Cesario sees that to bring off her performance she will need both an underlying wisdom (to conceive of the role in the first place) and then the tactical wisdom of wit to bring it all off. That is, as she says of the Clown, "He must observe their mood on whom he jests, / The quality of persons, and the time; / And like the haggard, check at every feather / That comes before his eye" (III.i.59–62). Earlier, perplexed by the complications multiplying around her, she had surrendered to the test of time; she now sees that a jester-fool, with his wit, can also use time, at least to some degree, quickly perceiving the immediate and passing emotions of his audience, the social standing of the persons present and even, like a young hawk being trained for hunting, forego the lesser birds for the game birds. "This is a practice / As full of labor was a wise man's art; / For folly that he wisely shows is fit; / But wise men, folly-fall'n, quite taint their wit" (III.i.61–65). Viola has learned that *Sophia*, the wisdom of the truth of nature, needs the protection of *phronēsis*, practical wisdom or wit, if only to notice the audience to whom one speaks of the higher wisdom. The Clown has taught her that with practical wisdom she doesn't need to be the victim of fate, of shipwreck by sea or in love, if she pays attention to persons (without necessarily 'respecting' them, as neither fools nor gods ever do), and if she exercises good timing in her wit's exercise.

Her newly calibrated wit immediately faces a test, as Olivia enters the garden. Dismissing her retinue, the Countess engages Cesario in another private conversation. Olivia describes another bear-baiting but this time her honor is the bear, Cesario's thoughts the unmuzzled dogs that torment it at the command of 'his' "tyrannous heart" (III.i.117). When Cesario expresses pity, Olivia calls that a step toward love, which Cesario denies, as "we oft pity enemies" (III.i.122). *What do you think of me?* Olivia asks. I think that, "You do think you are not what you are," Cesario answers (III.i.136); *you are my enemy, without knowing it.* What is more, Cesario tells her with equal honesty, "I am not what I am" (III.i.138). She has mastered the Clown's art of words. She can tell the truth while keeping it concealed.

Placed in the Duke's position of loving unrequitedly, his female counterpart-ruler seeks to overbear her beloved as he had attempted to do, by strength of will and of passion. Whatever ambiguity words related to 'being' may have, "I would you were as I would have you be" (III.i.139). Swearing by "the roses of the spring," which must be gathered timely, and by "maidhood, honor, truth, and everything," she confesses her love which, despite "all my pride" neither wit nor reason can hide (III.i.146–47). Unlike Maria, who would restrict Sir Toby's drunkenness within civil limits, unlike

Malvolio, who would limit merriment within civil limits austerely tight-
ened, Olivia asks Cesario to fetter 'his' reason with reason itself, as "love
sought is good, but given unsought is better" (III.i.153)—an argument
Duke Orsini might well have used, had he wooed directly, not through an
intermediary who unwittingly precluded the success of his suit.

Cesario answers the suit by protesting 'his' innocence. "By innocence,
I swear, and by my youth, / I have one heart, one bosom, and one truth, /
And that no woman has; nor never none / Shall mistress be of it, save I
alone" (III.i.154–57). 'His' reason practices self-government, not submitting to the rule of another's passion, however good that passion may be—
relative to another passion. Cesario/Viola's reason follows nature, not the
appearance she has contrived. In her use of ambiguous words, she never
loses sight of the nature words may reveal or conceal.

Cesario promises not to bring the Duke's impassioned "tears" to Olivia
again (III.i.159). Olivia can only invite 'him' to come again, "for thou mayst
move / That heart which now abhors to like his love"—more specifically,
his beloved (III.i.160–61). In truth, Viola would like *his* love very much
were it directed to herself, according to nature.

Meanwhile, indoors at Olivia's, the comical men contrive their own
plot to match Maria's plot. Sir Toby and Fabian scheme to make gulls out
of Sir Andrew and Cesario. They urge Sir Andrew, who still entertains the
remote hope that he might win Olivia, to challenge his rival to a duel. This
would set up another love triangle, substituting Sir Andrew for the Duke
but retaining Olivia as the beloved and Cesario as the middle-'man'. A
letter will advance this plot, too, although this time they will induce the
gull to write the letter himself.

Out on a street in town, Sebastian is thanking "my kind Antonio"—
'kind' being another word with more than one meaning, namely, compassionate or natural, that is, specific to a species—for his loyalty and
friendship. He is right. The sea-captain compassionately intends to guide
the young man, inexperienced in travel and friendless in Illyria; he is a true
friend, and he is indeed of Sebastian's kind or type, a man of virtue. When
Sebastian says he wants to look around the town, to see "the memorials and
things of fame / That do renown this city" (III.iii.23–24). This worries Antonio, however, who once fought a sea-battle against the Duke's galleys in
a piratical mission. Antonio will retire to an inn called The Elephant, named

after the animal which never forgets—a sort of memorial to memorials, and a reminder that memories may be of base things as well as noble ones. Meanwhile, he tells the young man, by all means visit the sights of interest here, "feed your knowledge" on those tokens of Illyrian virtue (III.iii.41). To know what the citizens of a city esteem is to know something important about them, and about those who rule them. More, take my purse with you, in case you see something you might wish to buy. With that gesture of liberality, another measure of friendship and trust, they agree to meet again at The Elephant.

In Olivia's garden of temptation, of testing, Olivia and Maria must listen to Malvolio's love-prattle—a test of their patience, if nothing else. Quoting from the letter he believes she wrote, thanking Jove for his good fortune, he finally elicits Olivia's verdict: "This is very midsummer madness" (III.iv.53). She leaves him to the tender care of Sir Toby, to that gentleman's delight. As Fabian puts it, "If this were play'd upon a stage now, I could condemn it as an improbable fiction" (III.iv121–122). He keeps his eye on the purpose, however: "Why, we shall make him mad indeed" (III.iv.127).

Things get even better for the plotters when Sir Andrew arrives, letter in hand. He reads it aloud, with Sir Toby remarking on its one strength: in view of the illegal character of dueling, it contains no culpable evidence of a challenge. He promises to deliver the inanely written document to Cesario, but because it is too foolish to intimidate that gentleman, he elects to deliver the message orally, in his own words. Given Sir Andrew's imbecility and cowardice and Cesario's slightness and effeminacy, he predicts that no blood will come of their confrontation; they will likely only stare at one another like basilisks, except that human looks don't kill.

Olivia and Cesario enter the garden, Olivia complaining of Cesario's heart of stone. It is "my fault" to have "laid my honor to unchary out," but "such a headstrong potent fault it is / That it but mocks reproof" (III.iv.191–95). Her garden-Eden features the temptation seen in the biblical one, but stubborn, original sin has never been absent from it. "With the same 'haviour that our passion bears / Goes on my master's griefs," Cesario replies (III.iv196); Olivia has sought equality and she has achieved it, but hardly in the form she wanted. That is often the way with the desire for equality. Cesario continues to insist that the only way for Olivia to regain her honor, to be redeemed from her fault, is to feel "true love for my master"—thereby remaining loyal to 'his' master's command, although if Cesario succeeds Viola will lose him. When Olivia tries to trap 'him' with logic—"How with mine honor may I give him that / Which I have given to you?" (III.iv.203–04)—Cesario replies as one elevated to the position of a judge: "I will acquit you" (III.iv.205). Turning her heel, Olivia calls 'him' a fiend, casting herself as Eve in her garden psychodrama. She very much prefers to be the ruler, not the ruled, but her love has made that impossible.

Olivia's departure frees Cesario for the role Sir Toby has assigned 'him' in his own play. First, Sir Toby warns Cesario that there is a real devil in the garden, Sir Andrew, "a devil in a private brawl" (III.iv.225). After that "devil" appears, Sir Toby then confidentially tells him of Cesario's prowess; "they say he has been fencer to the Sophy" (III.iv.266)—that is, to the Persian Shah, although she's also been learning to be a verbal fencer in defense of the nature *Sophia* knows. Both principals are intimidated, Cesario confessing "I am no fighter" (III.iv.231) but "one that would rather go with Sir Priest than Sir Knight" (III.iv.258–59), Sir Andrew proposing that he bribe the fencer with a horse if 'he' will decline combat. This time, Cesario/Viola can appeal not to Time, which isn't on her side in this case, but to God, who alone can defend her, she thinks, as "I lack as a man" (III.iv.23). Manhood is a natural thing, and Time may test and reveal it; salvation is an immediate thing, and at this moment it seems that only God can deliver her.

But this is no divine comedy. Instead, a human savior, Antonio, arrives. Mistaking Cesario for 'his' twin, Sebastian, he offers to defend 'him' against the challenger. This offends Sir Toby, whose plot is being marred by the intruder, but before any damage can be done, officers arrive to arrest the sea-captain. Antonio asks Cesario for the purse he'd given to Sebastian, evidently so that will be able to pay bail. When 'he' cannot produce it, Antonio assumes he's been betrayed by his friend. The officers take him away, but not before he calls Cesario "Sebastian." This tells Viola that her brother may have survived the shipwreck and is in Illyria. If so, "Tempests are king and salt waves fresh in love!" (III.367–68). Viola can't reveal her true nature quite yet, but time and nature have indeed come to her rescue, giving her far greater scope for her wisdom and wit.

Act III has seen the education of the two noblewomen. Viola has learned from the Clown how to understand the relation of wisdom, wit, and words in meeting the exigencies of Fortune in the course of time. Olivia has learned, or is beginning to learn, the limits of a ruler's power when it comes to matters of love, nature's heart.

The Clown enjoys a noteworthy form of freedom. Most of the time, he manifests himself when and with whom he chooses, saying whatever he wants to say, without punishment. Sebastian has arrived in front of Olivia's house, and the Clown is there to greet him—this time, however, on orders from the Countess, who has sent him out to bid Cesario to speak with her. But just as the two rulers are ruled, now the fool is fooled. He mistakes Sebastian for Cesario, attempts to give him the message from Olivia. When nonplussed Sebastian dismisses him, the Clown indignantly appeals to the reality of names, forgetting his own teaching on the ambiguity of words: "Your name is not Cesario; nor this is not my nose neither"—overlooking the difference in degree of self-evidence between a word and a thing (IV.i.7–8). Indeed, "Nothing that is so is so" (IV.i.8). Even, and especially, the trickster relies on knowing what reality is, on what (as a U.S. president famously intoned) *is* is. How does this fellow Cesario so blatantly deny the reality of himself, which the Clown sees in front of him?

Sebastian would get rid of him by paying him off, treating him as the court fool that he is. Sir Toby and Sir Andrew arrive before Sebastian can leave, and they too mistake him for Cesario. Sir Andrew and Sebastian scuffle, with Sir Andrew threatening his rival with a lawsuit, once Sir Toby has safely restrained the surprisingly fight-ready 'Cesario.' "I'll have action of battery against him, if there be any law in Illyria. Though I struck him first, yet it's no matter for that" (IV.i.31–33). Shakespeare's audience of judges and lawyers have undoubtedly encountered such plaintiffs before.

Sebastian breaks free of Sir Toby's grip, and they are about to fight when Olivia, alerted by the Clown, intervenes, pronouncing Sir Toby an "ungracious wretch / Fit for the mountains and the barbarous caves" (IV.i.46–47). She orders everyone away, except for her 'Cesario.' To him she pleads, "Let thy fair wisdom, not thy passion, sway / In this uncivil and unjust extent / Against thy peace" (IV.i.51–52). She invites him into her house, so that he can hear accounts of "the many fruitless pranks / This ruffian hath botched up, that thou thereby / Mayst smile at this" (IV.i.54–55). Let laughter replace your rage, comedy replace incipient tragedy. Curse his soul "for me," because "He started one poor heart of mine, in thee" (IV.i.57–58).

Olivia intervenes first on the grounds of civility and good order, against outlaw dueling, however farcical; she doesn't know it's farcical, any more than Sebastian does. Sir Toby's comic plot was about to spin out of his control because his anger was overbearing his sense of fun. He is, after all, a 'Sir,' a knight, a man of the warrior class, however self-abased he has become with eating and drinking and pranking. Olivia prevents the comedy from turning tragic by banishing the men she calls the "rudes," the uncivil, those unworthy of a place in civil society (IV.i.49), those who act beneath their conventionally rightful places in that society because their nature prevents them from living up to such places.

She next appeals not to 'Cesario'/Sebastian's civility but to his reason, to his nature rather than his sense of civil propriety. She knows Cesario has the kind of nature that can draw itself back from anger to reason, a nature that can recall itself into civil society, and indeed (as she continues to hope) into her household. Like a deer, a hart, her heart leaped in fear when she saw him endangered by the sword in the hand guided by the damnation-worthy soul of her unregenerate uncle. She hopes 'Cesario' will enter her household out of compassion for that fear, a sure token of her love.

If this 'Cesario' were Viola, the impasse would recur. 'He' would excuse himself, faithfully respecting the Duke's authority. But Olivia has committed a right error. When it comes to reason, Sebastian has every reason to think that either all these people are mad or he is—and if not mad, then dreaming. But crucially, unlike Viola/Cesario, Sebastian/Cesario by nature looks at Olivia and very much likes what he sees. The man who loves memorials and would lodge at an inn named for the never-forgetting Elephant now tells himself, "Let fancy still my sense in Lethe steep / If it be thus to dream, still let me sleep!" (IV.i.58–59). "Would you be ruled by me?" Olivia asks (IV.i.60). "Madam, I will" (IV.i.61). To Olivia, suddenly her reluctant beloved has consented to her suit. The stern judge who had fiendishly acquitted her of responsibility for loving 'him' now acquits himself nobly in the role she wills for him. 'Acquit' is yet another word with more than one meaning. The play's alternate title, *What You Will*, also has a double meaning: the audience assumes it means 'as you like it,' 'what you want.' The rulers in the play, however, being rulers, have been habituated to obtaining what they will, and love has frustrated them in that. Her beloved having replied in accordance to her will, Olivia has every reason to believe her will has finally prevailed, her just rule restored, her regime well-ordered again.

Over at the prison, Malvolio has been thrown into a lightless cell, darkness being considered a cure and a punishment for madness, an imitation on earth of the evil soul in Hell. Maria, Sir Toby, and the Clown still aren't done with him. Another plot, another disguise: Maria dresses the Clown as a curate, "Sir Topas." "Topas" might be a pun on *topas*, the word for a traditional theme or topic in rhetoric. The fake curate who pays Malvolio a visit does 'treat' him according to the conventions of the time, pretending to perform an exorcism to free the prisoner from the Satanic forces that the plotters pretend are controlling him. Since Malvolio can see nothing, the Clown only needs to change his voice to manifest himself as himself, as well—his wit making himself into twins. Malvolio associates darkness with ignorance and with Hell; he is indeed plunged into the one and may as well be in the other. He insists on his sanity, but neither of the Clown's personae will credit him with it. Whereas in his ignorance Sebastian, being sane, had sanely doubted his own sanity, and is said rightly to be civil, ignorant Malvolio, equally sane, but only conventionally civil, never doubts but is lyingly said to be mad. Or is it a lie? *His* version of civility was humorless, too pure (and too Puritan) for this world. He has been sanely mad, ill-willed. 'As you will,' directed at him, would lead men and women into a sort of prison. In that way, his punishment is just.

Sir Toby, chastened by the Countess' scolding and banishment from the household, decides that the pranking play has played itself out. He fears Olivia's continued displeasure with his antics. The tormentors withdraw, but not before the Clown promises to bring him light, pen, and paper, so Malvolio can write to the Countess. The Clown sings a taunting farewell ditty about vice, madness, and the devil.

Out in "the glorious sun" and air, Sebastian soliloquizes in the garden (IV.iii.1). He is filled with "wonder" at a gift from the Countess, a pearl; unlike much else preying upon his mind, he can touch and feel the pearl; it is real. And it symbolizes other realities. The pearl is the only gem that isn't a stone, but the product of a living thing. It is also the only gem that needs no polishing, no cutting, no human artisanship to make it more beautiful. It comes from the sea, where life on earth originated, and from which Sebastian has come to Illyria. In ancient Illyria, as in nearby Greece, it was associated with Aphrodite, the goddess of love; in Christian iconography it symbolized another form of love, chastity before marriage. And in the Book of Matthew the pearl of great price symbolizes the Kingdom of God, for which a wise merchant would sell everything else he has. The pearl, then, is a natural thing betokening the divine regime, and the Christian marriage Olivia hopes for is a sacrament, a human token of the divine regime.

Sebastian also wonders at the absence of Antonio, whose "counsel now might do me golden service" (IV.iii.8). All of these things, he sanely and reasonably thinks, may not be madness at all, in himself or in the others, but only the result of "some error" (IV.iii.10). He doubts that the Countess could be mad; if she were, "she would not sway her house, command her followers," with "such a smooth, discreet, and stable gearing, / As I perceive she does" (IViii.17–20). When Olivia comes to him, priest in tow, she invites him into the nearby chantry, where, "before him, / And underneath that consecrated roof," he may "plight me the full assurance of your faith, / That my most jealous and too doubtful soul, / May live at peace" (IV.iii.24–28). For his part, Sebastian consents to the ceremony of betrothal and, "having sworn truth, ever will be true" (IV.iii.33). He has seen her beauty as a woman and her virtue as a ruler, and that knowledge of the nature of her body and soul is good enough for him.

The Clown, Fabian, the Duke, his attendant Curio, and Cesario convene in front of Olivia's house. At last the Duke has come to make his suit in person, without intermediary. The Clown pleases the Duke by saying that he, the Clown, profits more from enemies than friends because enemies help him gain self-knowledge, while friends only flatter. In this play of disguises, of doublings, from costumed bodies to natural twins to ambiguous words, self-knowledge opens the pathway to knowledge simply. The Duke calls this Socratic lesson "excellent" (V.i.21). He promises payment to the Clown if he will announce his presence to the Countess and bring her out to parley with him.

Some officers lead Antonio by. Cesario recognizes him as 'his' rescuer. The Duke also remembers him as the captain of the pirate ship, a man so brave in battle that the "very envy and the tongue of loss / Cried fame and honor on him" (V.i.52–53). Cesario would have the Duke pardon him, as he offered to defend Cesario when endangered in the duel. The Duke wants to know why he dared to come to Illyria; Antonio explains that it was out of friendship for Sebastian, whom he takes Cesario to be. He endangered his own life for that friend, after rescuing him from "the rude sea's enrag'd and foamy mouth" (V.i.72). But when he in turn had needed his friend to return his money, the man betrayed him, "not meaning to partake with me in danger" (V.i.81). Out of cowardice, Antonio charges, 'Sebastian' failed to repay a double debt: life and purse.

Cesario does not know how this can be, but as a wise judge in the case before him, the Duke asks the pertinent question, having to do with time: When did you come to Illyria? When Antonio says it was today, the Duke sees that his testimony is somehow false, as Cesario arrived prior to that. Before he can inquire further, Olivia and her attendants emerge from her house. "Now heaven walks on earth," the Duke exclaims, unknowingly referring to the theme symbolized by the pearl Olivia has given to his unknown rival. No longer wishing to bother with Antonio, he dismisses him by saying that Cesario has attended upon him for the past three months. As Viola had hoped, time has redeemed her, although not in a way she could have anticipated.

Seeing Cesario and wondering at 'his' continued allegiance to the Duke, the Countess accuses: "You do not keep promise with me" (V.i.97). As for the Duke, if music is the food of love, she will not dine with him: If you have come to sing "the old tune" to me, it will sound in my ears like "howling after music" (V.i.102–04). To this the Duke can only fulminate at "you uncivil lady," ungrateful for his faithful love, deserving no less than death at his hands, "had I the heart to do it" (V.i.106–11). But since he knows she prefers Cesario to himself, he will kill Cesario, "sacrifice the lamb that I do love / To spite the raven's heart within a dove" (V.i.124–25). Incomprehensibly to Olivia, Cesario consents. "I, most jocund, apt, and willingly, / To do you rest, a thousand deaths would die." (V.i.126–27). "Have you forgot yourself?" (V.i.135), Olivia gasps. Calling Cesario her husband, she summons the priest as her witness, a claim Cesario finds equally incomprehensible. When she denies the betrothal, Olivia repeats the charge Antonio had leveled; Cesario is a base coward. "Fear not, Cesario, take thy fortunes up; / Be thou know'st thou art, and then thou art / As great as thou fear'st" (V.i.142–44). Cesario of course knows 'himself' to be other than what Olivia supposes. Like the Duke, the Countess esteems self-knowledge and, like him, has not yet fully achieved it. Both mistake the nature of Cesario, the object of their contention, and thus mistake themselves. The priest affirms the "contract of eternal bond of love" the couple (as he thinks) entered into, in his presence. In fewer than fifty lines, Shakespeare has brought together the themes of his play: fidelity, contract, civility, rage, love, self-knowledge, sacrifice, courage and cowardice, rule—all of them symbolized by doubleness, shadowed by duplicity.

The play has veered straight toward tragedy, again. Cesario begins to protest, but when Sebastian arrives the perplexities begin to dissolve, and comedy reclaims the plot. He begins by apologizing to Olivia for injuring her kinsman, Sir Toby, he could have "done no less with wit and safety," even had he been "the brother of my blood" (V.i.202–03). Looking back and forth between Sebastian and Cesario, the Duke exclaims, "One face, one voice, one habit, and two persons! / A natural perspective, that is and is not" (V.i.208–209). A "perspective" is a mirror; in the mirror and the one mirrored we see the real, what is, and its reflection, what is not but is identical to what is. *This* perspective is natural, as the twins are both real, neither an image. The Duke again speaks Socratically, inasmuch as it's Socrates who remarks that $1 + 1 = 2$—that is, two things become one, a pair. And they do so without violating the principle of non-contradiction. Olivia responds as Socrates might want his interlocutor to respond: "Most wonderful!" (V.i.217). Up to now, all had assumed that it could not possibly be the case that Cesario and Sebastian were distinct; such a thing seemed to defy logic. But not so. Knowledge is beginning to satisfy wonder, the desire to know.

The twins themselves find all this hard to believe because the thought of each has been based on the false premise that the other had died. When Cesario worries that 'he' is seeing a ghost, Sebastian responds as Plato's Socrates would: "A spirit I am indeed, / But am in that dimension grossly clad / Which from the womb I did participate" (V.i.228–30). That the ideas "participate" in matter, giving them their physical shape, explains how he can be a spirit and a body at the same time, dual in one way, one in another.

There is only one remaining problem of self-contradictory duality to solve. Cesario isn't a woman, as far as Sebastian and the others can see. "Were you a woman, as the rest goes even, / I should my tears let fall upon your cheek, / And say 'Thrice welcome, drowned Viola!'" (V.i.231–33). "Thrice" because their identity as a pair is real, and their dualities as male and female, and as brother and sister, are also real. Cesario has the solution to this problem. "I am Viola" (V.i.244), as I can prove by admitting my disguise and by the testimony of one member of another pair: the Illyrian sea-captain who rescued her, as distinct from Antonio, the sea-captain who rescued Sebastian.

Sebastian can now turn to Olivia to say, "So comes it, lady, you have been mistook" (V.i.251). But not through any malicious plot. It was "nature in her bias" that "drew in that" (V.i.252). The innocent joke on her is that "You are betrothed both to a maid and a man" (V.i.255), both to Cesario/Viola, with whom you first fell in love, supposing her a man, and to me, the real thing. As for the Duke, he has seen Viola's fidelity unto her prospective death, and now he only wants to see her in women's clothing. "Since you called me master for so long, / Here is my hand; / You shall from time be / Your master's mistress" (V.i.314–16). Those two will also become one.

As it happens, Viola reports, she had entrusted her clothes to her savior-captain, who is now in prison because Malvolio had sued him. The Countess assures her that she will order Malvolio to free him; the difficulty is that Malvolio himself is not only in jail but said to be "much distract" (V.i.272). This brings another potential legal dispute to the attention of the lawyerly audience. The Clown had withheld Malvolio's letter to Olivia, now giving the excuse that "a madman's epistles are no gospels" (V.i.278–79). The lie, an artificial and misleading mirror of the truth, is quickly 'seen through' when Olivia commands the Clown to give the letter to Fabian, who reads it aloud; the Duke in his capacity as judge hears, and says, "This savors not much of distraction" but of sanity (V.i.304).

With both the Duke and the Countess in agreement regarding Malvolio and, more importantly, with the disentanglement of the love triangle in accordance with nature and reason, not Fortune, deception, or convention, they can reach a politic settlement, which the Countess now proposes. "My lord, to please you, these things further thought on, / To think me as well a sister as a wife, / One day shall crown the alliance on't, so please you, / Here at my house and at my proper cost" (V.i.306–09). "Madam," the Duke replies, "I am most apt t'embrace your offer," as he no longer feels any need to embrace Olivia herself (V.i.310). Twin brother and sister have each gained a spouse; each spouse has gained a 'twin' sibling. These natural pairings parallel the spiritual pairings according to the Christian doctrine of marriage, whereby husband and wife are spiritually and physically bound together as 'one flesh' in their covenant with one another, before God—as two in 'one flesh.' One plus one equals two, which is one. Moreover, a brother-in-law, a sister-in-law, Christianly considered, become spiritual brother and sister. This will form the foundation of their political alliance. They already have begun to rule, together, not as the Duke originally had ruled but in accordance with both natural and Christian love, which cannot be willed, but with which one's will ought to be aligned.

At the Countess's command, Fabian brings Malvolio before them. Malvolio accuses her of wrongdoing, since she wrote a letter to him, courting him, and this was the efficient cause of the events ending his imprisonment in the dark as a madman. Examining the handwriting on the letter signed with her name, Olivia pronounces it counterfeit—a false or unnatural twin—and identifies its real author, Maria, whose 'hand' she knows. She promises Malvolio that when a full investigation has been completed, "Thou shalt be both the plaintiff and the judge / In thine own cause" (V.i.344–45).

This prospect is more than enough to alarm Fabian into both confessing and turning state's evidence. (He is, after all, named for the Roman general who defeated the mighty Hannibal by avoiding direct battles.) "Let no quarrel, nor no brawl to come, / Taint the condition of this present hour" (V.i.346–47). "I most freely confess" my own and Sir Toby's "device against Malvolio here" (V.i.349–50). He hastens to add that they so devised in retaliation of "some stubborn and uncourteous parts / We had conceived against him" (V.i.351–52). Maria only forged the letter at the urging of Sir Toby, so she is at most an accessory to the crime, "in recompense whereof he hath married her" (V.i.354)—indeed a punishment that fits the crime. But, as Fabian pleads in his and Sir Toby's defense, their "sportful malice" should provoke laughter, not revenge "if the injuries be justly weighed / That on both sides passed" (V.i.355–58). For his part, the Clown mounts his own defense, pointing to Malvolio's conceit and will-willed insults directed at himself, in front of the Countess. "Thus the whirligig of time brings in his revenge" (V.i.363).

The whirligig of time recalls Viola's reflection, her reliance on time to reveal the nature Fortune disrupt. Self-righteous Malvolio will not offer a reciprocal confession, despite the Countess's compassion ("Alas, poor fool, how have they baffled thee!" [V.i.359]). Unlike the others, he cannot accept having been fooled by the duplicity of appearances; he cannot laugh at himself. "I'll be revenged on the whole pack of you!" (V.i.367) he vows, stalking off. The Puritans would indeed prove difficult to integrate into the English regime, and they would take their revenge, less than a half-century after Shakespeare put those words into Malvolio's mouth. Malvolio may be, as Maria said, more an *ambitieux* than a Puritan, but in civil society and politics, it would sometimes be difficult to see the difference, insofar as some Puritans' souls lacked self-knowledge.

The Countess nonetheless continues to pity her abused steward. The Duke commands that he be pursued and offered a peace settlement, since "he hath not told us of the captain yet"—the holder of the proper woman's garments he wants his future wife to recover (V.i.370). Once that is settled, "and golden time convents"—that is, convenes—"a solemn combination shall be made / Of our dear souls" (V.i.368–70). Time, as revealer of nature, is indeed golden; what Viola had said resignedly about the goodness of time her future husband can now say with joy. And he, who had expected the hunter Cupid's arrow to strike Olivia's heart, now sees that slow Time is still more golden than Cupid's swift arrow, that the truer love may come in the longer time in which nature reveals itself. Gold is the color of royalty, of crowns, of ruling. The judges and lawyers in Shakespeare's audience will recognize "convents" as a term in law, meaning the action of a legal authority who summons a person to present himself in court. The Duke has found a way to reconcile human beings and citizens, nature and law, as made known to him in time. In this final scene, Curio is present for the third time, but this time he remains silent and has nothing to do. The Duke's curiosity and his love, his mind and his heart, have been satisfied.

Once Cesario's proper garments have been delivered, he shall address her no longer as Cesario but as "Orsini's mistress, and his fancy's queen" (V.i.374). There is justice in the whirligig of time because there is justice in nature, which at times decrees revenge, at other times reconciliation. The near-tyrant's fancy needs a queen to rule it, or at last to share in self-rule; the cure of love isn't music but a good beloved. Having come, seen, and conquered as Cesario—conquering first, unintentionally, a woman who mistakes her for a man, then conquering a man who finally sees him as a woman after testing her loyalty while she still seemed a man—Viola can now reassume her real name, a word not for a piece of music but for an instrument that makes music—in her case, music made by nature. Her brother's name, which he shares with their late father, means venerable, revered; with Olivia as his bride, he can now live up to that name despite, but also because of, the shipwreck Fortune meted out.

Shakespeare nevertheless gives music the last lyrics. All leave except the Clown, who sings for the first time to the audience. When a little boy, he tells them, "a foolish thing was but a toy"; when a man, I needed to attend to serious things, defending my household "'gainst knaves and thieves" (V.i.377,381). "But when I came, alas! to wive.... By swaggering could I never thrive" (V.i.383,385). The swagger, the pride, that intimidates evildoers, the strong, overbearing will that makes all the world a battlefield, and even the house of one's beloved a castle to be besieged, must give way to reciprocity, to the humility of ruling and being ruled, to the politic relationship of husband and wife, one flesh ruling one household. "A great while ago the world begun" (V.i.391); the need to conform to one's will to nature exists, is a reality not an illusion, because nature is the setting, the stage, on which human beings, the last beings created, must live. To know themselves, in households and in cities, they must know that. "But that's all one, our play is done; / And we'll strive to please you every day" (V.i.393–94). Will you will that? Will those at the Inns of Court, who rule according to the rule of law, understand and walk along the natural paths the law serves to delineate for the instruction and restraint of impassioned men and women who often prefer to step away from those paths?

PART THREE
THE COMEDY OF MORALS

Morality can be stern, a matter of command, of impartial and unfeeling law. Its enforcers risk giving too much sway to the 'thumotic' or spirited part of their souls—demanding retribution for offenses against it, up to and including a pound of flesh. When so spurred, they stand in need of the comic punishments meted out in The Taming of the Shrew *and sometimes redirected toward love, erotic or agapic, as in* As You Like It.

CHAPTER SIX
TAMING OUR SHREWISHNESS

In front of an alehouse on a heath—a wild place in a wild place—the indignant hostess confronts Christopher Sly. A tinker or itinerant pot-maker, Sly lives up to the reputation of his profession, then held to be an occupation for drunks. He doesn't live up to either part of his name, except in the way he puns off the name of his family: "Let the world slide" (Induction i.5). But as to the rest, he is neither a providential nor a provident man. Not Christlike—innocent as a dove, prudent as a serpent—not Machiavellian—vulpine and lion-like—he could not be less a ruler than he is. Incapable of rule, including self-rule, he seemingly cannot be ruled, at least not by the poor Hostess, whom he refuses to pay for some ale glasses he broke. Unjust, a man who will not pay his debts, like all drunks he harbors too much anger as well as too much appetite in his soul. Aristotle might call him the least political man imaginable, and therefore not fully a man at all, since man is the political animal.

A better ruler, called only "Lord," chances by, with his retinue and his hunting dogs. [1] Seeing poor, passed-out Sly, he likens him to a swine but recognizes him as human, a "drunken man" under the Circean spell of ale (Induction i.34). But as a true ruler, the Lord not only judges men aright, he knows what to do with them. Take him back to my home (out of the wild, into civil society) and make him "forget himself" (which is indeed a favor, given the character of the Sly 'self') (Induction i.38). Like a stage director of a play, the Lord directs his men to hang "his fairest chamber" with "all my wanton pictures"; "balm his foul head with warm distilled waters"; scent the air by burning "sweet wood"; when he awakes, have music ready, "a dulcet and heavenly sound" (Induction i.44–49). Sight, touch, smell, hearing: four of the five senses will 'argue' for a new identity; eroticism, especially, brings a man out of himself, redirects his thoughts to the loved one (or ones, as there is more than one wanton picture). The Lord does not appeal to Sly's taste, inasmuch as it inclines to the taste of ale. Let *that* sleeping swine lie.

"If he perchance speak"—show a telltale sign of humanness—tell him a noble lie (Induction i.50). Address him as His Honor, ask him for a command; will you wash yourself, will you dress yourself, and how? Tell him he is a hunter, a horseman, a husband whose lady "mourns at your disease," which is lunacy—a dreamlike condition from which he has just now awakened (Induction i.60). The Lord induces his men to look at his plot as an amusement, "pastime passing excellent, / If it be husbanded with modesty" (Induction i.65–66). Husbandry or agriculture works with nature; modesty or moderation works with care.

With fine comic timing, a troupe of actors arrives, looking for work. The Lord is happy to provide it, inviting them to join in with "some sport in hand / Wherein your cunning can assist me much" (Induction i.89–90). He instructs his page, Bartholomew, to dress as a woman and pretend to by Sly's wife, and to tell him he's been deathly ill for seven years. (Later, one of the Lord's servants more than doubles the number to fifteen.) As to the players, above all the Lord needs them never to act 'out of character' in his play, lest his stagecraft fail. And as to his other servants, "Haply my presence / May well abate the over-merry spleen, / Which otherwise would grow into extremes" (Induction i.135–36). The true ruler's presence moderates the passions of the ruled, civilizes them. The Lord rules by natural means (water, sweet scent) and mostly by art (wanton pictures, music, a play). Sly is very far from being ready for a real and civil life. He needs a comprehensive moral education.

The Lord and his men carry out this plot. Awakened but far from 'woke,' the patient asserts his identity: "I am Christopher Sly; call me not 'honor' nor lordship" (Induction ii.5). Reverting to his favorite appetite, he swears he "never drank sack in my life," sherry being a gentleman's drink, unlike his preferred ale, the beverage of the people (Induction ii.7). For food he wants salt beef, salt being a spur to more drinking. He even gives his lineage, far from aristocratic, dating back only so far as his father, plain Burton Heath, a name that suggests the wild and inhuman part of nature where Sly was found. Son Christopher has been something of a changeling—peddler by birth, card-maker by "education," a keeper of a tame bear "by transmutation," and "by present profession a tinker" (Induction ii.16–19). "Score me up for the lying'st knave in Christendom" (Induction ii.23–24)—English Christendom's finest example of the Cretan liar. To this, the Lord adjures him to, "Call home thy ancient thoughts from banishment, / And banish these abject lowly dreams" (Induction ii.29–30). He calls for Apollonian music, the opposite of Dionysian drunkenness. And the Lord states, with judgelike authority, "Thou art a lord, and nothing but a lord," with "a lady far more beautiful / Than any woman in this waning age" (Induction ii.59–61).

That arrests the man's attention, begins to reform his self-knowledge. "Am I a lord and have I such a lady?" (Induction ii.66). Do I dream now or have I been dreaming? Surely, "I do not sleep: I see I hear, I speak; / I smell sweet savours, and I feel soft things" (Induction ii.68–69). With a boost from wishful thinking, his senses convince him, as planned, even as common sense could not—he having little of that to work with. He calls for ale again, but now only the weakest kind. The Lord's men ignore that, instead bringing him his 'wife,' Bartholomew, who tells him that the doctor has left instructions for 'her' not to share his bed with him, lest his illness recur. Instead, the players will cure his understandable melancholy at having his eros first aroused, then denied. They will stage a play, "The Taming of the Shrew." This play-within-the-play will have its own play (or plays) within it, as the several levels of noble lies are arranged to lead not only a drunkard but all of Shakespeare's audience through our senses but beyond them. Since each of us is likely drunk with some impediment to wisdom and the other virtues, the play bids to cure Shakespeare's audience of the shrewishness underlying our drunkenness. It operates by having us, first, look down on and laugh at Christopher Sly, supposing that we are in on the joke, even as Shakespeare and his players play a salutary joke on us.

Let the game begin. In the play we meet Lucentio ("Light") and his servant Tranio. They have journeyed from Lombardy (specifically the city of Pisa, "renowned" for its "grave citizens" [I.i.2]). Lucentio would leave the home of a merchant father, foregoing citizenship for the liberal arts, the way to the philosophic life. "Here let us breathe, and haply institute / A course of learned and ingenious studies" (I.i.8–9), especially the study of "Virtue and that part of philosophy" which "treats of happiness / By virtue specially to be achiev'd" (I.i.18–20)—the philosophy found in Aristotle's *Nicomachean Ethics*. Ah, but as Tranio may know, the *Ethics* might lead to

the *Politics*, or, if not to politics, then to Stoicism. "Let's be no Stoics nor
no stocks"—restraints—he prays, "Or so devote to Aristotle's checks"—his
moderation—"as Ovid be an outcast quite abjured" (I.i.31–33). Logic, yes;
rhetoric, very well; "music and poesy" by all means, even mathematics and
metaphysics: But 'pray' "Fall to them as you find your stomach serves you
/ No profit grows where is no pleasure ta'en" (I.i.38–39). Epicurean Tranio
has a mind rather like an American college student; he likes a curriculum
with as many 'electives' as possible. "In brief, sir, study what you most af-
fect," what you want (I.i.40). If you would flee political life, select from
Aristotle's books as you please, but avoid the stern apoliticism of the Stoics
and embrace the pleasurable apoliticism of the Epicureans. In Plautus' play,
Mostellaria, from which Shakespeare borrows him, Tranio is a clever slave,
as indeed he is here; a man of wit, a fixer, but of 'slavish' character—low,
pleasure-loving, given to manipulating the low side of other souls, bending
them to his own inclinations. "Gramercies, Tranio, well dost thou advise,"
Tranio exclaims, inclining toward becoming a genteel version of Sly (I.i.41).

An object for erotic desire immediately appears. A Paduan gentleman,
Baptista Minola, has two daughters—Katherine, "rough" and shrewish elder
to studious, beautiful, and modest Bianca. They are accompanied by Hortensio and Gremio, suitors of Bianca. Of the two, Hortensio is the more eligible, as Gremio is a comical old man— stock figure in Italian comedy.
Unfortunately for them, Baptista will not marry his younger daughter until
he finds a husband for undesirable Katherine. Upon seeing Bianca, Lucentio falls in love, too; upon hearing her dedicate herself to her books, in the
likely prospect that her sister will never wed, his mind becomes as entranced
with her as his eyes. In what might be a kind of love test, Baptista asks
Hortensio and Gremio to find tutors for her.

When the Minolas go into their house, the suitors immediately hit on
a more practical object of recruitment, a suitor for Katherine. Rivals for
Bianca, they are allies on that. For their part, Lucentio and Tranio devise
their own 'play' or plot to win her. Lucentio will present himself as a tutor
in order to gain access to her. Meanwhile, Tranio will assume Lucentio's
identity in Padua, a plausible imposture because faces alone don't distinguish master from manservant. Nature makes no such distinction, at least
physically; they can change clothes, even as a clothing change was part of
the 'play' on Sly, and even as actors in plays change into their costumes,

into their assumed identifies—to sleep, perchance to dream, not of some Hell but of a person and of things outside their ordinary selves. And so, perhaps, to learn. Shakespeare himself served in his company as plotter, ruler, and player. And he learned as he went, from histories and light comedies to tragedies and *The Tempest*. Lucentio announces that he has another purpose to his plotting but does not disclose it.

This is to say that the Lord presents the changeling Sly with a play about changelings played by changelings. The play will invite Sly to change, to reorient, his soul, even as his condition has been changed for him by the Lord. Off to one side, now in a newfound role of theater critic, Sly does indeed approve of the play, although he cluelessly wonders if it's now finished. No, his 'wife' assures him, it has just begun; his cure has many scenes to go.

Veronese gentleman Petruchio and his servant Grumio (not to be confused with old man Gremio) have arrived in Padua to visit Petruchio's "best beloved and approved friend," Hortensio (I.ii.3). (The root of "Hortensio" means "garden"; there is perhaps a hint of apolitical Epicureanism in this university town). His father having died, Petruchio seeks in Padua not the liberal arts but a fortune and a wife, preferably in the same person. Hortensio tells him he knows a prospect, unfortunately "shrewish and ill-favored" (I.ii.58) but "rich, and very rich" (I.ii.61). As manly and thumotic as Lucentio is ardent and 'intellectual,' Petruchio replies that "wealth is the burden of my wooing dance" (I.ii.66). Therefore, "Be she as foul as was Florentius' love" (an old hag who nonetheless turned into a beautiful woman, by magic), or "old as Sibyl," or even "as curst and shrewd / As Socrates' Xanthippe or a worse"—philosophy lingers in the background, even with Petruchio—all's well that ends well, wellness being defined by him as wealth. [2] He too has a plot: He will disguise himself as a music teacher to gain access to Baptista's household, then take things from there.

Lucentio (having assumed his new identity as tutor "Cambio") and his new patron, old Gremio, pass by the two friends and Grumio. Gremio expects the tutor to advance his suit by reading love poetry to Bianca while pleading Gremio's case to her. Not knowing that the others have overheard the conversation, Gremio tells Grumio that the "schoolmaster" is here to tutor "the fair Bianca" (I.ii.163). Hortensio introduces Petruchio as a suitor to Katherine. But does he know how shrewish a lady she is, Gremio asks.

Petruchio is happy to discourse on Katherine, "an irksome brawling scold" (I.ii.184) whom he nonetheless intends to woo: "Have I not in my time heard lions roar?" *And the winds howl at sea?* Seen the "angry boar chafed with sweat" and "the great ordinance in the field," indeed "the greater thunder in the sky"? (I.ii.196–201). Hunter (like the Lord), soldier, perhaps unfearful of Heaven's lightning itself, why should Petruchio fear "a woman's tongue"? (I.ii.204). He will proceed to vindicate his boast. For their part, Hortensio and Gremio understand that his suit, if successful, will clear the way to Bianca.

Lucentio's servant Tranio enters, playing Lucentio. He claims to be yet another suitor of Bianca, but proposes that he, Hortensio, and Gremio deal with one another "as adversaries do in law— / Strive mightily, but eat and drink as friends" (I.ii.275–76). It is a fine proposal for a comedy, also setting up Tranio's two gulls for the deception needed to give his master the decisive advantage in his secret contest to win the lady.

Baptista's house is the setting for the beginning of Petruchio's celebrated taming of Katherine, who's been acting insufferably toward her father and Bianca. Suspecting her blameless sister of desiring Hortensio, rich old Gremio, or both, she strikes her; when Baptista reprimands her, she turns on him, accusing him of favoring Bianca and vowing revenge. Baptista's deranged household thus consists of a weak father, a rebellious and unsisterly older daughter, and a decent younger daughter who for now must suffer them both. Padua, a city of liberal learning, features serious deficiencies in at least one of its ruling families. Families being the foundations of cities, of political life, Padua may be a university town with a government problem.

The several suitors present themselves at the Minola household, and Petruchio executes his strategy, which is to contradict Katherine at every turn. Goading her by calling her by the diminutive, 'Kate,' he taunts her by raising her as pleasant, gamesome, courteous, slow in speech, yet "sweet as springtime flowers" (II.i.239). Thickening the irony still more, he lauds "her princely gait" (II.i.252) and her likeness to the virgin goddess Diana— the way of a princess ambitious for rule but unfit for it, an impediment to the continuation of her own family and therefore in contradiction with her own ambition. He turns romantic language, the language of courtly love, into a vehicle of infuriating mockery. For once, the lady is at a loss for words, speech being the coin of politics. She can only sputter, as her father offers her hand in marriage. She recovers her speech sufficiently to protest to him, objecting to this impending marriage to a man she judges a "half lunatic," "mad-cap ruffian," and "swearing jack" (II.i.280–81). Her taming has just begun; Petruchio exits, off to Venice to buy wedding clothes, but not before describing his betrothed as "temperate as the morn," the virtue associated with wise rulership in the play's Induction. As Hiram Caton observes, Petruchio proceeds with Katherine very much as the Lord did with Sly, in principle if not in practice: To tame the immoderate and unruly soul, he subjects it to the opposite of what it wants, contradicting it at every turn, upending its sense of reality. [3] Unlike the Lord, he does not do so gently, as it were behind the back of his 'student.' Public shaming, not private illusion, must be the way to amend a soul drunk not on ale but on the will to power.

Gremio and Tranio (as "Lucentio") end the scene by arguing over which of them deserves Bianca, appealing to Baptista's love of wealth by describing their riches, real and alleged, respectively. Tranio outbids Gremio, but now he needs to produce the rich father he's claimed. The two secret suitors, the real Lucentio (as tutor "Cambio") and Hortensio (calling himself "Litio," playing the role of a music-master), will make their approaches to the daughter. Both men pass love notes to Bianca in the course of 'teaching' her. She prefers "Cambio," who rightly strikes her as the truer man, beneath the disguise. Hortensio proves the accuracy of her judgment by immediately plotting to shift his love to someone else.

Long before the actress-queen in *Hamlet*, Katherine shows herself a woman who protesteth too much, chafing at Petruchio's absence after having tried to order him to go away. It is this hitherto well-submerged sense that she hasn't been living well in her father's household, that she somehow wants and needs a husband stronger than her father, that makes her curable, that will enable Petruchio's strong medicine to work. When he returns, disheveled and insouciant, his servant Tranio begs him "to see not your bride in these unreverent robes," to "go to my chamber, put on some clothes of mine" (III.ii.108–09). Petruchio is not a man to be 'dressed' by another, advised by a very clever but less prudent (and less manly) man. The lady will be marrying him, not "my clothes," he replies (III.i.113). What she sees will be what she gets. Tranio suspects method in this madness, which continues at the wedding, when Petruchio avers to be "master of what is mine own," a wife who "is my goods, my chattels," and "my house"—indeed, his household stuff, field, barn, horse, ox, ass, "my any thing" (III.ii.225–28). Because she is his own, however, the man of military valor will defend her as his own, against all comers: "Kate, I'll buckler thee against a million" (III.ii.235). He rules her by virtue of his nature, not by the dubious virtue of 'clothes,' that is, of convention, of changeable appearance. Moderate Bianca, who needs no such taming, remarks that her sister, "being mad herself," has been "madly mated" (III.ii.240). Thumos has yielded to the superior thumos.

Nor is Petruchio done. The shrew has yielded, but perhaps not wholeheartedly—and if not wholeheartedly, then not for long. As a military man he knows the difference between truce and surrender. Reversing the tactic of the Lord, he takes Katherine from the city to the country. Sly is a human being 'countrified' by ale, a drunk passed out on the heath—in a 'state of nature,' as later writers would put it. He needs to be civilized gently, by means of seductive illusions, removed to civilization to live a noble lie for a time, in order to learn the truth about his real nature. Katherine, an uncivilized denizen of eminently civil, indeed liberal-artsy, Padua, needs not the gentle atmosphere she has learned to exploit but roughness, exposure to harsh truths, crushing defeat by someone who plays her own game better than she does. She needs exposure to a state of war. Petruchio abuses the servants; she pleads for them, thereby getting out of herself, as did Sly under the rule of the Lord. As one of the servants remarks, "He kills her in her own humor," even as the Lord kills Sly with kindness (IV.i.169); indeed, he later tells the servant, "this is a way to kill a wife with kindness" (IV.i.192), using nature against her anti-nature. Like Sly, she "sits as one new risen from a dream" (IV.i.170). In both cases, it is a dream induced in order to bring the patient back to reality. "Thus have I politicly begun by reign," Petruchio replies (IV.i.172). Unlike Lucentio, unlike the Lord, Petruchio is a political man, not merely a military one. But Caton is wrong to think him a Machiavellian. [4] Petruchio rules her not as a tyrant, for his advantage alone, but for her own good. That is, he rules her as a parent rules a child, replacing her hapless father in founding a new household. "Amid this hurly I intend / That all is done in reverend care of her" (IV.i.187–88). Here he reveals his true nature; he had claimed to be interested only in a rich wife, but now we know he wants a good one. Right rule is a kind of practical wisdom: "He that knows better how to tame a shrew, / Now let him speak; 'tis charity to show" (IV.i.194–95). Like his near-namesake Petrarch, Petruchio knows how to address a woman. Courtly Petrarch knows how to address a gentlewoman; Petruchio knows how to address an ungentle and indeed unkind one.

He soon teaches her how to beg, instead of her habitual commanding. He starves her body, taunting her by offering and then taking away both food and clothing—again in contrast with the Lord's treatment of Sly. [5] Enforced bodily suffering requires recourse to the mind, and indeed, as Petruchio instructs her, "'Tis the mind that makes the body rich; / And as the sun breaks through the darkest clouds, / So honour peereth in the meanest habit" (IV.iii.68–70). Her *thumos*, misdirected toward prideful *libido dominandi*, must be redirected toward the natural honor of a human being, founded in its distinctive nature, the capacity to reason. "O no, good Kate; neither art thou the worse / For this poor furniture and mean array" (IV.iii.175–76). As with Sly, she must learn her true 'identity,' her nature, removed from the conventions to which she has become accustomed. When she continues to murmur in rebellion, Petruchio even 'makes' time stand still: "It shall be what o'clock I say it is" (IV.iii.191). (Newton supposes time a constant, but Petruchio anticipates Einstein.) He soon makes her call the sun the moon, and then the sun again. Like the Lord, he bends his patient's perceptions of nature to his will, so as to break her ill-will, and by so doing to see her nature right.

Back in the city, in front of Baptista's house, Tranio finds in an elderly "Pedant" passing by the perfect type for the needed role of Vincentio, Lucentio's 'rich father.' As a smart casting director, he gives the old fellow motivation, gulling him into believing that his life's in danger, telling him that he must assume the role of Vincentio for safety's sake. Pedants and the elderly alike tend to have timid souls. His master and Bianca plan elopement; this is the additional plot Lucentio had hinted at, earlier, as he deployed the decoy 'Lucentio' to distract Baptista's attention from the doings of the real one with Baptista's daughter. But his, their, plot takes a twist when his real father meets Petruchio along the road and learns from him of the impending marriage. The elopement proceeds, but the young marrieds must now return to Padua, and to their fathers, neither of whom is a happy man for the deceptions. Petruchio and his Kate (herself now openly in love) can now watch the show with amusement, as the quiet, seemingly docile couple have made themselves the center of controversy.

The principals gather not at father Baptista's house but at Lucentio's; as the Bible and nature both command, the newly-married couple cleave to one another, form a new household. There, Lucentio can offer his guests hospitality, bring "our jarring notes" to "agree" (V.ii.1). "Feast with the best, and welcome to my house" (V.i.8). (At last, Kate will be fed.) "Pray you, sit down; / For now we sit to chat as well as eat" (V.ii.10–11). This is the first time anyone in the play sits, comes to rest. To eat is to serve the body; to speak is to exercise the mind; the jarring notes of body and soul can now agree in the newly and rightly constituted household, where the newly and rightly constituted household of spirited Petruchio and Kate are welcome guests. When Baptista, Petruchio, Lucentio, and Hortensio (successfully married to a rich widow) make a playful bet on whose wife is the most obedient, Petruchio wins; Kate's love of victory, redirected, can now contribute to a better household than the one she left for marriage.

She makes her victory speech to the ladies, when commanded by Petruchio to "tell these headstrong women / What duty they owe their lords and husbands" (V.ii.135–36). This she proceeds to do, but not in her former way, by her once-characteristic habit of berating. She reasons with them. Her rhetoric depends upon an account of human nature. She teaches them that nature, shared by men and women, has also differentiated them. She will prove a better Paduan lecturer than many a university professor, then and there, now and here.

"Unknit that threatening unkind brow" (V.ii.136). As always in Shakespeare, "kind" means natural, as in grouping natural objects according to their kind, their species. Some parts of nature are also kind in our sense, but not all—as for example the heath from which the Lord rescued Sly. Why is a threatening brow unnatural in a wife? Kate offers four reasons: It wounds your husband, your rightful ruler; it blots your beauty; it ruins your "fame," your reputation; it is neither "meet" nor "amiable" (V.ii.140–41). Like a dirty fountain, no one will drink from it. That is, if a wife will share a household with her husband, any attempt to rule by fear will fail, if he is a real man, the kind you want for a husband. Your way with him must go through attraction, through your beauty and your amiableness.

You will be better off if respected by him, and by others; your honor, even the honor of your family, depends on it.

Properly, your husband is your sovereign, but both a gentle and a kind one, one who "cares for thee" (V.ii.147). He does this by committing his body to "painful labor both by sea and land" (V.ii.147). You stay "warm at home secure and safe" V.ii.151). In justice, you owe in return for his care and protection "love, fair look, and true obedience," the duties a subject owes his prince (V.ii.153). Why so? To disobey "his honest will" makes the wife a "graceless traitor to her loving lord" (V.ii.158–60). But why are these sharply distinct 'roles'—our own contemporary term suggests playacting—*natural*? By nature, women's bodies are "soft and weak and smooth," ill-fitted for painful labor both by sea and land, at least in comparison to the bodies of men. Undermine your husband and you weaken his ability to defend you and the household you share with him. The bodies of women are fitted for living in soft conditions, not for "toil and trouble in the world" (V.ii.166). Our hearts should be correspondingly soft, Kate urges—harmonized with those of caring husbands, as the Apollonian music heard by Sly might do to his shrewish, unruly soul. Therefore, she reasonably concludes, wives should curb their willfulness and do their own natural duty, even as husbands do theirs.

"Why, there's a wench!" Petruchio rightly exclaims (V.ii.180). He commands a kiss and receives one. "We'll to bed" (V.ii.184), as their marriage is now of a kind as may prove a just, natural, secure foundation for a family.

As for his brother-in-law Lucentio, in victory Petruchio can be magnanimous, great-souled: "'Twas I who won the wager, though you hit the white"—punning on Bianca's name—"And being a winner, God give you good night!" (V.ii.186). Whereas thumotic Petruchio presents the matter in terms of victory, Lucentio presents it in terms of thought: "'Tis a wonder, by your leave, she will be tam'd so" (V.ii.189). Philosophy begins in wonder. Lucentio came to Padua to study philosophy, the crown of the liberal arts. Tranio has failed to side-track him. Lucentio needs the example of his spirited, shrew-taming brother-in-law to spur him to philosophy, away from a slack epicureanism. Fortunately, his own wife will need no taming, so the young Socrates, if that is what he is, will have no Xanthippe to harass him. In forming an alliance, and by forming it at Lucentio's house, Petruchio and his new friend will strengthen the city or cities in which they live. They have formed an alliance between philosophic reason, practical reason, and spiritedness that mirrors not only a well-ordered regime but a well-ordered soul.

What can ale-soaked but now dried-out Sly learn from this play? He can learn how to order his soul rightly. He can learn to tame his inner shrew, the anger that lies beneath his drunkenness, the anger that must have made his soul drunk before he touched a drop of the brew. He can learn to get out of his own passions and appetites, away from his longtime identity, aspire to self-rule instead of self-indulgence, make a change that puts an end to his changeling ways. Although men and women have very different ways, by nature, as human beings they struggle with the same anger, the same *libido dominandi*, while remaining capable of the same capacities to reason and to love, justly and wisely. There is the foundation, in families, for good cities. If Sly heeds the lesson, he will no longer let the world slide, but join in the task of ruling it well, if only by ceasing to be unruly.

More broadly, it may also be that many in Shakespeare's audience will benefit from having 'taken the cure.'

Notes

1. See Hiram Caton: "On the Induction of *The Taming of the Shrew.*" *Interpretation: A Journal of Political Philosophy*, Volume 3, Number 1, Summer 1972, 53.

2. Florentius appears in Chaucer's Wyf of Bath's Tale, a tale about the proper role of a wife. A young knight and "lusty bachelor" in King Arthur's court, Florentius rapes a maid and faces death by beheading. Arthur's wife, Guinevere, calls the king to an act of just mercy: He consents to her 'plot,' that Florentius will have a year and a day to discover "what thing is it that women moost desiren." Florentius goes on the quest, but eventually despairs, as some women tell him they want riches, others honor, or "jolynesse," or freedom (meaning to do as they like), and so on. There is no consensus. Near the end of his period of reprieve, he comes upon more than two dozen ladies dancing in the forest, 'in nature'; they vanish, leaving behind an "old wyf" foul as she can be—worse than the much-married Wyf of Bath herself. She agrees to tell him the answer to the queen's question, in exchange for his promise to grant her a wish. The answer, he will tell Guinevere, is "Wommen desire to have sovereynetee / And for to been in maistre him above." All women, or at least "worldly women,"

harbor this libido dominandi, the passion Katherine exhibits openly. In exchange for this answer, which Guinevere approves as the correct one (Arthur acceded to it in granting her original request), the old wife demands marriage to Florentius. Understandably, the young knight resists, at which point the old wife offers him another bargain: You can have me "foul and old" but true and humble or young and fair and take your chances. Having now learned what women really want, Florentius leaves the decision up to her: She rewards him by changing into a woman both "fair and good." They seal their marriage with a kiss, as indeed Petruchio and Kate will do at the end of the play.

3. Caton, op. cit., 53.

4. Ibid. 57–58. Both the Lord and Petruchio aim at the good of the one they govern, not simply at their own good, as does Machiavelli's prince.

5. Michael Platt has discovered that Petruchio treats Katherine as a falconer does in training a wild female falcon. "The wild mature female is the most beautiful, the most hard to tame, and for both the reasons, the most prized of all falcons. The ways, including deprivation of light and food, are among those Petruchio tames his prized shrew Kate with." (Michael Platt: *Mighty Opposites: Machiavelli and Shakespeare Match Wits.* Self-published, 2021, Part VI, p.112, n.3.). Platt learned this the old-fashioned way, by talking with a falconer.

CHAPTER SEVEN
WHAT DOES SHAKESPEARE MEAN WHEN HE SAYS, "AS YOU LIKE IT"?

In the orchard at Oliver's house, his younger brother, Orlando, converses with Oliver's elderly servant, Adam. If Adam's name suggests the original 'Vetus Homo,' and an orchard suggests fruit, we might take this to be a new Eden. It isn't—or if it is, the Serpent rules it.

Orlando's late father, Sir Rowland de Boys, provided for him in his will. The lad is to receive either a gentleman's education or one thousand crowns. So far, he has received neither. Although Oliver has sent the middle brother, Jaques, away to a school that befits a gentleman, he keeps his youngest brother "rustically at home" (I.i.6–7)—rustically, because without an education he might as well be a bumpkin. Or worse: Orlando likens himself to an ox in a stall; his brother's "horses are bred better" (I.i.9–10). Instead of the good breeding of a gentleman, Orlando receives poorer breeding than an animal. Oliver undermines "my gentility with my education" (I.i.18–19)—which is no education at all—and thus "bars me the place of a brother" (I.i.17–18). That is, Orlando is by nature his brother, sharing the same father, but unnatural in his refusal to treat him in a brotherly way; in so refusing, he disables Orlando from achieving his mature nature through education. He also disqualifies him from his rightful place in the gentry class by means of the same bar. Oliver violates his brother's nature not only as a brother but as a human being, treating the youth as if he were an animal, ineducable—training him for a life of servility, the life of a beast of burden, when he should be educated to join with his brothers and with other gentrymen as a ruler.

But that isn't his nature at all. "The spirit of my father, which I think is within me, begins to mutiny against my servitude" (I.i.20–21). The thumotic character of the natural, and not merely conventional, aristocrat stirs in his soul. A human ox would be a beast ruled by his appetites, what Aristotle calls a natural slave. Orlando begins to be ruled by his spiritedness. What he lacks, so far, is the development of the naturally ruling element of his soul, his reason, stunted by his lack of education and perhaps his lack of experience, both of which could hone his innate capacity for *phronesis.* Hence, he laments, he can find "no wise remedy" for correcting his servitude (I.i.22). As yet, he can only chafe against it. But he has enough self-knowledge to appreciate his own nature, both its strengths and its (current) limitations.

Sir Rowland de Boys surely intended to exercise his own prudential wisdom in preparing his will, providing for his sons. He rightly judged that his eldest son would treat Jaques well. He wrongly judged that he would treat Orlando well. Does this suggest the limits of prudential wisdom, or merely the limits of *Sir Rowland's* prudential wisdom? Why does Oliver tyrannize over his father's youngest son?

Oliver enters the garden. Orlando complains of his treatment. He argues as follows: Oliver violates both convention and nature. "Courtesy"—the customs of the aristocracy, worldwide—requires the younger brother to defer to the eldest, the first-born (I.i.42); by the same courtesy, the same courtly, ruling convention, the older brother owes the young brotherly treatment. Orlando demands that he be given a gentleman's education or the thousand crowns their father willed him. He then goes further, arguing not only from convention but from nature: "I have as much of my father's blood in me as you" (I.i.44–45). By order of birth (one sort of nature, but one determined by fortune), I am your inferior, but by a more fundamental order of nature I am your equal.

This latter claim infuriates his brother, and he strikes Orlando; Oliver detests the claim that his brother is his equal in any way. They fight; Adam intervenes, asking them to remember their father, just as Orlando had remembered their father's will. If Orlando shows himself a natural aristocrat in the spiritedness he shares with his father, Oliver shows that spiritedness perverted into tyranny. Oliver proves this by calling old Adam a dog; the tyrant in his anger seeks not to establish proper subordination in accordance with courtesy, the rules of which he should have learned in the course of his own gentleman's education. More, he abuses both his brother and his father's longtime servant, now his own servant, whose name means 'Man,' to level of animals. Hegel would say that slave-Orlando has engaged in a struggle for recognition with his master-brother. No optimist who supposes the laws of something called History will dictate the slave's vindication in the eyes of the master, Shakespeare has the struggle issue only in a redoubling of the master's attempt to secure his tyranny. Unable to subdue his brother by abuse of convention, unable to subdue him in animal-like natural combat, Oliver will now seek to use his 'practical reason' not wisely but cunningly—and murderously. And it may well be that Oliver's apparently unreasoning rage against his younger brother erupts from an underlying fear, the source of which isn't hard to see.

For it transpires that a parallel but also different circumstance exists in the larger dukedom where Oliver's house stands. Duke Frederick has usurped the office of his brother, Duke Senior; in this case, the younger brother has rebelled successfully against the legitimate elder. Oliver may be terrified that the same thing might happen to him. Fortune has sent Oliver a man named Charles—a wrestler employed by the usurper duke. Oliver asks Charles for news of the new court, the new regime. He learns that several loyal lords of the dukedom have joined Duke Senior in exile; Frederick let them go, as this gave him what he takes to have been the good fortune of adding their lands to the holdings he had previously seized. Duke Senior's daughter, Rosalind, has stayed behind in Frederick's household because Frederick's daughter, Celia, raised alongside her from infancy, doesn't want to part from her. Oliver asks Charles about Rosalind; since young men seldom inquire about young ladies for no purpose, one may be confident that he has taken an interest in her.

Duke Senior has retreated to the Forest of Arden, which means Forest of Love—another intimation of Eden. But this Eden is no apolitical society consisting of a man and a woman. Although Charles does liken Arden to "the golden world" (I.i.111) it has a decidedly political and even potentially military cast. "Many young gentlemen flee to him every day" (I.i.109–10); supposedly attracted to the 'careless' forest itself, the gathering reminds Charles of Robin Hood and his merry men—not merely *esprits libres* but outlaws who, under the command of the exiled duke, might someday threaten the unjust regime from which they have exiled themselves. Usurper Frederick has cause to worry.

Charles has come to tell Oliver that Orlando intends to come into

Frederick's presence tomorrow, to wrestle the Duke's champion. That is, Orlando, without prospects in his brother's household regime, seeks to make his fortune at the higher level of the dukedom. Charles doesn't want to hurt the lad, whom he has every reason to suppose is taking a foolish risk. He asks Oliver to stop him; "for your love, I would be loath to foil him" (I.i.120–21). *Not at all*, Oliver replies. Probably lying, he says he knew about his brother's intention, and "labored to dissuade him from it" (I.i.130). But the lad "is the stubbornest young fellow of France" (I.i.131–32) and "a villainous contriver against me his natural brother" (I.i.134). Therefore, "I had as life thou didst break his neck as his finger" (I.i.135–36). Appealing to the wrestler's fear, he suggests that it's kill or be killed: If Orlando can't win, he'll find some way to poison Charles; the conniving youth will never leave "till he hath ta'en thy life by some indirect means or other," for "there is not one so young and so villainous this day living" (I.i.140–42). "I speak but brotherly of him" (I.i.143)—that is, I know him for what he really is, I know his true nature. Far from speaking brotherly of Orlando in the fraternal sense of the word, Oliver conceives of his brother's nature as if his brother were already dead: "Should I anatomize him to thee as he is, I must blush and weep, and thou must look pale and wonder" (I.i.143–45). Blush, because his gentleman's honor is shamed in having such a creature for a brother; weep, because I myself am a man of compassion, even for irredeemably lost souls. You, Charles, must be pale, fearful, and wondrous, uncomprehending at such a monster. It would not occur to Oliver that a man might be courageous and animated by the love of theoretical wisdom, the wonder that can lead to philosophy, to which the gentleman's education Orlando seeks would be the door; or, more frequently, that a man might be courageous and animated by the love of practical wisdom, the virtue most needful in a ruler—again the thing to which a gentleman's education would be the door. Instead of rewarding his brother with the natural and courtly recognition he deserves, Oliver sends an assassin to murder a man he could not beat.

Charles leaves and Oliver soliloquizes: "My soul, I know not why, hates nothing more than he," Orlando (I.i.151–52). Oliver lacks self-knowledge, but at least seems to know that he does not know. This would be a promising state of soul, this knowing what's unknown. But he does know. Orlando is esteemed among "my own people" (I.i.156). He poses a threat;

aristocracy, rule of the many by the few, must always concern itself with the many; unorganized, they pose no threat, but organized under the rule of another aristocrat and they will ruin you. Orlando might prove another Frederick, another usurper, although in this case his 'usurpation' would be just by nature, if not by nature, given Oliver's tyranny, which will not stop at murder to preserve itself. Rulers set examples for citizens and subjects; the example Duke Frederick has set makes even a legitimate ruling brother suspicious of his younger one.

Friends and cousins Rosalind and Celia meet not in an orchard but on a lawn in front of Duke Frederick's house. A lawn isn't fruitful; it is a place for play, for the friendship family members should enjoy. Today, Rosalind is too melancholy to be playful, despite Celia's coaxing. Like Orlando, she is remembering her father. Celia criticizes her for what she takes to be Rosalind's self-love, for loving her less than she loves Rosalind. *If I were in your place*, she says, *I would have learned to love Duke Frederick as a new father*. The argument fails, first because Frederick has done unjust injury to Rosalind's father, and because Rosalind's father is worthy of his daughter's love, as Frederick is not. Were Celia in Rosalind's place, she might be able to love her 'new father' if he were Rosalind's father, the good Duke Senior, but could she love her 'new father' if he were her real father, the bad Duke Frederick? Indeed, will she love her real father if he puts her love to the test, now? Rosalind takes care to teach Celia not to confuse nature with Fortune. "Fortune reigns in the gifts of the world, not in the lineaments of Nature" (I.ii.38–39).

The test comes in the person of the Duke's fool, Touchstone, who arrives with a message from Frederick, summoning Celia to him. The resulting badinage reflects the political circumstance of the dukedom under her father's rule. When Celia tells him that he may be whipped someday for the annoyance he causes, the fool replies, "The more pity that fools may not speak wisely what wise men do foolishly" (I.ii.80–81). In his usurpation, worldly-wise Frederick has been not only unjust but imprudent. Celia replies, "By my troth, thou sayest true; for since the little wit that fools have was silenced, the little foolery that wise men have makes a great show" (I.ii.82–84). The dukedom's right order has been upended because practical or prudential wisdom has deserted the souls of its ruler. Celia passes the first test, showing that she knows something is wrong in the way the dukedom is ruled. The second test is tougher.

A courtier of Frederick's arrives, bearing more news. Charles has defeated three men, breaking their bones. And now another match will occur, here on the lawn: Charles versus Orlando. When the entourage appears, the ladies attempt to persuade the handsome young man not to wrestle, Celia saying he does not know himself—your "spirits are too bold for your years" (I.ii.156–57), causing your reason to fail to judge rightly. Rosalind joins in, saying that his honor, his "reputation," be not injured if he withdraws from the contest to "embrace your own safety" (I.ii.162). This is no foolish assessment, as Orlando himself knows the limitations of his wisdom. But what has he to lose? "Punish me not with your hard thoughts" (I.ii.167–68) but "let your fair eyes and gentle wishes go with me to my trial" (I.ii.169–70). "If kill'd, but one dead that is willing to be so. I shall do my friends no wrong, for I have none to lament me; the world no injury, for in it I have nothing; only in the world I fill up a place, which may be better supplied when I have made it empty" (I.ii.170–73). Rosalind's melancholy, heartfelt lament, the melancholy of words, meets Orlando's melancholy of action. "Pray heaven I be deceiv'd in you!" she exclaims (I.ii.195). As he locks up with Charles, she thinks him an "excellent young man" (I.ii.195). She loves him for his mood, which matches hers, and for his excellence, his courage—which, in her own way, she will match.

To the astonishment of all, Orlando proves more than a match for Charles. He knocks the bragging speech out of the Milos Gloriosus, who is ignominiously carted off, unconscious. But when Frederick asks his name, curiosity and new respect turn sour. Sir Rowland de Boys was esteemed honorable by "the world," but "I did find him still mine enemy" (I.ii.206–07). You are a gallant youth, but your lineage is wrong; to Frederick, a man's innate nature is as nothing compared to a man's nature-by-lineage. This, despite his own willingness to overturn the rank of nature-by-fortune by betraying his elder brother, usurping his dukedom. He leaves.

Orlando avers that he is "more proud to be Sir Rowland's son" than "to be adopted heir to Frederick" (I.ii.213–15)—perhaps thereby revealing his intention in challenging Charles at the duke's court. To Rosalind, however, his lineage confirms his excellence: "My father lov'd Sir Rowland as his soul, / And all the world was of my father's mind" (I.ii.216–17). As for Celia, her eyes are opened, too. "My father's rough and envious disposition / Sticks me at heart" (I.ii.222–23). "Your mistress shall be happy," sir, "if you keep your promises in love / But justly as you have exceeded all promise!" (I.ii.224–26).

When Rosalind gives him a chain from her neck ("Wear this for me," as I too "am out of suits with fortune" [I.ii.227]), she fells Orlando almost as soundly as he felled the wrestler. As the ladies walk away, he can speak only to himself, saying, as "my better parts / Are all thrown down" (I.ii.230–31), even as she for her part walks back to say, "You have overthrown more than your enemies" (I.ii.233–34). His better parts are his courage and his human ability to speak to others. "O poor Orlando," he says, watching them depart for a second time, "thou art overthrown" by your "passion," which "hangs these weights upon my tongue," preventing the reason which no longer rules him from forming so much as a word to say (I.ii.236–38).

A spectator at the wrestling match, Frederick's attendant, Le Beau ("the Beautiful") returns to the scene to make a handsome gesture in reasoned speech. "I do in friendship counsel you / To leave this place," as the Duke "misconstrues all that you have done" (I.ii.242–46) and also now "hath ta'en displeasure 'gainst his gentle niece," Rosalind (I.ii.259). Le Beau adds, "Hereafter, in a better world than this, / I shall desire more love and knowledge of you" (I.ii.265–66). He is likely thinking of Heaven, but one tyrant doesn't necessarily make a world—even this world.

Alone, Orlando reflects on needing to return "from tyrant Duke unto a tyrant brother" (I.ii.269). Like Le Beau, he thinks of Heaven, or more precisely a glimpse of it on earth, "heavenly Rosalind!" (I.ii.270). Rosalind, indeed: hated, as he and his father's memory are, by the tyrant Duke, and now loved by himself and, in all likelihood, by his tyrant brother.

In the Duke's palace, to which they have withdrawn, the ladies deliberate. "O, how full of briers is this working-day world!" Rosalind begins (I.iii.10–11). With "his eyes full of anger" (I.iii.36), as Celia describes them, the Duke enters, calling Rosalind a traitor and exiling her under penalty of death if she refuses to remove herself from her court. Why? "I trust thee not" (I.iii.36). Recalling her long residence at the palace and her long friendship with his daughter, Rosalind replies, "Your mistrust cannot make me a traitor" (I.iii.52). Frederick then shifts from 'subjectivity' to 'objectivity': "Thou art thy father's daughter" (I.iii.54). When Celia defends her, the Duke exposes his real thought. The people of the dukedom sympathize with Rosalind. You, Celia, "art a fool" for trusting her (I.iii.76). You will "show more bright and seem more virtuous when is gone" (I.iii.76–78). Without the daughter of the exiled former duke in the dukedom, a perpetual reminder of the deposed man's virtues, the lesser but real virtues of his daughter will serve to reflect well on himself. The people will no longer incline in the favor of the deposed aristocrat and will then incline in the favor of the new one, securing his authority. 'As you like it,' indeed. Like Oliver, Frederick misuses his reason, making it into calculation, which he mistakes for prudential wisdom.

Two who do not like it are the faithful friends. Rosalind will go into exile, but where? The Forest of Arden is far away, and between the dukedom and the forest many dangers menace a traveling lady. Celia chooses true friendship over a false, unfatherly father. She will go into exile with her friend. Rosalind has her own counterplot, a prudential counterplan to answer Frederick's calculated policy. As she is tall, she will disguise herself as a man in order to intimidate would-be thieves. They agree to bring Touchstone with them, as they find him to be the touchstone (or perhaps the whet-stone) to their wits and "a comfort to our travel" (I.iii.127)—providing entertainment and perhaps at least a modicum of manly protection, however unimpressive. [1] Celia affirms that they go "to liberty, and not to banishment" (I.iii.134); sensible lady that she is, they'll bring their "jewels and their wealth" with them (I.iii.130).

With the conclusion of the First Act, Shakespeare's audience can conclude two things about the "you" in the play's title. They know that they are the "you" who are promised a play they will like. 'The few'—in this case, the playwrights—know that they must please 'the many'—the playgoers—if they are to continue to write plays for a livelihood. The people also may suspect that "you" means the people in a political community, who hold the balance of power by consenting to the rule of those whom they deem legitimate, authoritative. Some rulers will attempt to wipe out consent by making them fearful, but such rulers are themselves fearful—of them, and of rivals of ruling status and character, whose very virtues make them the more dangerous to tyrants and more appealing to the people. In both instances, the many hold the real power, and the few know it. The few must therefore reason, prudentially; some will reason calculatedly, instead.

In the Forest of Arden, Duke Senior tells his allied lords, his "brothers in exile," that "old custom" has "made this life more sweet / Than that of

painted pomp" (II.i.3–4). The forest is less dangerous, free of peril, as they
no longer feel "the penalty of Adam" (II.i.3–4). Here the winter wind, harsh
but free of malice, "bites and blows upon my body" (II.i.18) but with none
of the breezy, more dangerous flattery of the court. Nature's winds "feelingly
persuade me what I am" (II.i.11)—not, like flattery, what I am not. "This
our life, exempt from public haunt, / Finds tongues in trees, books in the
running brooks, / Sermons in stones, and good in everything" (II.i.15–17).
Lord Amiens (which means "friend") finds him happy in so "translat[ing]
the stubbornness of fortune / Into so quiet and sweet a style" (II.i.19–20).

The Duke feels compassion for the deer they kill for food, "poor dap-
pled fools" dressed in nature's motley (II.i.22). Another of the allied dukes
tells him that Duke Jaques (not to be confused with Sir Rowland's middle
son) suffers a melancholy fit over the deer, calling the Duke a worse usurper
than his brother, for killing them. Like the Duke, Jaques is alienated from,
made-foreign to, court life but unlike him he cannot find solace in nature,
in Arden, as nature requires humans to usurp and tyrannize, killing stags.
Jaques rebels against life itself. The Duke would seek him out, as "I love to
cope him in these sudden fits," when "he is full of matter" (II.i.68–69).

Back at the usurper Duke's palace, Frederick rages about the runaway
ladies. One of his underlings suggests that since they are enamored of Orlando they may be in his company. Frederick sends for Oliver; he will command him to find Orlando. But Orlando isn't with the ladies; he is in front
of Oliver's house. Adam intercepts this "young," "gentle," and "sweet master," this "memory of old Sir Rowland" (II.iii.2–14). Your very virtues, he
tells him, are "sanctified and holy traitors to you" (II.iii.13), bringing not
only exile but the possibility of death. Having heard of Orlando's victory
over the court wrestler, knowing that it has stirred admiration of him
among the people, Oliver would burn Orlando's room with him in it. "O,
what a world is this, when what is comely / Envenoms him that bear it!"
(II.14–15). This old Adam knows a venomous snake when he sees one. He
offers Orlando his life savings in exchange for the privilege of continuing
to serve him in exile. He will prove no burden, as "my age is a lusty winter"—a human nature parallel to the good non-human nature Duke Senior
has found in the forest—"frosty but kindly"—"kind" being a synonym for
natural (II.iii.52–53). He knows the reason for his health: He has practiced
moderation throughout his life. If Orlando's leading virtue is courage,

Adam's leading virtue is moderation. This Adam has learned the lesson of Eden, which is not to reach too eagerly for forbidden fruit, however good it may look to eat.

Orlando sees in this "good old man" an example of the virtue of 'the ancients'—of "the constant service of the antique world, / When service sweat for duty, not for meed!" (II.iii.56–58). In the modern world, men sweat only for promotion, for reward. "We'll go along together" (II.iii.66), fellow men of antiquity, the time when man lived closer to nature and accepted its limits as lessons in humanity. Adam replies, "Fortune cannot recompense me better / Than to die well and not my master's debtor" (II.iii.75–76). He counts loyal service to a worthy master not merely as duty but as a kind of privilege, which he has paid for in advance by tendering the savings he earned in service to the worthy father back to the worthy, true, natural son. They will head for the forest.

Rosalind, Celia, and Touchstone are already there. Rosalind too is a figure from the ancient world, telling Jupiter of her weariness of spirit. For her part, Celia's weariness is bodily. They rest. They meet two shepherds, old Corin and young, love-sick Silvius (whose name means "woods"). Rosalind sees in Silvius the mirror of herself. Touchstone observes that, "We that are true lovers run into strange capers; but as all is mortal in nature, so is all nature in love mortal folly" (II.iv.50–52). Rosalind agrees, seeing that nature sets limits, even to seemingly unending love-sickness.

When they learn that the shepherds have no food to share because the local landowner is "of churlish disposition" (II.iv.75), refusing to offer hospitality to travelers, and in fact intends to sell his farm, Rosalind tells Corin that if he will buy it she will pay him back. The ladies like the forest, would settle there, within the malice-free limits nature imposes. Elsewhere in Arden, Orlando and Adam have found the same thing; Orlando goes in search of food for his servant—serving his servant.

Meanwhile, the self-pitying courtier Lord Jaques takes a certain pleasure in exile. He finds his contentment in melancholy—although, like Duke Senior, he understands that in the forest he has no enemy but "winter and rough weather" (II.v.8). The Duke can't find him, wondering if he has "transform'd himself into a beast" (II.vii.1)—as in a way he has, a maudlin pitier of deer rather than a human hunter of food necessary for life. As fortune would have it, Jaques finds the Duke, or rather wanders in on him, having met a fool (presumably Touchstone) in the forest. The fool, he reports, moralized on the reality of time, whereby "from hour to hour, we ripe and ripe, / And then, from hour to hour, we rot and rot" (II.vii.26–27). Jaques took delight "that fools should be so deep contemplative" (II.vii.31). He would be one: "Motley's the only wear" (II.vii.34). "I am ambitious for a motley coat" (II.vii.43) like that of fool-men and fool-deer. Duke Senior is confident that "Thou shalt have one" (II.vii.44).

Jaques explains that he would be a fool because as a fool he'll have liberty "to blow on whom I please" (II.vii.49). Since by his nature a fool won't be taken seriously by anyone, and especially by the powerful, like nature's wind he can whip all alike, with salubrious effect. "Invest me in my motley; give me leave / To speak my mind, and I will through and through / Cleanse the foul body of th' infected world, / If they will patiently receive my medicine" (II.vii.58–61). Having lost his trust in dubious promise-makers upon having been deposed, Duke Senior will give him no such leave, knowing him to have been "a libertine" in civil society, too, "as sensual as the brutish sting itself" (II.vii.65–66). To such a man, liberty would be nothing more than "license" to "disgorge" his sins on a world that's bad enough now (II.vii.68–69).

Jaques' 'hurt' rebuttal of these suspicions is mercifully interrupted by Orlando, sword drawn, who challenges the men to a fight if they refuse to give him food. The Duke calms him: "Your gentleness shall force / More than your force move us to gentleness" (II.vii.102–03). Upon seeing that he's stumbled upon gentlemen in the forest (albeit ones described as having dressed as "outlaws"—presumably to deter such attackers), Orlando apologizes, confessing to incivility but explaining that necessity, and not only his own, motivated his threat—a right statement of the natural law.

After Orlando departs to fetch Adam, Duke Senior takes the opportunity to offer Jaques some needed instruction—moral necessity being as real as physical. "Thou seest we are not all alone unhappy; / This wide and universal theatre / Presents more woeful pageants than the scene / Wherein we play in" (II.vii.130–31). This enables Shakespeare to give Jaques one of the playwright's most celebrated speeches—the one beginning "All the world's a stage, / And all the men and women merely players"—describing the "seven ages" of man (II.vii.139–43). Two things need remarking on these ages or "acts" on the world stage, ranging from the inarticulate ("mewling and puking") infant to the "whining school-boy" to the "sighing" over to the honor-loving soldier "seeking the bubble reputation" to the well-fed, latitudinarian judge to the broken-down dotard, a senile wreck in his "second childishness" on the brink of "oblivion," "sans teeth, sans eyes, sans taste, sans everything" (II.vii.144–66). First, this gamut (or gauntlet) puts in motion and places in time the three parts of the soul as described by Socrates in Plato's *Republic*: appetite, spiritedness, and reason. But it does so in an entirely un-Socratic way. Jaques denigrates both the life of the spirited soldier—the reputation, the honor he seeks is nothing, a bubble—and the practical wisdom of the judge, "full of wise saws and modern instances" (II.vii.156), a platitudinous fool. Second, man begins in feebleness and resentment (mewling, puking—rejecting even food—and whining), ends in like feebleness followed by death, nullity. That is, Jaques' melancholy derives from or produces a sort of nihilism based on a denial of anything much more than the body, itself only temporary.

Duke Senior does not refute this Epicurean claim. Orlando does. He does it in action, not words—his liberal education having been denied by his unbrotherly brother. Orlando returns with the Vetus Homo, old Adam. While just as mortal as Jaques or any man, Orlando proves himself nonetheless loyal, compassionate for a man instead of deer, and just. Always courageous, his experiences in the forest have strengthened more virtues, virtues as needful as courage in a man, a woman, a ruler. Duke Senior, whose hospitality contrasts with the tight-fisted landlord (to say nothing of his murderous landlord-brother), welcomes them, invites them to dine, calls for music. The singer sings of the winter wind's superior kindness, naturalness, to ungrateful men, most of whose friendships and most of whose love bespeak "mere folly" (II.vii.181). Insofar as this is so, Jaques is right. But it isn't entirely so. The Duke tells Orlando, "I am the Duke / That lov'd your father" (II.vii.195–96). He invites him and "the good old man" (II.vii.197) to tell him their stories, so that he may "all your fortune understand" (II.vii.200). All men want to know, Aristotle writes; all political men want to know the fortunes of potential allies. Duke Senior is both political man and man, simply.

From tyranny in the family and tyranny in the dukedom, from just disobedience in the family by Orlando and in the dukedom by Rosalind, in the First Act, to harsh, malice-free, and just nature's regime in the Second

Act, a regime where friendship and genuine civility can rekindle, Shakespeare now takes us to the heart of his play, the Third Act, whose theme is love. Love animates families and dukedoms, whether they are just or unjust, natural or unnatural, because there are several kinds of love, ranging from the self-love that would ruin all others in the scramble for domination to the self-sacrificing agapic love of Christ on the Cross. For Shakespeare, erotic love infuses the finest friendships and marriages, but it is erotic love inflected by agapic love, a love neither selfish nor selfless but mutual, and good for both lover and beloved. If politics is ruling and being ruled, loving and being loved gives politics life, whether in a family or a dukedom, because true lovers want the good for themselves and for the ones they love.

But first, the haters. Act III begins in Frederick's palace, to which the usurping Duke has summoned the lesser tyrant, Olive. God loves by His grace; the Duke presents his listeners with a false *imitatio Dei*, proclaiming that he embodies "the better part made mercy" (III.i.6). He orders Oliver to find his brother and bring him back, "dead or living" (III.i.6). As a precaution, he will hold Oliver's lands as guarantee of his fidelity. When Oliver tries to assure him that "I never lov'd my brother in my life" (III.i.14), Frederick replies, "More villain thou" (III.15)—true, both as regards Oliver and himself. When Oliver leaves, he has his officers "of such a nature" (III.i.16)—villainy—to make an assessment of the lesser tyrant's house and lands, preparatory to seizing them. After all, any man who matches the tyrant's villainy might endanger the tyrant's rule as surely as an association of good men in exile does. The greater tyrant's self-love ruins subjects and soul alike, stealing from subjects and blocking self-knowledge by corrupting his natural 'self' or soul, the soul that would have loved his brother, the true Duke. One might say that Shakespeare here gives a portrait of a man who has made the Machiavellian exchange of soul for self.

True lover Orlando hangs a paper with a poem on it on a tree in the forest of Arden. His poem praises his beloved, testifying to "thy virtue" (III.ii.8). His love must be pure, entirely non-manipulative, because he has no reason to think she will ever see it; it is rather his witness to any who might pass by. After he departs, the first to see it will be good old Corin and the roguish court-fool, Touchstone. Corin asks Touchstone, "How like you this shepherd's life?" (III.ii.13). This elicits a sophistical and self-contradictory non-answer culminating in a patronizing, intendedly satirical counter-question: "Hast any philosophy in thee, shepherd?" (III.ii.21). Corin has enough to know the causes and effects that anyone can see, that fire burns and rain wets, and to have common sense; "he that hath learned no wit by nature or by art may complain of good breeding, or comes of a very dull kindred" (III.ii.26–28). Evidently, the shepherd has enough philosophy in him to know how to frame an ironic rejoinder to a snobbish fool. Quite possibly sensible of the wound he has received, Touchstone declares Corin "a natural philosopher" (III.i.29), asking him if he's ever been to court.

The natural philosopher's response recalls Socrates' critique of Greece's natural philosophers. They attempted to understand nature directly, failing to see that their impressions of nature might be twisted by their own opinions, by what we would call their 'assumption.' The way to philosophize is not, Socrates says, by naïve observation of dumb rocks and trees, but by examining the opinions of fellow-citizens and foreign visitors to one's native city. *Political* philosophy is the gateway to knowledge of nature, and especially of human nature. Touchstone would touch the philosopher's stone by bidding the natural philosopher to come to court, to consider politics.

But what kind of politics does Touchstone know, if not the corrupt politics of Frederick's dukedom? Rosalind and Celia have used him philosophically, as a whetstone for their wit, as Socrates (called "the Athenian buffoon" by one humorless German) did with many a clod in Athens, but has any of the ladies' wit rubbed off on clownish Touchstone?

Not so. Still hoping to dominate the conversation, Touchstone claims that if Corin has never been at court he can never have seen good manners; without having seen them, his manners must be wicked; and since wickedness is sin and sin is damnation, "Thou art in a parlous state, shepherd" (III.ii.40). But it is Corin who understands the Socratic distinction between nature and convention: "those that are good manners at the court are as ridiculous in the country as the behavior of the country is most mockable at court" (III.ii.41–43). His example is the courtly custom of kissing hands, which "would be uncleanly if courtiers were shepherds" (III.ii.44–45). Ignoring this pointed example, Touchstone demands additional ones, which Corin supplies, rewarded only with more entertaining sophistries in reply. As a court jester, Touchstone is a good entertainer; as a philosopher, he is the buffoon sober-sided citizens say Socrates is. "You have too much courtly

wit for me" (III.ii.62), Corin allows, probably recalling his distinction between court and country and applying it to shows of wit, a natural virtue
that requires apprehension of circumstances to be well-aimed. [2] As for
himself, "I am a true laborer: I earn what I eat, get what I wear; owe no
man hate, envy no man's happiness; glad of other men's good, content with
my harm; and the greatest of my pride is to see my ewes graze and my lambs
suck" (III.ii.65–68). Relentless Touchstone jibes that this makes him a
worse sinner still, a bawd to cattle and sheep. *Beatus illi*: Happy or blessed
is the man who lives in the country, working his own land with no landlord.
In Horace's classic statement of this theme, irony pervades the presentation,
as the man who speaks is a usurer. In Shakespeare's version, the countryman
praises his way of life without irony, the court-jester provides the sarcastic
denials. It may be significant that Touchstone touches twice on the religious
theme of sin, attempting to make Corin, whose name derives from the
word for 'heart,' cringe before him in guilt. His heart sound in the midst
of nature, Corin refuses the bait.

Rosalind unwittingly puts a stop to the dialogue. Dressed as Master
Ganymede (she had, after all, prayed to Jupiter), supposed brother of
Aliena, she enters, holding one of Orlando's poems, which she found on a
tree-branch. "Let no face be kept in mind / But the fair Rosalinde," she
reads (III.ii.84–85). This pledge, a faithful act of mind, Touchstone answers
with a parody which reduces love to physical terms and animal-imagery,
after which he derides "the very false gallop of verses" (III.103). 'Ganymede'
calls him a "dull fool" (III.ii.105)—it may well be that the matter of
whether the verses 'scan' isn't paramount in the lady's mind—to which he
replies, "Let the forest judge" (III.ii.111). Indeed, in time nature will judge
who is the fool, who the wise.

Celia enters, another of Orlando's poems in hand, one praising Rosalind as Nature's distillation of all the best features of classical heroines, and
again citing virtues of the mind—reading, teaching—in verses acknowledging the human pilgrimage in time, recalling Jaques' speech but ending
with a vow of loyalty instead of a counsel of despair. Dismissing Touchstone
and Corin, Celia confides that she has found not only the poem but its author. The man himself comes along, accompanied by Jaques; the ladies hide,
listening. Jaques wishes Orlando would "mar no more trees" by carving
poems in them (III.ii.244)—his exaggeration, since while Orlando may

have carved his beloved's name in trees, he has damaged no trees by hanging papers inscribed with poems. As always, Jaques' compassion, his feelings toward nature, veer toward the maudlin and misanthropic.

No friendship arises between them, nor could it; the lover and the melancholic are ill-suited to one another. Genuine friendship calls for virtue in both parties, but "the worst fault you have is to be in love," Jaques charges (III.ii.265)—a 'vice' Orlando will not correct in himself. Jaques judges him a fool; Orlando judges him a Narcissus, a self-regarding lover of his own reflection. Both men are lovers, then. Who is the greater fool? Nature will judge.

After Jaques leaves, Rosalind/Ganymede discovers herself. Her witty remarks show her a superior substitute for caviling Jaques. Remarking his good grooming, she challenges his claim to be a lover. Lovers are disheveled, she says. He seems to love himself more than any other, an unconfessed Narcissus. She subjects him to a courtly love-test, here in nature. Steering the conversation to his poems, she induces him to confess that he wrote them and then, calling love "merely a madness" (III.ii.368), promises to cure him of it if he will pretend that 'he' is Rosalind. She will then drive the madness out of him by driving him mad with her contradictory moods. But, the patient insists, "I would not be cured, youth" (III.ii.389). Oh, but "I would cure you, if you would but call me Rosalind, and come every day to my cote and woo me" (III.ii.390–91). Does Orlando now guess the ruse? For he agrees to go.

The central scene of this central Act is a comedy within the comedy, the natural equivalent to Shakespeare's device of presenting a play within a play. Touchstone has found himself a country girl and woos her, as sarcastic Jaques trails behind, eavesdropping and commenting as they go. Touchstone asks Audrey if his features content her, prompting her to ask, "What features?" (III.iii.4). What, indeed? Touchstone compares himself to the "capricious poet," Ovid, poet of changelings, of a nature without a nature, a nature of metamorphoses effected by gods more capricious than any poet (III.iii.6). Audrey doesn't know what 'poetical' is. "Is it honest in deed and word? Is it a true thing?" (III.iii.14–15). Truly, not, Touchstone tells her, as "the truest poetry is the most feigning, and lovers are given to poetry; and what they swear in poetry may be said as lovers they do feign" (III.iii.16–18)—Rosalind's worry about Orlando, the reason she puts him to the test.

Punning on "honest," Touchstone says he wishes Audrey were poetical because he would not have her be honest—honorable, chaste—unless she were ugly (III.iii.21–22). Honesty "coupled to beauty is to have honey a sauce to sugar" (III.iii.25–27); he would have his beauties incautious with their honor. Melancholy Jaques calls him "a material fool" (III.iii.28); he means that Touchstone gets right to what's on his mind, sexual conquest. Playgoers may hear another sense of "material"—physicality, neither rational, spiritual, nor honorable. In this Touchstone does serve as the touchstone for Jaques' nature, he the equal materialist (and, one recalls, the equal or even greater libertine) and the sadder man for it.

Touchstone proposes marriage, saying that the nearest vicar, Sir Oliver Martext, can do the dubious honor. And Shakespeare (in his usual guise as Fortune) causes that gentleman to walk by; when asked to perform the ceremony, however, he requires that there be someone to give the bride away. Jaques steps forward to volunteer, but advises Touchstone to marry not in nature but in a church with "a good priest who can tell you what marriage is" (III.iii.74–75); "this fellow" will mis-join the two of you, mar the text of the ceremony (III.iii.75). Touchstone tells the audience in an aside that he prefers not to be married *well*, as that "will be a good excuse for me hereafter to leave my wife" (III.iii.81). In this he is Ovidian-capricious, a would-be metamorphoser of himself. Nonetheless, he goes off with Jaques, in search of a more courtly, less natural, priest, leaving Vicar Martext not to have been "flout[ed] out of my calling" by either "fantastical knave" (III.iii.93–94).

This comedy in the middle of the comedy embodies in farce the themes of the more (as it were) serious comedy that frames it. The lover's folly, the question of trust—which cannot exist if nature is metamorphic and language metaphoric, 'dishonest'—the nature of love itself (mindful or only physical?), and the legitimacy, the lawfulness, of the marriage, the reliability of the vows, the words, central to the marriage ceremony: here they are.

All these matters, material and immaterial (in both meanings of both words), stir the two ladies. They are now frustrated because Orlando has failed to fulfill their promise to visit them. But faithful Corin appears instead, telling them to come with him "If you will see a pageant truly play'd / Between the pale complexion of true love / And the red glow of scorn and proud disdain" (III.iv.47–49). Rosalind/Ganymede can hardly resist, as "the sight of lovers feedeth those in love"; "I'll prove a busy actor in their play"

(III.iv.53–55). The "pageant" consists of Corin's young friend Silvius court-ing his beloved shepherdess, Phebe. She is playing hard to get. When the youth complains of the wounds inflicted on him by her scornful eyes, she (another materialist) demands to know how eyes can have wounded him, how eyes can wound anyone, as they have no weight and cannot injure like a hurled stone. One recalls that Rosalind/Ganymede has seen in Silvius a mirror of herself, and she does indeed busy herself as an actor in the play, reproving the girl for her "proud and pitiless" rejection of a good suitor (III.v.40). Phebe promptly falls in love with 'him'. Promptly, because (she burbles), "Who has loved that lov'd not at first sight?" (III.v.81). Even if eyes could not wound souls they can serve as portals to them, portals open to love's arrows. The hard armor of the girl-materialist proves less solid than she has imagined. In this, love humbles the proud, who suppose themselves invulnerable to it. 'As you like' is one condition, 'as you love' quite another.

The center of *As You Like It* and its follow-on scenes suggest that love metamorphoses all. But it metamorphoses them back to nature, which is steady, the right foundation of fidelity, although twisted by bad forms of rule in family and polity. How will love realign families and polities here?

Rosalind (still as Ganymede) and Jaques dialogue while Celia listens. Rosalind offers an Aristotelian critique of Jaques' melancholy: like its oppo-site, giddiness, it is an extremity; melancholics are "worse than drunkards" (IV.i.6). Jaques admits, "I do love it better than laughing" (IV.i.3), claiming it is "good to be sad and say nothing" (IV.i.7). "Then, 'tis good to be a post," the lady ripostes (IV.i.8)—somewhat inaccurately, since though posts do say nothing, they are never sad. This gives Jaques a chance to contradict himself by saying something—explaining that his melancholy isn't that of a scholar, a musician, a courtier, as soldier, a layer, a lady, or a lover (which combines the qualities of all the other kinds), but "a melancholy of mine own, com-pounded of many simples, extracted from many objects, and, indeed, the sundry contemplation of my travels; in which my often rumination wraps me in a most humorous sadness" (IV.i.15–18). One might be tempted to call Jaques a comparative political scientist, but Shakespeare likely means that he is worldly, and world-weary. Rosalind/Ganymede will have none of that. Exiled, she quickly purchased a new home. "I fear that you have sold your own lands, to see other men's; then to have seen much and to have nothing is to have rich eyes and poor hands" (IV.i.19–22).

Is that so bad? Jaques replies. "Yes, I have gain'd my experience" (IV.i.23). Before they can converse further, in a dialogue that might lead to philosophizing, Orlando enters. The lady posing as a young gentleman gains a dialogic partner of greater interest to herself, one who seeks not to philosophize but to establish a household, to love her country (you "disable all the benefits of your own country"), and to feel gratitude to her God (you "almost chide God for making you that countenance you are") (IV.i.31–34). A lover of her own, and of he whom she wants for her own, she dismisses Jaques' experience as saddening, preferring "a fool to make me merry than experience to make me sad—and to travel for it too" (IV.i.25–26). She turns from the melancholy fool-from-experience to the ardent fool she prefers.

Apparently still fooled by her disguise, Orlando addresses Ganymede as Rosalind, as per their agreement to stage a sort of play-within-the-play. Since Jaques' speech on the six ages of man, time has run its course as an undercurrent throughout the play. Rosalind tells him that if he arrives late for a promised appointment again, "never come in my sight more" (IV.i.37). She relents soon enough (in comedy as in love, timing is everything), and they soon co-produce a play-marriage. But marriage, she tells him, doesn't solve the problem of time: "Men are April when they woo, December when they wed: maids are May when they are maids, but the sky changes when they are wives" (IV.i.134–36). They exchange witticisms on infidelity; when it comes to sharpening her wit, fool Orlando proves a superior touchstone than Touchstone. But when Orlando tells her he must end their repartee and leave to dine with the Duke, 'Rosalind'/Ganymede makes his prompt return from that dinner a test of fidelity in the course of time. Indeed, she says, "Time is the old justice that examines all such offenders, and let Time try" (IV.i.183–84). If men and women, especially husbands and wives, often change over time, time will judge, separating the faithful from the unfaithful, identifying those whose characters are firm enough to satisfy the vows they make to others concerning what they will do and not do, in future times. The soundness of families and dukedoms alike depends on that.

As Rosalind and Celia await Orlando's return, Silvius delivers a love-letter from Phebe. Rosalind sends him back to her with the command: "If she loves me, I charge her to love thee" (IV.iii.71–72). At this point, her ruling powers seem secure, having repelled an unwanted suitor and welcomed the better one. But now her capacity to rule men and events, and even herself, gets thrown into hazard, again, in the person of Oliver.

The audience must assume that he has arrived in his hunt for his brother. He carries a "bloody napkin" (IV.iii.94), which he presents to Rosalind as Orlando's. He tells how it was bloodied. "A wretched ragged man, o'ergrown with hair"—the opposite of Orlando, well-groomed or civilized, even in the forest—"lay sleeping on his back," with a green and gold snake wrapped around his neck, preparing to slither into his open mouth IV.iii.107–11). This man was himself, who has indeed spoken serpentine words, outside the Forest of Arden. The satanic reptile would enter its own home. "Seeing Orlando, it unlinked itself, / And with indented glides did slip away / Into a bush" (IV.iii.112–14). In the shade under the bush was a lioness, waiting for the man to move, "for 'tis / The royal disposition of that beast / To prey on nothing that doth seem as dead" (IV.iii.117–19). The queen of beasts in this forest is the predator preying upon the predator-brother. In the forest, the bush doesn't burn; not God but beasts that are enemies of man make use of it. Lioness and snake are the only deadly females in the play, and the only deadly animals. The forest needs the virtue of human beings to rule the animal-evil that does dwell in it. Human beings cannot rule when asleep, and neither can they mis-rule.

This gave wide-awake Orlando a choice to make. He could let his lying and lying-down brother lie and die. Celia first wants to know if the sleeping man was Oliver, Orlando's "most unnatural" brother (IV.iii.123). "I know he was unnatural," Oliver confesses (IV.iii.125). He reports that his brother nearly walked away. "But kindness, nobler ever than revenge, / And nature, stronger than his just occasion, / Made him give battle to the lioness," which he killed (IV.iii.129–31). "I awak'd" (IV.iii.133). In saying all this, Oliver must have trusted his brother to have given him a true account—a trust reinforced, as it must have been, by the sight of the dead lioness. If kindness is nobler than revenge, then Orlando had proven himself more the gentleman than his brother, to his brother. If nature is stronger than an opportunity to act justly, then the overall framework of human judgment has prevailed over the occasion—the larger understanding over the smaller.

Celia now wants to know if the man before them is the unnatural brother himself. "'Twas I; but 'tis not I," Oliver replies (IV.iii.136). Past and present, the difference time can make, when a just action is timely within the 'space' of nature, the forest: Asleep in sin, Oliver woke up to his true nature. "I do not shame / To tell you that what I was, since my conversion, / So sweetly tastes being the thing that I am" (IV.iii.137–39). This is a metamorphosis not out of Ovid but out of Plato and the Bible—the turning-around of the human soul towards the ideas, when a prisoner of the cave of political conventions begins the journey to philosophy, and the conversion of the sinner to citizenship in God's regime. It is classical eros inflected by Christian agape.

The brothers didn't stay out in the woods. They returned to the house of "the gentle Duke," who "gave me fresh array and entertainment, / Committing me to my brother's love" (IV.iii.143–45). Civility requires clothing (in this case, new clothes for a renewedly human man) and leisure; it also requires faithful, declared bonds betokening shared brotherliness in a family and shared citizenship ruled by a man whose gentlemanliness contrasts with the savagery of his own unnatural brother, the usurper-tyrant whose uncivil society he fled.

All of this points to the cause of the blood on the cloth. In combat with the lioness, Orlando lost blood. He sent me here, Oliver says, to tell you why he couldn't keep his promise to return, "that you might excuse / His broken promise" in light of this physical evidence of his continued fidelity to me and to "the shepherd youth / That he in sport doth call his Rosalind" (IV.iii.154–57).

At this, 'Ganymede' faints, then recovers sufficiently to request that she be taken home. That is, unlike homeless, ever-traveling Jaques, she continues to fix her attention on, seek comfort in, the household. Oliver cannot understand why a man lacks "a man's heart" (IV.iii.165). Honestly enough, 'Ganymede' confesses that it is so; 'he' does lack one of the manly virtues. Nonetheless, Rosalind has recovered her wit with her consciousness, asking Oliver to tell Orlando that she only counterfeited her swoon. Oliver recognizes the noble lie as a lie but will do as she asks.

Love begins the transition from nature to civil society with plotting. If wrongly directed, the plots of lovers amount only to scheming, as Frederick and Oliver demonstrated. If rightly directed, toward mutual good, the plots of lovers prove reasonable pathways to consummation in marriage. Rosalind's well-intended and reasonable, if comically elaborate plot almost fails when she loses her reason for a moment, fainting dead away. But she recovers and sticks to her story, which now moves toward its end.

The final Act sees the lovers binding themselves firmly to one another. This begins with the unlikely pair of Touchstone and Audrey. A rival appears, the shepherd William. Touchstone interrogates him. He asks him several questions of ascending difficulty: How old are you? What is your name? Where were you born? Are you rich? And finally, are you wise? William says he is wise, upon hearing which claim Touchstone recalls "a saying, 'The fool doth think he is wise, but the wise man knows himself to be a fool'" (V.i.30–31). Like Socrates, the wise man knows that he does not know; he loves wisdom, without supposing he has it in any comprehensive, godlike way. William fails the Socratic test. Touchstone then cites "the heathen philosopher" who, "when he had a desire to eat a grape, would open his lips when he put it into his mouth; meaning thereby that grapes were made to eat and lips to open" (V.i.31–34). Perhaps more Aristotelian than Socratic, this simple example of teleological design illustrates what nature is. It is an instance of humanly achievable knowledge, the acquisition of which makes of one somewhat less of a fool than before. Two more questions for William: *Do you love this maid? Yes:* that is, he desires to eat the grape. Are you "learned" (V.i.35)? *No.* Self-described as wise but ignorant, then. That being so, William, learn this: *Pour a full cup of water into the glass and the cup will be empty, no longer holding the water. I now possess Audrey and you do not. And, not to put too fine a point on the matter, now go, or I will kill you.* Audrey joins in urging him to go, joining the long line of women who cause nice guys to finish last. On a decidedly less noble level, Touchstone loves his own, as Rosalind loves her own. They understand that love is exclusive, not cosmopolitan. Now he's as ready to marry as a man like himself will ever be.

Owing his life to the brother he set out to kill, Oliver has transformed their relationship from suspicion to intimacy. To Orlando's astonishment at the sudden love between Oliver and 'Aliena,' Oliver simply asks for his approval of their marriage—effectively treating Orlando as an older, at least equal brother. He will give their father's land and revenue to Orlando, set up his household in the forest, and "die a shepherd" with his presumed shepherdess-bride (V.ii.12). "Ganymede' arrives to assure Orlando that the couple really did experience love 'at first sight,' that experience of time compressed. On hearing this, and having learned to trust 'Ganymede's' prudent wit, Orlando agrees to the marriage, wasting no time himself: "They shall be married tomorrow; and I will bid the Duke to the nuptial" (V.ii.40–41). He only feels "heart-heaviness" because he won't be marrying Rosalind (V.ii.44). When 'Ganymede' volunteers to substitute for her, he refuses; "I can no longer live by thinking" (V.ii.48). If the fool thinks he is wise, as the saying goes, then the playacting lover may well prefer to give up thinking, give up his pretend-beloved, his beloved-in-thought alone. Only the real person will do. If he has seen through Rosalind's disguise, he wants her to stop playing and reveal herself, in action.

In another sense, to give up thinking is to give up philosophizing, or the attempt to philosophize. Neither Orlando nor Rosalind is a philosopher. They are, however, candidates for the activities of marriage, for the household rule animated not by the love of wisdom but the love of their own home, family, country. Where would nature be, without them? Or cities?

Rosalind, who never loses sight of reality and is nobody's fool, now knows the truth of what she tells him: "You are a gentleman of good conceit" (V.ii.51)—that is, of good thought—and I "can do strange things" (V.ii.56–57). Concocting yet another noble lie, she tells him that since the age of three she's "convers'd with a magician, most profound in his art and yet not damnable" (V.ii.57–59)—a practitioner of 'white magic'—and so tomorrow 'he' will use the power he has learned to bring him Rosalind herself, "without any danger" (V.ii.63–64). You can then marry her, "if you will" (V.ii.68), even as your brother marries 'Aliena'.

The next couple to arrive are Silvius and his still-recalcitrant Phebe. No philosopher, either, Silvius nonetheless offers a sound definition of love derived from his experience, and therefore according not to thought abstracting from particulars but according to an analysis of love's sixteen components. They are: sighs and tears, faith and service, fantasy, passion and wishes, adoration, duty and observance, humbleness, patience, purity, trial, and obedience. Adoration and duty are the central components of love, and because love's components are sound, loving is not blamable, no matter what his beloved says.

While not blaming misdirected love, Rosalind does intend to put the several lovers here on the right tracks, the ways befitting the nature of each. To Silvius, she promises to "help you if I can"; to Phebe, she says, "I would love you if I could" and "I will marry you if ever I marry woman, and I'll be married tomorrow"; to Orlando, she promises that "I will satisfy you if ever I satisfied man, and you shall be married tomorrow" (V.ii.104–08). Reason enables her to be true and false, without self-contradiction, thanks to her mastery of the capacity of words for ambiguity and even paradox or seeming contradiction. That mastery is her true art, a magic both illusory in its capacity for telling plausible noble lies and it power to redirect human thoughts, passions, and actions toward constituting a good regime.

Missing from this meeting, Touchstone and Audrey are still in the forest, where she tells him that she has preferred him to rustic William because she wants to become "a woman of the world," a poor shepherdess no longer (V.iii.4). They too intend to marry tomorrow, so it won't be long before she will learn if better social standing will be the consequence of the marriage she plans. Two pages from Duke Senior's household come by and sing the happy couple a love song celebrating spring as the time for love. Predictably, Touchstone complains about their artistry, or the lack of it, but one page insists, "We kept time, we lost not our time" (V.iii.36–36). As in comedy and love, in music timing is everything, as it is in nature itself. Music plays over time, unfolding in time, and it depends on timing both in the harmonies it consists of and in the performers who play it. If it is to be good, their timing needs to be well-judged, prudent. Music, like comedy and love, requires right rule.

The next day, right-ruling Duke Senior, his friend and ally Lord Amiens, Jaques, Orlando, Oliver, and 'Aliena' await 'Ganymede.' 'He' arrives, with Silvius and Phebe in tow, commending patience, preeminently the virtue tested by time. The Duke agrees to give his daughter Rosalind in marriage to Orlando, if Rosalind does appear. 'Ganymede' extracts from Phebe a promise to marry Silvius if Phebe refuses to marry 'him,' 'Ganymede,' a promise she makes easily because she makes it unsuspectingly. And Silvius as easily consents to marry Phebe, "if she will" (V.iv.17). 'Ganymede' and 'Aliena' then depart, replaced by Touchstone and Audrey; the jester amuses the Duke, delivering a comic account of the ways of courtly quarreling and a satire on courtly chivalry based on a typology of lies. Having been deceived by lying courtly courtesies, the Duke takes the point. Touchstone, he observes to Jaques, "uses his folly like a stalking-horse, and under the presentation of that he shoots his wit" (V.iv.100–01). Exotericism has its virtues, a truth Rosalind will demonstrate, upon her return.

Undisguised, Rosalind and Celia return with Hymen, the god of marriage. Hymen hymns, "Then there is mirth in heaven, / When earthly things made even / Atone together" (V.iv.102–04). Atone: Might this be Rosalind's discreet apology, put in the mouth of a god, for her benign ruses? In comedy, justice and repentance harmonize on earth, as they do in Heaven. Rosalind recovers her father, gains a husband, and loses an unwanted lover who, now knowing the reality, bids "my love adieu" (V.iv.115). Hymen hymns again: "Whiles a wedlock-hymn we sing, / Feed yourselves with questioning, / That reason wonder may diminish, / How thus we met, and these things finish" (V.iv.131–34). This isn't the theoretical reason of philosophy but the practical reason of right ruling. Hymen sings on: "'Tis Hymen peoples every town, / High wedlock then be honored. / Honor, high honor, and renown, / To Hymen, god of every town!" (V.iv.137–40). Marriage is the foundation of the family, family the foundation of the town. Hymen is a god of the civil religion everywhere, as universal as nature itself in its generative power. Having learned from nature, these now fully civilized men and women will bring what they've learned into a civil society that they will now establish. Duke Senior had founded a band of brothers, but by nature brothers cannot generate a lasting political community. That takes a settlement which includes women on the right terms, the terms of human nature, which exhibits reasoned speech in conditions of shared justice and mercy.

This happy ending ignores one massive threat. The rulers of the new *polis* have made no provision for foreign policy. Internally sound, their community is externally at hazard from the regime of the usurper-tyrant whose evil rule its citizens have escaped. But there is still one more person to make his appearance. We recall that there are two Jaques—one the melancholy traveler, the other the second son of Sir Rowland de Boys. Jaques de Boys now enters, with news from the court of Duke Frederick. "Hearing how every day / Men of great worth resorted to this forest," Frederick has mounted a military expedition of "mighty power" to attack the exiles (V.iv.148–50). Poised to enter the forest, he met "with an old religious man"—the only one we've met is the Vicar Martext—who "converted" him "both from his enterprise and from the world" (V.iv.153–55). Frederick has ceded the crown back to Duke Senior, restored all lands to those he dispossessed, and entered a monastery—spiritual exile from the Kingdom of Man. For the man of extreme *libido dominandi*, for the tyrannical soul, only the most extreme form of turning away from the world will suffice.

These are welcome, well-timed wedding gifts. Oliver and Celia will return to live on his restored estate. The Duke will return to his rightful throne. His son-in-law Orlando will return as heir to the "potent dukedom" (V.iv.163), with wise Rosalind at his side to tender counsel. All of Duke Senior's friends and allies will "share the good of our returned fortune, / According to the measure of their states," that is, according to justice (V.iv.168–69). Before returning to our newly-restored "dignity," the Duke happily commands, forget its restoration for the moment and "fall into our rustic revelry" with music and dance, human harmonies consonant with those of the nature around them, and now in them (V.iv.170–71). Music is the imitation of the natural harmonies, speaking to the soul, dance the action of the body in accord with music. [3] Soul and body are the last pair to be reconciled, as right rule, the soul's thoughts and sentiments, now accord with the body's actions.

Regimes are exclusive; not everyone can or would be reconciled to one. The melancholy Jaques will imitate Frederick's self-exile; like him, he has no wife, no place within the harmonies of civil society. Love harmonizes, but it also excludes those who neither love nor are loved. Duke Senior invites him to remain, but Jaques prefers to retire to the Duke's soon-to-be-abandoned cave. He has gone from libertine to world traveler to melancholic and now to isolato. For him, however, none of his metamorphoses has changed him into a person who can participate in a civil society animated by natural sentiments, the principal of which is an entwining of erotic love, especially love of one's own. Jaques is an egoist who doesn't even love himself. His cave isn't even the Platonic-Socratic cave of human convention. It is a cave not beneath but outside the cave, warmed neither by the love of God, as a monastery might be, or love of neighbor, as a civil society might be. It is the cave of misanthropy, the end of apolitical epicureanism. Shakespeare has delivered each soul to its rightful place.

The plot of the play so concluded, Rosalind steps forward to speak to the audience in a kind of play outside the play. "It is not the fashion," the convention, "to see the lady in the epilogue" (Epilogue 1). Having consistently shown how to navigate between such convention and nature, she will not falter now. "If it be true that good wine needs no bush, 'tis true

that a good play needs no epilogue" (Epilogue 4–5); since a "bush" was
what the vine tavern owners would hang to advertise the wine they had on
offer, she means that a good play, like a good wine, needs no advertising; it
will win customers by 'word of mouth,' as they liked it. The only other
"bush" mentioned in *As You Like It* is the one retreated to and the lion hid
under. Bushes may conceal the bad as easily as they may publicize the good.
Predatory animals seek cover to do evil; human beings with rightly ordered,
harmonized souls seek the good without being drawn to it with ballyhoo.
They do need to be told about it.

Rosalind will not beg the audience to like the play. Rather, "My way is
to conjure you" (Epilogue 10), the way of the magician of words, of speech
and reason, under whose beneficial spell you may be. She conjures them
with her words one last time, asking both men and women to like the play.
Perhaps her spell, her lessons about love, marriage, fidelity in family and
country will remain with this real-world audience after they leave the theater of thought Shakespeare has made, even as his characters will return to
civil society re-grounded in nature.

As you like it: Indeed, how do you like it, and what is it? How will you
know yourself well enough to become a loyal brother, a good friend, a faithful citizen, a true lover, husband, wife? To know yourself you will need an
education, and absent the sound, liberal, gentlemanly and gentlewomanly
education of rulers, you may need to learn what is humanly natural from
nature itself and from what is kindly artificial—noble lies taught by a benevolent plotter or playwright, blending well-timed speeches and action with
artful costume designs, well-ordered music, song, and dance, all of them
protecting good souls and redirecting bad ones toward nature, toward
human nature in its capacity for reason, love, and right reverence.

Notes

1. Harold C. Goddard observes that a touchstone is a type of black sandstone
    that tests the purity of gold and silver when a merchant rubs the precious
    metal on it. The small streak of metal on the stone can then be analyzed. "Not
    precious itself, it reveals preciousness"—or, it might be added, the lack of it—
    "in what touches it." (Goddard: *The Meaning of Shakespeare*. Two volumes.
    Chicago: The University of Chicago Press, 1967 [1951], I.290.) Goddard,
    who finds great fault in Touchstone, doesn't sufficiently reflect on the fact that

a bit of precious metal rubs off on him; this may be what Duke Senior sees in, or at least on, him.

2. Scholars have suggested that "Corin" is short for "Corinthians," and here are reminded of Paul's observation that God has chosen the foolish things of the world to confound the wise.

3. C. L. Barber writes, " *As You Like It* seems to me the most perfect expression Shakespeare or anyone else achieved of a poise which was possible because a traditional way of living connected different kinds of experience with each other," a "humorous recognition… of the limits of nature's moment." (C. L. Barber: *Shakespeare's Festive Comedies.* Cleveland: World Publishing Company, 1963 [1959], 238.) However, nature isn't only a moment, even if living 'out in nature,' in the forest, is. Rather, members of the renewed political society will take nature's lessons back to the potent dukedom.

PART FOUR

THE COMEDY OF POLITICS

One dimension of political comedy can be found in rhetoric, speech intended to persuade others of the veracity of the speaker's thoughts, and to move them to act according to those thoughts. As All's Well That Ends Well *demonstrates, such persuasion may deceive not only others but the speaker.* Love's Labour's Lost *addresses another form of deception—the attempt not to rule according to nature but to master it, to turn a kingdom into a sort of academic cloister, an unnatural regime in which the rulers forgo love in pursuit of knowledge. Zeal so misdirected will ruin any regime. That Shakespeare does not commend the opposite, Dionysian, way of life may be seen in* The Winter's Tale, *where the Delphic Apollo passes judgment on a jealous king.*

CHAPTER EIGHT
IS ALL WELL THAT ENDS WELL?

The young Count Bertram of Rousillon, his mother the Countess, Helena (a gentlewoman and ward of the Countess), and elderly Lord Lefeu converse in the Count's palace. A setting for a comedy not a 'history play,' 'Rousillon' isn't exactly the real Roussillon. Claimed by Charlemagne and his heirs among the French kings during the Middle Ages, by Shakespeare's time the real Roussillon had been ruled by the Spanish Hapsburgs since 1516 and would remain under their rule until the French king obtained it in the Treaty of the Pyrenees in 1659, following a long war. There hadn't been a count of Roussillon since the twelfth century. Shakespeare's "Rousillon" anticipates the future French conquest in the sense that the Count in his play owes allegiance to France. One letter short of the fact, Shakespeare's 'Rousillon' serves the purposes of comic semi-fiction.

As so often in Shakespeare, the play doesn't begin comically. The Count has been called to the King's court, and his widowed mother regrets it: "In delivering my son from me, I bury a second husband" (I.i.3). The play begins with a paradox—delivery, a metaphor for birth, described in funeral terms. Lafeu attempts to console her and her departing son, saying that the King's virtue will make of the King a husband to her and a father to the young Count. But the King's kind step-fatherly status won't last long, it seems; he is mortally ill and his physicians can do nothing for him. The Countess believes that Helena's father, a physician "whose skill was almost as great as his honesty," could have prolonged the King's life "so far" that he "would have made nature immortal" (I.i.17–18). But this physician evidently could not heal himself, as he too has died, leaving Helena under the Countess's protection. Lafeu knew the man, saying, "he was skillful enough to have liv'd still, if knowledge could be set up against mortality" (I.i.26–27). LaFeu discreetly reminds the Countess of the limits of what we now call 'scientific' knowledge, which can indeed be set up against mortality but not eternally. God might make nature immortal, but physicians cannot.

The Countess claims another kind of knowledge, moral knowledge. Helena has inherited honesty and, more generally, goodness from her father. "The remembrance of her father never approaches her heart but the tyranny of her sorrows takes all livelihood from her cheek" (I.i.43–44). Perhaps alerted by the word "tyranny," LaFeu makes bold to correct the Countess and her protégé. "Moderate lamentation is the right of the dead; excessive grief the enemy of the living" (I.i.48–49).

Bertram interrupts their philosophizing. "Madam, I desire your holy wishes" (I.i.52). His mother blesses him, exhorting him to "succeed thy father in manners, as in shape!" (I.i.54–55). "Thy blood and virtue / Contend for empire in thee, and thy goodness / Share with thy birthright!" (I.i.55–57). That is, a young aristocrat's spirited "blood," which elevates him above commoners, may rival his moral virtue as he reaches the age of self-rule. Accordingly, she gives him moral advice that may strengthen his virtue against his "blood." "Love all, trust a few, / Do wrong to none; be able for thine enemy / Rather in power than use, and keep thy friend / Under thy own life's key; be check'd for silence, / But never tax'd for speech. What heaven more will, / That thee may furnish, and my prayers pluck down, / Fall on thy head!" (I.i.57–62). Reduced to simple English, her advice is sound. Christianity commands us to love all but to trust God; humans may be trusted provisionally, after testing. Be just, and match your enemy's powers but not his customs, his habits—the practices that make him your enemy. Guard your friend with your life. Speak but do not chatter. Beyond that, God will do as He will do, and I shall pray that His blessings will fall upon you.

Countess, Count, and LaFeu depart, leaving Helena alone. We learn that in truth her sentiments align with LaFeu's wise precept: she "think[s] not on my father" (I.i.73). "I have not forgot him; my imagination / Carries no favor in't but Bertram's" (I.i.76–77). Her tears and her pallor are for his departure to the royal court, not for her father's departure from this earth, six months earlier. In her mind she has followed the Biblical injunction to leave her father and join with her husband, but as with 'Rousillon' itself, imagination isn't reality. Nor is it likely to become reality, as Count Bertram is "far above me"—a commoner—like a star above the earth (I.i.81). Her "blood" does not equal his. For this reason, her love, like the funereal "delivery" the Count to the King by the Countess, contradicts itself. "Th' ambition in my love thus plagues itself; / The hind that would be mated by the lion / Must die for love" (I.i.84–85). Helena initially takes the "blood" of aristocratic birth to be a part of nature; aristocrats are a different 'species' than commoners, and to contradict nature only invites nature to enforce this natural limit by killing the thing which contradicts it. Like her father, Helena has contracted an illness that threatens to be fatal, although in her case she might cure herself by refusing to dream of marrying above her putatively natural limit. Her own nature, however, makes that supremely difficult for her to do, as she loves him.

The question, then, is, what is her natural limit? Should she love him? Is social and political rank more natural than virtue? Is her beloved's virtue worthy of her love? Is her virtue worthy of his love? She admits to herself that she loves him for his body, not his soul—for "his arched brows, his hawking eye, his curls" (I.i.88). She knows she indulges in "idolatrous fancy," idolatry being precisely devotion to bodies instead of souls and, worse, the divinization of the inanimate (I.i.91). She calls into question her own virtue, which is now tested.

Tested in the person of Parolles, Count Bertram's attendant. Helena says, "I love [Parolles] for his sake"—for Bertram's sake—yet "I know him a notorious liar" and "think him a great fool, soley a coward" (I.i.93–95). The pun is apt: Parolles' soul will indeed prove entirely pusillanimous. Parolles' name means 'speech'—highly suspect speech, in Helena's opinion; in this she follows the Countess's admonition about the right and wrong use of speech and silence. Parolles immediately proves himself an ironist, addressing her as "fair queen" (I.i.100)—with a likely pun on 'queen' as 'whore,' a false wish that has fathered the evil thought. He proceeds impudently but not Socratically, asking if she's "meditating on virginity" (I.i.105). In a way she has been, so she answers by taking up his theme while rejecting his imputation, replying, "Man is enemy to virginity; how may we barricade it against him?" (I.i.107–08). After some punning and suggestive badinage, Parolles speaks his mind: "It is not politic in the commonwealth of nature to preserve virginity. Loss of virginity is rational increase; and there was never virgin got till virginity was first lost. That you were made of is metal to make virgins. Virginity by being once lost may be

ten times found; by being ever kept, it is ever lost. 'Tis too cold a companion, away with't," being "against the rule of nature" (I.i.120–125,127). All
true enough. Scarcely in favor of perpetual virginity, Helena then asks, now
speaking *her* mind, how might a woman "lose [virginity] to her own liking?" (I.i.141). Parolles doesn't answer her question, instead urging her to
abandon her virginity in haste.

With perfect equanimity, Helena doesn't respond to his suggestion, instead turning the conversation to Parolles' "master" (I.i.154)—thereby reminding him both of his station and his duties. She worries that when
Bertram gets to the King's court he'll have "a thousand loves" and therefore
a mind whose attention will divide itself in many directions, from friends
to enemies and, most pertinently in her own mind, "a mistress," "a traitress,"
and "a dear" (I.i.154–58). He will become self-contradictory, a man of
"humble ambition" and "proud humility," a being of "jarring concord" and
"discord dulcet" and "sweet disaster"—in sum, no fit master at all (I.159–
61). She has given Parolles every reason to suspect that she worries less that
the Count will be a fit master for him as that she can never be a fit mistress
for his master. The arrival of a page, advising him of his master's summons
to accompany him to the King's court, has the welcome effect of removing
Parolles from her presence and thereby rescuing her from any further self-
betrayals and unwanted advances. In their farewells, she distracts him by
ridiculing his self-proclaimed warlikeness, to which he can only rejoin that
he intends to "naturalize" her upon his return (I.i.195), unless she gets herself "a good husband" before then (I.i.200–01). Indeed, she will try.

Helena's dialogue with oily Parolles, her only true rival for the Count's
affections, has roused her fighting spirit and with it her capacity for reasoning, both 'theoretical' and practical. Alone again, she no longer mopes
over the impossibility of reaching to the star that is her beloved. The stars
do not rule us. "The fated sky / Gives us free scope; only doth backward
pull / Our slow designs when we ourselves are dull" (I.i.203–05). The power
that "mounts my love so high," enabling me to see him even when he isn't
here, also enables me to distinguish fortune from nature (I.i.206). The distance between us is a matter of fortune, a thing of the fated sky, but nature
enables her not only to imagine but to think. "Who ever strove / To show
her merit that did miss her love?" (I.i.212–13). I know how to cure the
King's disease, and I therefore can justify my own presence in his Court.

At the Court, in Paris, the King of France has made a geopolitical decision. Two Tuscan city-states are at war—Florence and Siena. And indeed they were, throughout the decade of the 1550s. At that time, France was resisting the ambitions of the Holy Roman Emperor, Charles V who was also Charles I of Spain. The Hapsburgs ruled Roussillon, although the native Catalans remained restive under their rule. In search of allies, France sided with the Lutherans in Germany and the Ottomans; in 1555 Pope Paul IV tilted toward France, ruining the Hapsburg's hopes for a worldwide empire. In the following year, Charles divided his kingdom between the Spanish Hapburgs (headed by his son, Philip II) and the Austrian Hapsburgs (headed by Charles's brother, Ferdinand). Siena would lose its war with Florence and be surrendered to Spain, Florence's ally.

In the play, the French King knows he will receive a request from his cousin, the Austrian Hapsburg monarch, to deny aid to Florence. This means that the Austrian Hapsburgs are indirectly opposing the ambitions of the Spanish Hapsburgs. The King, who must know that many of the residents of Siena are of French origin, intends to go along with his cousin's request, but, hedging his bet, will allow French gentlemen to fight on either side, as they choose. As one of the King's attendants observes, this "may well serve / A nursery to our gentry, who are sick / For breathing and exploit" (I.ii.15–17). That is, the young aristocrats grow restive; abroad, they will hone their battle skills against foreigners and (it might be added) not against the King at home; those who survive will return better officers in the army of France.

Count Bertram, Parolles, and Lafeu arrive at the King's Court. In terms of the history of the time, this is anomalous not only because there were no more Roussillian counts but because Roussillon was ruled by the Hapsburgs, owing no allegiance to France and indeed forming part of Spain, France's rival. However, it may be that these men, all of whose names are French and therefore feel stronger loyalty to the King of France than to any Hapsburg.

The King greets the young Count cordially but with prudent caution. He is no Helena, his judgment swayed by physical appearance. "Youth, thou bear'st thy father's face," a face well formed by "frank nature"—the word "frank" meaning both vigorous and Frankish, French (I.ii.19–20). Nature is "curious"—that is, careful—never working "in haste"; that is why his face is so "well-compos'd" (II.ii.20–21). But the King knows that a face is only a face. "Thy father's moral parts / Mayst thou inherit too!" (I.ii.21–22). Having served in battle with the Count's father, the King judges him as having been "Disciplined of the bravest" (I.ii.28); his father's wit was equal to that of today's "young lords," but unlike them he exhibited neither "contempt nor bitterness" (I.ii.33,36). "His honor, / Clock to itself, knew the true minute when / Exception bid him speak, and at this time /His tongue obey'd his hand" (I.ii.38–41). In all this, and especially in "his humility," he "might be a copy to these younger times" (I.ii.44–46). Merely speaking of him is medicine to the ailing King; "it much repairs me" (I.ii.30), even as his example, if followed by young French aristocrats, would considerably improve them and repair France. Unfortunately, the "judgments" of today's young are often "mere fathers of their garments," and their "constancies / Expire before their fashions" (I.ii.61–63). Finally, the memory of the long-lived Count reminds the King of the Count's physician, Helena's father, who might have cured the King, had he still lived.

Back at the Count's palace in Rousillon, the palace clown, Lavache, asks the Countess's blessing to marry Isbel, a commoner lass with a regal Spanish name. "I am driven on by the flesh" (I.iii.28), and as a sinner "I do marry that I may repent" (I.iii.35–36), as marriage is a sacrament. What is more, marriage may gain him friends, which he has not now. And if cuckolded, why then he will profit, as the lover will cherish his wife, who according to the Christian teaching is of 'one flesh' with her husband. Cuckoldry unites even Puritans and Catholics, "howsome'er their hearts are sever'd in religion, their heads are one" because their cuckolds' horns tangle together like jousting deer in a herd. He even has a ballad to celebrate the thought: "Your marriage comes by destiny, / Your cuckoo sings by kind" (I.iii.59–60). Marriage may be destined but cuckoldry is natural; destiny is really chance, as the odds of drawing a good woman in the marriage lottery are, he estimates, one in ten. "La Vache!" in French slang is an expression of astonishment, as in the English phrase immortalized in America by Phil Rizzuto, "Holy Cow!" Offended and amused at this perpetually surprising man, the Countess sends him to fetch Helena. Before he goes, Lavache compares her to Helen of Troy, whose "fair face" may have caused the Greeks to sack Troy after the young Trojan prince, Paris, had seduced her and carried her off from her husband, King Menelaus of Sparta

(I.iii.67). But this Helen has already resisted the advances of Parolles, although she does intend to go to Paris.

The palace steward reports that he has heard Helena talking to herself about her love for Bertram. The Countess is not surprised, and is in fact pleased, regarding the nature of Helena to be sound. Helena understands her nature to be the nature of youth, when "love's strong passion is impress'd" (I.iii.124). The Countess calls her in and teases her by saying, "I am mother to you," knowing that if she really were Helena's mother Bertram would be the girl's brother, and unmarriageable (I.iii.128). It takes some doing, but she extracts the confession, "I love your son" (I.iii.185). Unworthy of him by convention, by social standing, "I follow him not / By any token of presumptuous suit, / Nor would I have him till I do deserve him," but I "never know how that desert should be," and so "love in vain" (I.iii.188–92). Why then do you intend to go to Paris and the King's Court? Because "my father left me some prescriptions / Of rare and prov'd effects, such as his reading / And manifest experience had collected / For general sovereignty" (I.iii.212–15). Among these is a remedy that can cure the King. In curing the King, she must think, she might prove herself worthy of the Count. The Countess blesses her mission, approving the young lady's ulterior motive.

In Paris, the King bids farewell to the young and older lords who are off to the Tuscan war; in victory, he assures them, they will be rewarded. "See that you come / Not to woo honor, but to wed it," so that "fame may cry you aloud" (II.i.14–15,17). And beware "the girls of Italy," who may make you "captives before you serve" (II.i.22). Bertram is judged too young to go, and is indignant at the King's decision. Parolles urges him to disobey the royal command, to "steal away bravely" (II.i.29), and Bertram intends to do so, "though the devil lead the measure," as Parolles self-revealingly intones.

The King next receives a different kind of rhetorician, one who would persuade him to be saved, not hazarded. Telling him that the esteemed physician Gerard de Narbon was her father, Helena describes the medicine he had researched, which can cure his illness. The King doubts this, since his own "most learned doctors" have failed, concluding "that laboring art can never ransom nature / From her unaidable estate" (II.i.115). He knows the peril he faces, and also knows that she has "no art," only a lesser sort of knowledge passed down from her good father (II.i.132). True, Helena concedes, but "what I can do can do no hurt to try, / Since you set up your rest 'gainst remedy" (II.i.133–34). More, "He that of greatest works is finisher / Oft does them by the weakest minister" (II.i.135–36). Unlike Parolles, Helena appeals to reason—the medicine can do no harm to a dying man—and piety—the God who can make all things end well can readily pour through a weak vessel. What is more, God is not only omnipotent but all-knowing; therefore, "Of heaven, not me, make an experiment" (II.i.153). I am willing to make it, on pain of death; if I fail, "with vilest torture let my life be ended" (II.i.173). It may well be that her faith is in nature, in the medicine, that her rhetoric of piety originates only from an intention to counteract the King's skepticism concerning her competence, but that is still more solid, and undoubtedly better-intentioned, than the rhetoric of Parolles, which is mere verbiage.

She has persuaded the King. "Methinks in thee some blessed spirit doth speak / His powerful sound within an organ weak; / And what impossibility would slay / In common sense, sense saves another way" (II.i.174–77)—reasoning founded on uncommon premises also persuades. He is especially impressed with her Christlike willingness to sacrifice her life after torture: "Sweet practiser, thy physic I will try, / That ministers thine own death if I die" (II.i.184–85). He hasn't reckoned on the serpentine prudence Christ commands along with dovelike innocence. "If I help," Helena ventures, "what do you promise me?" (II.i.188). And will you "make it even," repay my life-saving service to you with something equally vital to me? The King agrees. Very well: if my medicine cures you, "Thou shalt give me with thy kingly hand / What husband in thy power I will command" (II.i.192–93)—aside from a man of French royal blood, she assures him. The King again agrees.

Comic piety enters in, in a more obvious way, in dialogue between the Countess and her Clown. The Countess has a mission for him. "I shall now put you to the height of your breeding," she says (II.ii.1). "I will show myself highly fed and lowly taught," he promises, anticipating that she will send him to the King's Court (II.ii.3). The Countess demands to know what "makes you special," to suppose that he would have business there (II.ii.5). Why, because "I have an answer will serve all men," the highest as well as the lowest (II.ii.14). You mean "your answer [will] serve all questions," be "an answer of such fitness for all questions?" the Countess inquires

(II.ii.18,27). But of course, and he invites her to try him with questions. He answers each with "O Lord, Sir!" But what if your impudence leads to your whipping? "I ne'er had worse luck in my life in my 'O Lord, Sir!' I see things may serve long, but not serve ever." (II.ii.52–53). Not all appeals to God, or to human royalty, will answer all questions, especially if the appeal provokes corporal punishment. In this, the Clown is less than Christlike, although not altogether lacking in prudence. The irony is that the Countess does have business for him in the King's Court, namely, to deliver a letter to Helena, for whom she continues to care and whom she will continue to advise.

There, Helena's cure has worked, and the remaining personages in the palace marvel at it. Pious Lafeu remarks, "They say miracles are past; and we have our philosophical persons to make modern"—commonplace— and "familiar things supernatural and causeless" (II.iii.1–3). This causes us "to make trifles of terrors, ensconcing ourselves into seeming knowledge when we should submit ourselves to an unknown fear" (II.iii.3–5). This, Bertram and Parolles concede (Parolles a bit too volubly), puts into question the authority of the great physicians Galen and Paracelsus. Helena and the audience know that the fated sky gives us free scope, and evidently so does God, since the King's cure came from nature carefully searched by man.

In his grace, and according to his contract, the King grants Helena her choice of bachelors, one of which she takes to be the cure of her own illness, her love-sickness. "This is the man," she says, indicating Bertram, in an echo of the Gospel announcement of our Savior (II.iii.102). Bertram wants none of it. "Your Highness, / In such a business give me leave to use / The help of mine own eyes" (II.iii.104–06). In this he reveals his rebellious character to the King, apparently preferring his natural judgment to the King's obligation, but in fact objecting to Helena's inferior social standing ("A poor physician's daughter my wife! / Disdain / Rather corrupt me ever!") (II.iii.113–14).

But the King is the King. He can exalt those of low degree, grant noble status to Helena. It is, after all, only a convention, and one within his power to mend. *More seriously*, he continues, *you, Bertram, mistakenly rate convention over nature.* "Strange it is that our bloods, / Of color, weight, and heat, pour'd all together, / Would quite confound distinction, yet stand off / In differences to mighty" (II.iii.116–19). In nature, there is no such thing as 'blue' blood. "If she be / All that is virtuous—save what thou dislik'st, / A poor physician's daughter—thou dislik'st / Of virtue the name; but do not so" (II.iii.119–22). This was the King's initial question about Bertram and his handsome face, whether it fronted a noble soul.

Why should Bertram prefer virtue to social standing? "From lowest place when virtuous things proceed," the King says, "The place is dignified by the doer's deed; / Where great additions swell's, and virtue none, / It is a dropsied honor" (II.iii.123–26)—an honor as diseased as the King was, and as France still is. Being "young, wise, and fair," Helena is heir to nature, and her natural virtues "breed honor" (II.iii.129–31). To lack virtue is to dishonor honorable parents, and virtue exhibits itself in acts; "the mere word's a slave," a "lying trophy"—as Parolles would rather not believe, and as Bertram misleads himself insofar as he follows Parolles' advice (II.iii.135,137). "If thou canst like this creature as a maid, / I can create the rest/ Virtue and she / Is her own dower, honor and wealth from me" (II.iii.140–42).

It is an irrefutable argument, but Bertram rejects it: "I cannot love her, nor will strive to do't" (II.iii.143). In invoking his honor as a count, Bertram only provokes the King to involve his own greater honor. "My honor's at the stake, which to defeat, / I must produce my power" (II.iii.147–48). Bertram quickly seems to yield, and the King marries them on the spot.

Bertram nonetheless remains obdurate in thought if obedient in action. And his disobedient thought will carry into effective disobedience in action. Married, he determines to go to the wars "and never bed her," never consummate the marriage (II.iii.266). Parolles, unchastened by a severe scolding by Lafeu, presses him on, offering his version of practical wisdom: "A young man married is a man that's marr'd. / Therefore away, and leave her bravely; go, / The King has done you wrong" (II.iii.291–93). Wordy Parolles goes next to Helena to inform her that her husband will depart tonight "on very serious business" (II.iv.38). She contents herself to say only, "On everything I wait upon his will" (II.iv.52).

In the struggle for Bertram's mind and heart—and thus his will and his actions—Parolles seems to have won, twice calling Bertram his "sweetheart" (II.iii.261, 264). Just before his own departure for the wars Bertram tells the dismayed Lafeu that Parolles is "very great in knowledge, and accordingly valiant" (II.v.6–7). On the contrary, the elderly lord insists, in front of Parolles, Parolles is a liar and a coward. "There can be no kernel in this light nut"—no kernel of truth—the "soul of this man is his clothes; trust him not in matter of heavy consequence" (II.v.41–43), such as the war you are about to fight in. He walks away, Helena walks in, and Bertram refuses to kiss her goodbye—one last act of contempt, expressive of his mind and heart.

In Florence, the Duke receives two French lords, who head a troop of soldiers. They are brothers, the captains Dumain. As 'Parolles' means speech, words, 'du main' means 'of the hand'; these are men of deeds, not words. Given that "the fundamental reasons of this war" strike the lords as "holy," the Duke wonders why "our cousin France" does not support him (III.i.2,4). For reasons of state, the lords cannot disclose the reasoning of the King, who prefers not to offend his other cousin, the Austrian monarch who opposes Florence. They content themselves to observe that the young French lords, "that surfeit on their ease" (like the French King, they've been described as diseased), "will day by day / Come here for physic" (III.i.17–18). When Bertram arrives a short time later, the Duke makes him the general of his cavalry, whereupon the young Count swears by "great Mars" to "make me but like my thoughts," that "I shall prove / A lover of thy drum, hater of love" (III.iii.9,11). Indeed, he has already written to his mother to explain that while he has deferred to the French King's command to marry Helena he will never consummate the marriage and instead has gone to war.

The Countess is not amused. "This is not well," she tells the Clown, when her "rash and unbridled boy" takes it upon himself "to fly the favors of so good a king," angering him "by misprizing... a maid too virtuous / For the contempt of empire" (III.iii.26–27, 29–30). Bertram has gone so far as to lay down a sort of love-test for the woman who is already his bride: If she can remove the ring from his finger, "which shall never come off, and show me a child begotten of [her] body that I am father to, then call me husband; but in such a 'then' I write 'never'" (III.ii.55–58). The Countess blames her son's corruption on Parolles, "a very tainted fellow and full of wickedness" (III.ii.85). My son "can never win" on the battlefield "the honor that he loses" in turning his back on his king and his wife.

Faced with an apparently insurmountable challenge, Helena first prays (and not to Mars) that her husband will survive the war, feeling guilt at the thought that she has caused him to go (which is not true) and risk his life. She thinks that if she now leaves France, he will return to it, and to safety; in this, her love is selfless, a desire for what is good for him. She writes to the Countess, announcing her intention to set out on her own mission as a pilgrim to the shrine of Saint Jacques le Grand "with sainted vow my faults to have amended" (III.iv.7). Bertam is "too good and fair for death and me; / Whom I myself embrace to set him free" (III.iv.16–17). Upon reading this intention in Helena's letter, the Countess can only hope that this will indeed induce her son to return, and for Helena then to reverse her course and return as well.

It turns out that Helena will soon form other plans, if indeed she hasn't already done so. As before, she does not intend to leave matters entirely up to God. She heads not for the saint's shrine, west of Rousillon, but in exactly the opposite direction, to Florence. Outside that city, the elderly Widow Capilet, her daughter Diana, and their friend Mariana converse. Parolles has been courting Mariana, who rightly regards him as "a filthy officer" unworthy of her attention (III.v.15). She warns Diana against both Parolles and Bertram, whose words in her judgment are only "engines of lust" (III.v.18). Diana, named after the chaste goddess of the hunt, assures her: "You shall not need to fear me" (III.v.26).

Helena approaches them, ostensibly on the way to the shrine, and the widow invites her to lodge at her house. The lady also asks if she knows Count Rousillon and expresses pity for his new wife, as the Count has been courting Diana, rather in contradiction to his vow to Mars, not to mention his wedding vow. Not knowing that she is speaking with that wife, the Widow suggests that Diana may be able to do the wronged woman "a shrewd turn" (III.v.64).

With perfect comic timing, Bertram and Parolles appear, at the head of the army—Parolles in the aptly unheroic role of drummer. Playing along with her disguise, Helena asks her companions which one is "the Frenchman," the Count. Diana points him out, asking, "Is't not a handsome gentleman?" (III.v.77). "I like him well," Helena admits; "'Tis pity he is not honest," Diana ripostes, not intending to wound anything better than the Count's reputation. As for Parolles, "Were I his lady / I would poison that vile rascal" (III.v.81). The men march past, the women retire to the Widow's house.

Encamped in front of Florence, the French lords warn Bertram of Parolles. "He's a most notable coward, an infinite and endless liar, an hourly promise-breaker, the owner of no one good quality worthy your lord's entertainment" (III.vi.8–11). Bertram agrees to test him with a task less daunting than the one he assigned his wife. Parolles lost his drum during Florence's victorious battle with the Sejoys and has vowed to recover it. Let him try, then have him intercepted by a troop of Florentines; they will pretend to be Sejoys and interrogate him. "Be but your lordship present at his examination," at which Parolles will be blindfolded; "if he do not, for the promise of his life and in the highest compulsion of base fear, offer to betray you and deliver all the intelligence of his power against you, and that with the divine forfeit of his soul upon oath, never trust my judgment in anything" (III.vi.23–28). Having settled on this plan, Bertam confides to one of the lords that the fair Diana, though "wondrous cold"—having returned his love-letters—will receive a return visit from him (III.vi.103). The lord is eager to come with him and look her over.

The women will be ready for them. Helena admits to the Widow that Bertram is her husband. She enlists the lady's help. Since the Count "woos your daughter," let her consent to his suit but demand his ring as a token of his love (III.vii.17). This is nothing more than a "lawful" plot; your daughter will then deliver the ring to me and "herself most chastely absent," as her namesake the goddess would do (III.vii.33). With the ring in her possession, Helena will then be able to consummate her marriage in a dark bedroom. Her husband will intend wickedly while acting lawfully, prey to his wife's noble deception.

The deceptive plot Bertram is in on proceeds as planned, in Bertram's absence. On orders from the Second Lord, the men who seize Parolles will speak gibberish, deploying nonsense words that Mr. Words, Mr. Speech, cannot understand. One soldier will act as 'translator.' During the stakeout, the men hear Parolles talking to himself, trying to find the words with which he can conceal his failure to recover his drum. He wishes he hadn't promised to retrieve it in the first place. "I find my tongue is too foolhardy; but my heart hath the fear of Mars before, and of his creatures, not daring the reports of my tongue" (III.i.28–29). He has lied not only to others but even to himself: "What the devil should move me to undertake the recovery of this drum, being not ignorant of the impossibility, and knowing I had no such purpose?" (IV.i.31–33). The Second Lord wonders, "Is it possible he should know what he is, and be what he is?" (IV.i.41). It is. Clever but imprudent, Parolles out-talks himself, deceiving himself more than he deceives anyone other than those (like Bertram) whom he tells what they want to hear. Seized by men who evidently speak some foreign language he doesn't know, Parolles exclaims, "I shall lose my life for want of language," although he knows five languages (IV.i.66). For a man who depends upon mere words alone, there are not always words enough; Shakespeare himself was not only a playwright but an actor. "O, let me live," Parolles pleads with his captors, through the 'translator,' "and all the secrets of our camp I'll show, / Their force, their purpose" (IV.i.80–82). The Second Lord considers him a woodcock—a bird easily trapped, synonymous with a fool, a dupe. The con artist is a fool; in trying to fool others with words he won't live up to, he ends by fooling himself with those words and getting fooled by others with words that mean nothing at all.

Meanwhile, Bertram pursues his other, romantic, plot. At the Widow Capilet's house, he tries Diana with Parollian sophistries. "You should be as your mother was / When your sweet self was got" (IV.ii.9–10). "She was then honest," Diana says, irrefutably (IV.ii.11), adding, "My mother did but duty; such, my lord, / As you owe your wife" (IV.ii.12–13). Not so, the Count replies: "I was compell'd to her, but I love thee" (IV.ii.15). He vows loyalty based upon that loving consent. Diana ventures to doubt his honesty. "Be not so holy cruel," Bertram pleads, for "love is holy" and I am in love with you (IV.ii.33). Pretending to yield, the lady demands the ring, which he will lend her, not give her, as it is an heirloom "which were the greatest obloquy i' th' world / In me to lose" (IV.ii.44). Yes, well, "Mine honor's such a ring," and my chastity "the jewel of our house," the "greatest obloquy i' th' world / In me to lose," the lady rejoins. At this, Bertram gives up: "Here, take my ring; / My house, mine honor, yea, my life, be thine; / And I'll be bid by thee" (IV.ii.51–53). In mock betrothal, she gives him a ring off her own finger in exchange; it is really Helena's ring, given her by the King as a marriage gift.

Springing the trap, she tells him to visit her bedroom at midnight but to stay absolutely silent. I shall return your ring later on, with an explanation for this strange lack of speech among lovers, which the audience knows is necessary because Helena will be in the bed. The required silence is not only necessary but fitting. Bertram and Parolles talk too much. The plot against Parolles takes advantage of that. The plot against Bertram requires him to act silently in a good way, if with bad intent. If Judaism is said to be a religion of law and outward compliance with it, Christianity a religion of release from the consequences of bad actions combined with an insistence on right intentions, Helena's plot executes her rightful intention with respect to Bertram while duping him into acting in accordance with the law, against his own wrongful intention. After he leaves, Diana reflects that *Mother told me men talk and act this way*; quite understandably, she resolves to "live and die a maid" (IV.ii.74).

Back in the Florentine camp, the French ladies have learned that a peace has been concluded. The lords discuss Bertram, who has now received the letter of reprimand from the Countess. "There is something in't that stings his nature," the First Lord remarks; "for on the reading it he chang'd almost into another man," rather as conversion to Christianity changes a sinner into a new man (IV.iii.2–3). This is just, the Second Lord says, as "he has much worthy blame laid upon him for shaking off so good a wife and so sweet a lady"—especially by so "incur[ring] the everlasting displeasure of the King," the First Lord adds (IV.ii.5–7). Worse, he has "perverted a young gentlewoman here in Florence," giving her his ring (IV.ii.12); worst of all, he has caused his wife to die of grief (one of the lords has heard) at Saint Jaques le Grand. "I am heartily sorry that he'll be glad of this," the First Lord laments (IV.iii.60); "how mightily some times we drown our gain in tears!" (IV.iii.63–64).

Despite his courage on the battlefield, in love Bertram is as much a traitor as Parolles, and the Second Lord asks if it is not damnable in themselves to continue to cooperate in the plot against his vile adviser. The First Lord suggests that in doing so they serve justice, inasmuch as the Count has farther to fall than Parolles: "The great dignity that his valor hath here acquir'd for him"—something cowardly, all-talk Parolles has so conspicuously failed to acquire—shall "at home be encount'red with a shame as ample" (IV.iii.64–65). The Second Lord draws the moral: "The web of our life is of a mingled yarn, good and ill together. Our virtues would be proud if our faults whipt them not; and our crimes would despair if they were not cherish'd by our virtues" (IV.iii.69–72).

The Count arrives, announcing that of his remaining business in Florence, "the greatest" remains unresolved (IV.iii.86); he of course doesn't specify that this is his recently concluded tryst with Diana—in fact the un-witting consummation of his marriage to Helena—not knowing that the lords know exactly what he means. But now he would hear the continuing interrogation of Parolles. He listens as the blindfolded Parolles says he speaks truth regarding his estimate of the number of horsemen under the Count's command, and indeed he does, the Count confirms. "But I con him no thanks for't in the nature he delivers it" (IV.iii.144). That is, for once Parolles speaks truly, but the nature of his intent in doing so is false, treasonous. His treachery extends to Bertram's private affairs, as well; he's written to Diana, again quite truly, saying "the Count's a fool, and full of gold" (IV.iii.196).

Having decided that Bertram is to blame for his predicament (after all, he tells himself, he wouldn't have been captured if he hadn't been trying to impress the Count), he is happy to betray him. As he tells his interrogator, "I knew the young Count to be a dangerous and lascivious boy, who is a whale to virginity, and devours up all the fry it finds" (IV.iii.203–05). For his part, in calling Parolles a "damnable, both-sides rogue," Bertram also speaks the truth and not incidentally refrains from denying the truth Parolles has spoken (IV.iii.206). In learning the truth, the nature, of Parolles, Bertram begins to learn the truth of himself. He also begins to learn the truth about, the nature of, *parole*, of speech itself, which can be true or false, honest testimony or a both-sides rogue, subject to yet another form of speech, the speech of judgment, the speech of vindication and of damnation.

As Parolles rattles on, disclosing information on the number of foot soldiers in the army and slandering both of the French lords (cowards, rapists), the Second Lord finds him oddly entertaining. Parolles says of the First Lord, "He has everything that an honest man should not have; what an honest man should have, he has nothing"; "I begin to love him for this," the Second Lord admits (IV.iii.242–44). The man "hath out-villain'd vil-lainy so far that the rarity redeems him" (IV.iii.255). After assuring his cap-tors that he will readily betray both the Duke of Florence and Count Rousillon, Parolles has his blindfold removed. He sees the Count. "You are undone, Captain," the soldier-'translator' says—"all but your scarf," which is still knotted around his throat (IV.iii.300–01). The erstwhile empty suit has nothing left to wear but a sort of noose.

When his interrogators leave him alone, he soliloquizes. True to his nature, Parolles gives his truest confession yet: "If my heart were great, / 'Twould burst at this" (IV.iii.307–08). Since it isn't, it doesn't. "Simply the thing I am / Shall make me live," although he does draw a modest moral: "Who knows himself a braggart, / Let him fear this; for it will come to pass / That every braggart shall be found an ass" (IV.iii.310–13). "Parolles," he advises himself, "live safest in shame. Being fool'd, by fool'ry thrive. / There's place and means for every man alive" (IV.iii.315–16). Now knowing himself, he concludes that even rogues have their place in the natural order, in his own way echoing the Second Lord's moral. It isn't only speech, the distinctively human part of human nature, that's double-sided; nature is, too, an therein lies its comedy and its tragedy, both.

Helena sees this, too. Her plot successful, her marriage consummated without her husband's knowledge—a sort of just and lawful cuckoldry—she thanks her allies at the Widow's house, who will be rewarded when she receives the King's promised reward. There will be justice among the women. Not so much among men, however. She reflects: "O, strange men! / That can sweet use make of what they hate, / When saucy trusting of the cozen'd thoughts / Defiles the pitchy night" (IV.iv.21–24). But with her female allies at hand and their joint mission accomplished, "All's Well That Ends Well" (IV.iv.35). Reason, in line with nature, can make sense of nature's apparent self-contradictions and, if it guides human actions, share in its telos, which is served by many means, among them the natural increase that results from mating. The women will travel to Marseilles to meet with the King, who has stopped there on the way to Rousillon.

At the Count's palace in Rousillon, the Countess, Lafeu, and the Clown await the return of the prodigal son. They too have heard that Helena has died. Lafeu blames Parolles, whose villainy "would have made all the unbak'd and doughy youth of a nation in his color," which is the "saffron" yellow of cowardice (IV.v.2–3). The Countess agrees, saying that his machinations caused "the death of the most virtuous gentlewoman that ever nature had praise for creating" (IV.v.7–9). Consistent with the 'double' nature of nature, Lafeu turns the dialogue to comedy by engaging in badinage with the Clown, who plays on the fact that 'le feu' means fire by announcing himself to be in the service of the great Prince of this world, a prince even greater than the French King, the prince who "ever keeps a good fire"

(IV.v.55). The Clown tells LaFeu that any tricks he plays "are their own right by the law of nature" (IV.v.55)—the *concordia discors*, the law that admits contraries as servants of its telos, the end that is well.

Sending the Clown away, Lafeu confides to the Countess that he has asked the king to "speak in the behalf of my daughter," Maudlin, as a bride for the widower, Bertram (IV.v.64). The Countess approves. The King will arrive at Rousillon tomorrow. Bertram is there now, and they go to see him. For her part, having missed the King in Marseilles, Helena has sent a letter to him, a letter signed by Diana, who will further her plot.

Parolles is already in Rousillon, hoping that Lafeu will intervene mercifully in his favor. He runs into the Clown and describes himself as "muddied in Fortune's mood, and smell[ing] somewhat strong of her strong displeasure" (V.ii.3–5). The Clown is more than equal to a battle of words with Mr. Speech. "Fortune's displeasure is but sluttish, if it smell so strongly as thou speak'st of; stand aside, sir" (V.ii.6–7). "Nay, you need not stop your nose, sir; I spake but by a metaphor," Parolles protests (V.ii.9–10). "Indeed, sir, if your neighbor stink, I will stop my nose, or against any man's metaphor" (V.ii.11–12). The Clown, being a comedian, knows the doubleness, the ambiguity, of words very well. He understands Parolles, that living pun, that walking metaphor of the potential duplicity of speech.

Lafeu comes by, and Parolles turns to him. "I am a man whom Fortune hath cruelly scratched," he begins, altering his metaphor (V.ii.28). Lafeu is quick to defend Fortune's honor: "Wherein have you played the knave with Fortune, that she should scratch you, who of herself is a good lady and would not have knaves thrive long under her?" (V.ii.30–32). He knows all about the tale of the drum, mocking Parolles because of it. He does show mercy, however, telling Parolles, "Though you are a fool and a knave, thou shalt eat" (V.v.50–51). "I praise God for you," Parolles replies, in a rare show of piety (V.ii.52).

Lafeu is off to the Count's palace, where he meets with the King, the Countess, and the French lords, none of whom know Helena is alive. "Your son," the King tells the Countess, "as mad with folly, lack'd the sense to know / Her estimation home," that is, her true worth (V.iii.2–4). The Countess attempts to mollify him by attributing her son's misjudgment to "natural rebellion, done in the blaze of youth," when passion overcomes "reason's force" and burns the one who is impassioned (V.iii.6–7). She had warned her son of exactly this danger, how his "blood" contended with virtue for empire over his soul, but he heeded Parolles' tempting words instead of her parental ones. The King assures her of his forgiveness, and Lafeu observes that for all the injuries Bertram has done, he did "the greatest wrong of all" to himself (V.iii.14–15). And in answer to the King's query, Lafeu reports that Bertram has consented to marry Maudlin, in submission to the King's intention. The King mentions the Duke of Florence's letters of commendation; the young Count's soul has some important warlike virtues, virtues no king, no defender of the realm, would rightly overlook. This marriage serves France.

Bertram enters, repentant, pleading for mercy. The King grants it and asks if he remembers the daughter of Lord Lafeu. He does, "admiringly," as she had been his first choice in marriage—so much so, he claims, that he underestimated the beauty of all other women, including Helena. "Thence it came, / That she whom all men prais'd, and whom myself, / Since I have lost, have lov'd, was in mine eye / The dust that did offend it" (V.iii.5154). He thus radically changes his earlier story. Initially, he had argued that Helena was unworthy of him because beneath him in social standing, a mere physician's daughter. Helena had proved her merit to the King by curing him, by her knowledge of nature, a knowledge more valuable than any social convention. Now, if Bertram's account is to be credited, it transpires that his aversion was also natural, not conventional—an attraction to Maudlin's beauty which "warp'd" his perception of Helena's beauty, making her seem "hideous" (V.iii.49,52).

The politic King does credit, or at least says he credits, the Count's account. "Well excus'd," he judges (V.iii.55). As always, he draws a moral: "Oft our displeasures, to ourselves unjust, / Destroy our friends, and after weep their dust; / Our own love waking cries to see what's done, / While shameful hate sleeps out the afternoon. / Be this sweet Helen's knell." (V.iii.63–67). But for a king the dead past must bury its dead, lest those who continue to live under his rule be ruined. "And now forget her" (V.iii.67), he commands, and marry Maudlin. The Count consents, asking for heaven's blessing on his second marriage to his first love, without which divine blessing he would be better off dead, his "nature ceased" (V.iii.72). To sensibilities steeped in romance, the King's command and the Count's consent jar. But the romance in which 'we' have steeped ourselves, stemming from the courtly love of the Middle Ages and branching into modern Romanticism, ignores facts Shakespeare knew. In the courtly romances, love is a passion pursued outside marriage; married love was at best Christian-agapic, often politic, but seldom erotic-sentimental. For Shakespeare and especially for Shakespeare's monarchs and aristocrats, married love is less serious in 'our' sense, but much more serious in another way, a way 'our' modern understanding of politics and of love doesn't readily understand, except as a form of cynicism.

But not so fast. Lafeu asks for "a favor" from Bertram, a token of his love for his daughter, an engagement ring. Bertram gives him the ring Diana had given him in exchange for his own family heirloom. Lafeu and the King immediately recognize it as the wedding gift the King bestowed on Helena. His enraged Majesty demands, *How did you despoil Helena of that ring?* Not knowing about the gift-ring in the first place, the hapless young Count denies that it belonged to Helena, but his mother sternly corrects him: "I have seen her wear it; and she reckon'd it / At her life's rate" (V.iii.89–91).

Afraid to admit his (as he believes) tryst with Diana—one of those ladies in Italy Helena had rightly worried might attract him—Bertram claims that he obtained the ring from a lady in Florence who threw it from her window to him, wrapped in a paper with her name written on it. *But I explained my marital status to her,* he claims, *and although she dropped her infatuation, she nobly insisted that he keep her ring.* This utterly implausible tale, worthy of Parolles, scarcely convinces the King, who no longer extends his credence to the words of the young Count. He too had heard Helena say "she would never put it from her finger / Unless she gave it to yourself in bed" (V.iii.109–10). You must have murdered her. He orders the guards to take Bertram away; "we'll sift this matter further" (V.iii.123). In his own defense, Bertram rejoins, "If you shall prove / This ring was ever hers, you shall as easy / Prove that I husbanded her bed in Florence, / Where she never was" (V.iii.124–25). Right on the first part, wrong on the second.

The comedy sharpens more, as the King receives a letter from the Widow Capilet, denouncing Bertram as a seducer. The lady and her daughter then enter the King's presence, Diana claiming that she is Bertram's wife. Still trying to lie his way out, entangling himself further, Bertram calls her "a common gamester of the camp" (V.iii.186). Why would a prostitute have the ring? With fine irony, Diana calls none other than Parolles as her witness. But the man is "a most perfidious slave," Bertram sputters, a man "whose nature sickens but to speak a truth" (V.iii.203,205). A man of nothing but empty, deceiving words, Parolles' nature is so unnatural that it falls ill if forced to speak truly, the lying Bertram truly protests. In the event, Parolles testifies honestly that Bertram was indeed "mad for" Diana, although the King gets little more out of him and quickly dismisses him as worthless (V.iii.255).

But "she hath that ring of yours," the King suggests, the heirloom ring you would no more part with than Helena would part with the ring I gave to her (V.iii.207). Thinking quickly, Bertram concocts another word-invention. "Certain it is I lik'd her," he allows, "and boarded her i' th' wanton way of youth" (V.iii.208–09)—the excuse his mother had offered the King. But it was all her fault. Diana "did angle for me, / Madding my eagerness with her restraint"—truly a creature of "infinite cunning" (V.iii.210–11, 214). She received the heirloom in exchange for a commonplace ring such as one might purchase at market. When Diana identifies the ring His Majesty has in his possession, the one he gave to Helena, no ordinary ring at all, the pretense evaporates, and Bertram confesses.

This only leads to a new perplexity: How did Diana come into possession of Helena's ring? Knowing that Helena is waiting in the wings, Diana answers with riddles—exhibiting for one last time the ambiguity of words, even when deployed honestly. When in frustration the King orders her to prison, she calmly turns to her mother and asks her to post bail, then offers one last riddle—one that recalls the play's opening paradox of the "delivery" that is also a burial, but in reverse. "He knows himself my bed he hath defil'd; / And at that time he got his wife with child. Dead though she be, she feels her young one kick; / So there's my riddle: the one that's dead is quick— / And now behold the meaning"—the cue for living Helena to enter, pregnant (V.iii.293–98).

The King can only ask, "Is't real that I see?" (V.iii.299). So much to hear, so many lying, deceptive, metaphorical, words, some empty of content, others pregnant with meaning: Is seeing really believing? As always in this play, yes and no. "No, my good lord," Helena answers, focusing attention on the meaning of the phrase "is't" (V.iii.300). "'Tis but the shadow of a wife you see, / The name and not the thing" (V.iii.301–02). I am married legally, in words, but rejected by my husband. Bertram protests, "Both, both," we are married both in name and in reality, in convention and in nature. "O, pardon!" (V.iii.302). *As a matter of fact*, Helena says, *you are right: I have the heirloom ring and I also have your words in your letter, promising that when I get the ring from you finger and you gotten me with child, you can then call me husband, put the word on the thing.* Beaten, bewildered Bertram turns to the King. "If she, my liege, can make me know this clearly, / I'll love her dearly, ever, ever dearly" (V.iii.309–10). She can and doubtless will explain how she pulled them off—both the ring and the plot.

Critics who complain that the Count may still lack sincerity overlook the fact that this is a comedy. True romance isn't the point, and never was. Sure enough, good old Lafeu announces, "My eyes smell onions; I shall weep anon," asking Parolles, that man of mere cloth, to lend him a handkerchief (V.iii.314). Does he weep for the reconciliation, for his now-ignored daughter, Maudlin, or both?

The King too wants a coherent, step-by-step telling of the plot, "to make the even truth in pleasure flow" (V.iii.319). He makes amends to Diana, offering her the same opportunity he'd granted to Helena, to choose her husband; she will soon come over to the side of nature, leaving virginity behind but in legal, verbal propriety while securing her widowed mother's property, too.

All's well that ends well? The King remains prudent to the end: "All yet seems well; and if it end so meet, / The bitter past, more welcome is the sweet" (V.iii.326–27). Discord will serve concord, maybe.

This is the point of the Epilogue. "The King's a beggar, now the play is done" (E.1). That is, in the penultimate reversal of roles, yet another up-ending of convention, the King, who lives a life of command, can only hope for the best, having reached the limit of both rule by decree and rule by advice. "All is well *if* this suit be won, / That you express content; which we will pay / With strife [effort] to please you, day exceeding day" (E.2–4). Shakespeare, ruler of all words, himself depends upon something beyond his control: audience approval. "Ours be your patience, then, and yours our parts; / Your gentle hands lend us, and take our hearts" (E.5–6). We players, actors, are now the audience to your wordless, unambiguous action, your 'play,' which is your applause. With this final reversal of roles, of rulers being ruled, Shakespeare and his players are done.

Only if Shakespeare has persuaded his audience with words and plot they deem fitting, only if he has succeeded in ruling their sentiments with his reasoned, playful argument and action will they consent to judge his work as he wishes it to be judged. Judgment first came to light in the contrast between the authority of elders, with their advice, their piety, and their plans, and the passions and plans (often schemes) of the young, who seek to evade authority. Authority based on experience won over many years and on piety (the 'faith of our fathers') finds its criterion in nature. There is the authority of medical knowledge or 'physic,' rightful authority over bodily nature. There is also the authority of moral knowledge, authority over conduct—knowledge of the virtues that make men and women human or inhuman. Moral knowledge distinguishes 'blood'—thumoerotic passion, the fight for love and glory—from virtue. It distinguishes courage (Bertram, Helena) from cowardice (Parolles), prudence (the King, the Countess, Helena) from folly (Bertram, Parolles), justice (the women generally, the King, the French lords) from injustice (the young men, especially Bertram, with his failure to form a just estimate of Helena's worth), and finally moderation (Lafeu, the Countess) from immoderation (the young generally, gripped by their passions).

Speech, aimed at persuasion, rhetoric, may be true or false. Speech to oneself, soliloquy, may also be true or false, insightful or self-deceptive. Speech 'meets' or 'courts' action especially in love, in courtship. Helena deceives in her actions but usually speaks the truth, and for virtuous ends. Parolles speaks lies at the service of passions, finding a ready audience in Bertram. Helena and Parolles are love-rivals, seeking to win the heart of the young Count. Helena asks him the crucial, comic question: How to lose one's virginity to one's own liking? (And, therefore, to one worthy of your liking, else your liking will soon turn to disliking.) This is a question concerning physical bodies and the passions they arouse but also a moral question concerning good and bad. To answer it, you will need to confront the problem of appearance and reality, deception and unmasking, revealing. As a wise ruler, the King knows that already, but the young lovers need to learn it.

Nature raises the question of free will, and especially of reasoned choice, against fatality (fortune, chance) and perhaps divine providence. The clown Lavache sees this in his cynical or 'reductionist' way, by calculating the odds of a good marriage as one in ten. Helena sets her prudent plotting not so much against fate as within its framework. She is right to see that her beloved is 'above her' in conventional social status, but the overarching question is to know one's place within the order of nature, to have self-knowledge. More, as the French lord asks, as he considers vile Parolles, is it possible to know that one is a coward, a liar, and a fool, and still to be all those things? Evidently so, as Parolles illustrates. But he too knows his place in nature. If nature is a *concordia discors*, an order encompassing disorder, conflict, then even a knavish fool has his place. Virtue, a kind of strength, needs vice to test it, to 'prove' itself in both senses of the term.

All's well that ends well insofar as reason out-plots passion, bringing the convention of marriage into line with natural passion, in a condition of mutual correction. But reason's victories are temporary because the discord remains—as it must, if the virtue aiming at the good end is not to weaken. The comedy of *All's Well That Ends Well* sustains itself throughout because the audience knows that the wise plotters have the foolish scoundrels firmly under their rule. Any utopian tendency to suppose that this will always be so is wisely deprecated by the King, who has ruled too long, learned the limitations of wise rule too well, to think otherwise.

CHAPTER NINE
THE GEOPOLITICS OF LOVE

In the royal park of the King of Navarre, Ferdinand outlines a singular policy to his three principal attendants, the lords Berowne, Longaville, and
Dumaine. Ferdinand is modeled after Shakespeare's contemporary, Henry
III of Navarre. By the time Shakespeare wrote *Love's Labor's Lost*, Henry
had seized the throne of France and had been crowned Henry IV, the first
of the Bourbon line. Navarre was a Huguenot sanctuary, but after assuming
the kingship of France Henry adjured Protestantism for Catholicism as a
means of consolidating his authority in a predominantly Catholic country—famously remarking, "Paris is worth a Mass." As a reader and friend
of Montaigne, however, in 1598 he issued the Edict of Nantes, establishing
toleration of Protestantism in an attempt to assuage religio-political ani-
mosities in his kingdom. Shakespeare's Ferdinand is also poised to ascend
to the French throne, but by romantic rather than military means—means
appropriate to comedy.

Berowne is Charles de Gontaut, duc de Biron, a noted Protestant soldier called the "Thunderbolt of France." Henry made him Marshal in 1594,
but despite this distinction his loyalty remained suspect; he was beheaded
on charges of treason a few years after Shakespeare's play was first staged.
Longaville is Henry I d'Orléans, duc de Longueville, a Protestant soldier
who had defeated Catholic forces in a 1589 battle; Dumaine is Charles,
duc de Mayenne, an ardent member of the Catholic League and former
rival of Henry for the throne (they reconciled in 1595). Henry's court thus
consisted of aristocrats representing the two religious sects which had very
recently put down their arms after years of civil war. Ferdinand's court at
Navarre was already a miniature version of the French court at the time of
the play.

King Ferdinand needs to unite Navarre, especially its ruling class. For
this, he seriously proposes a Renaissance version of a plan devised (with

characteristic irony) by Plato's Socrates, who said that unless philosophers become kings, or kings truly and adequately philosophize, a just political regime will prove impossible to establish. As neither the king nor his attendants are philosophers engaged in reasoned inquiry into the conventions of their country, perhaps they can truly and adequately philosophize or, less ambitiously, become more thoroughly the liberally educated men Renaissance scholars and politicians alike esteemed.

If they are not philosophers, lovers of wisdom, why would they do such a thing? Why would they unite behind the King's unusual plan? The king appeals not directly to their *logos* but to their *thumos*. "Fame, that all hunt after in their lives, / Live regist'red upon our brazen tombs, / Th'endeavor of this present breath may buy / That honor which shall bate his scythe's keen edge, / And make us heirs of all eternity" (I.i.1–7). He proposes a vast war, a war of the soul, but most emphatically not the kind of soul-war which has wracked Christian Europe. He will redirect his aristocrats' souls toward becoming "brave conquerors" in the "war against your own affections," the "huge army of the world's desires" (I.i.8–10). With its royal court having subdued their appetites, with its population then imitating the court's high example, "Navarre shall be the wonder of the world" (I.i.12), both a place of wondering and a place wondered at, esteemed, a Jerusalem of learning. "Our court shall be a little Academe"—a modern version of Plato's school—"still and contemplative in living art" instead of roiling in war and vaunting in the art of war (I.i.13–14).

To this end, the king has ordained a comprehensive three-year fast, whereby he and his attendants—all young and unmarried—will abstain from strong drink, much food, and all women for the next three years. They will arm themselves for this *psychomachia* by pledging their honor with "deep oaths," now to be signed (I.i.23). The young king has a bit of the 'secularized' Calvinist about him.

Longaville and Dumaine readily consent. For these three years, "the mind shall banquet, though the body pine," Longaville avers, inasmuch as "dainty bits / Make rich the ribs, but bankrupt quite the wits" (I.i.25–27). Dumaine, too, pronounces himself "mortified" against "the world's delights," intent rather on "living in philosophy" (I.i.32). Berowne has reservations. "Not to see a woman" in three years (I.i.37)? Harsh sumptuary laws? Even sleep deprivation in order to spend more time studying? "O, these are barren tasks, too hard to keep" (I.i.47). His earlier, verbal oath he had "sworn in jest," but an oath in writing is a serious thing (I.i.54). "What is the end of study, let me know" (I.i.55).

Ferdinand answers that the end of study is "to know which else we should not else know" (I.i.56). You mean, Berowne asks, "things hid and barr'd...from common sense" (I.i.57)? Yes, "that is study's god-like recompense" (I.i.58). Oh, but of course, Berowne rejoins, I have no problem in swearing to do those sorts of things—to study where I might dine well, especially on days when I am forbidden to do so; or to "study where to meet some mistress fine, / When mistresses from common senses are hid"; "Or, having sworn too hard-a-keeping oath / Study to break it, and not break my troth" by some exoteric show of compliance (I.i.63–66). This is (following Socrates' own formula) to know what one doesn't know. "Swear me to this, and I will ne'er say no" (I.i.69). But mere book-learning will never do. "Study is like the heaven's glorious sun, / That will not be deep-searched with saucy looks. / Small have continual plodders ever won, / Save base authority from others' books" (I.i.84–87). You, King, may aspire to Platonism but you will end in Scholasticism. [1] There is no real glory or honor in that. Berowne thus plays the role of the girl who laughed at the philosopher who stumbled while gazing at the heavens. Such "earthly godfathers of heaven's sight"—the astronomers—"have no more profit of their shining lights / Than those that walk and wot not where they are. / Too much to know is to know nought but fame; / And every godfather can give a name" to a star he can never reach (I.i.88–93). The Christian-Aristotelian peripatetics—those Roman Catholics who couldn't beat the duc de Biron in battle—cannot make practical use of the phenomena they know merely by observation, in order to name. The end of the King's new regime is as little likely to be achieved as Socrates' *politieia.*

Ferdinand dismisses Berowne's common-sense critique of Scholasticism as a self-contradictory effort "to reason against reading!" (I.i.94), and his loyalists concur. Berowne replies with an argument founded on nature as it is, obedient to the cycles of time. The King conceives of time as a death-dealing scythe against which only fame can triumph, a fame which only a three-year 'regime' of study governed by a *uniform* code of conduct can win. But real nature is seasonal. "Why should proud summer boast / Before the birds have any cause to sing? / Why should I joy in any abortive birth?

/ At Christmas I no more desire a rose / Than wish a snow in May's new-fangled shows; / But like of each thing that in season grows; / So you, to study now it is too late, / Climb o'er the house to unlock the little gate" (I.i.102–09). The King would require book-study of four men, including himself, who should instead be thinking of marrying, then of producing heirs to their estates. (The real King Henry would indeed die childless.) "Study evermore is over-shot," Berowne comments, after reviewing the King's laws; "While it doth study to have what it would, / It doth forget to do the thing it should; / And when it hath the thing it hunteth most, / 'Tis won as towns with fire—so lost" (I.i.141–44). The King's war or fame or eternal life overlooks the conditions of life itself.

Nonsense, the King replies. He shall "of force dispense with this decree"; it will then rest "on mere necessity" (I.i.145–46). But, Berowne answers, such necessity will simply cause men in their weakness to fail in their compliance, "For every man with his affects is born, / Not by might mast'red but by special grace" (I.i.149–50). Spoken like a Protestant, but a prudent one. I shall sign your oath, my liege (Paul the Apostle also requires obedience to rulers), but I predict that I, who am the last to sign, "will last keep his oath" (I.i.158).

Meanwhile, Ferdinand offers a form of recreation to relieve his austerity regime. There is now in Navarre "a refined traveler of Spain," a "child of fancy," a man "in whom all the world's new fashion is planted," and so a fit object for courtly entertainment at his expense (I.i.161–62, 168). This Quixote, named Don Adriano de Armado, will serve as our court jester. Berowne and Longaville relish the prospect of mocking such a comical land-armada of a man.

But first the court must deal with the first arrested violator of the King's decree, the rustic Costard, who arrives in the custody of Constable Dull with a letter from Armado. Costard has been caught speaking with a country wench, Jaquenetta; "such is the simplicity of man to hearken after / The flesh" (I.i.211–12), he confesses. The King reads aloud Armado's verbose letter, in which he witnesses to Costard's crime while professing to be "besieged with sable-colored melancholy" (I.i.225). Amused into mercy, Ferdinand sentences the malefactor to a week of bran and water and to the rule of Armado. Considering the evidence before him after the King and the other two attendants have left, Berowne tells Costard, "I'll lay my head to any good man's hat / That oaths and law will prove an idle scorn," to which the rustic can only reply with similar humor, "I suffer for the truth, sir; for true it is I was taken with Jaquenetta, and Jaquenetta is a true girl" (I.i.287–91).

Costard won't become Armado's Don Pancho, as he already has one—his page, Moth. Armado wonders at his own melancholy; much badinage later (all of it to Moth's advantage), he answers his own question, confessing his love for "a base wench," none other than Jaquenetta (I.ii.57). His complaint against Costard was simply an attempt to eliminate his rival, a rival soon to be returned to him as a servant, despite his intention to get him out of the picture. That is, far from uniting the country, the King's plan has led to dissent in his court and to backstabbing among his people. Meanwhile, he begs Moth for examples of "great men" who "have been in love" (I.ii.63). The examples the boy offers—Hercules and Samson—should be far from comforting. When Moth tells him that Samson's beloved Delilah had a green complexion (for jealousy) and "a green wit" (an immature one), Armado insists that "My love is most immaculate white and red"—the colors symbolizing purity and modesty (I.ii.86–87). This should be no source of confidence, master, as such colors mask "maculate thoughts" (I.ii.88). To illustrate, he breaks into a lyric, singing that blushing cheeks betoken faults, whiteness fear of their discovery. "A dangerous rhyme, master, against the reason of white and red" (I.ii.103). Moth is well aware of his master's hypocrisy. Rhyme or poetry sets prudent limits on a too-schematic rationalism that readily ossifies into convention.

When Constable Dull delivers Costard (Berowne evidently having delegated that duty), Armado decides to impose a fast on his rival and to take Jaquenetta to the royal park, where she'll be the "day-woman" or dairymaid (I.ii.125). He confesses his helplessness against Cupid, the boy-god whose "glory is to subdue men" (I.ii.167)—even men of physical strength such as Samson and Hercules, even a man of wisdom, Solomon. He can only appeal for strength to "some extemporal god of rhyme," lest he "turn sonnet" (I.ii.169–70). Ex-temporal: beyond time. Turn sonnet: become transformed, as in an Ovidian poem, not into another form of nature but into a poem. Only prudence can save him now—a virtue absent from his moral repertoire. Elsewhere in the royal park, a delegation has arrived from France, headed by the king's daughter. The Princess (a fictional character, given the real Henry III's childlessness) is accompanied by attendant ladies Rosaline, Maria, and Katharine, Lord Boyet and two other lords. She has come to negotiate a dispute over the neighboring French province of Aquitaine, described tellingly by Lord Boyet as "a dowry fit for a queen" (II.i.8). Given the King of Navarre's edict, she cannot approach him without permission, so she sends Boyet to request an audience. The princess views Boyet with some suspicion, deprecating his flattery and telling him, when he says he is "proud of employment" in the mission, "All pride is willing pride, and yours is so" (II.i.35).

She prudently asks her attendants for character assessments of the principal members of the King's court. Each has encountered one of them previously. Maria judges Longaville to be "a man of sovereign parts, peerless esteem'd / Well fitted in arts, glorious in arms" (I.i.44–45), if a bit too sharp-witted—a man "whose edge hath power to cut" and does so too readily (II.i.50). Katharine considers Dumaine "a well-accomplished youth," but one who has "most power to do most harm" because "least knowing ill" (II.i.56–58)—a certain hazardous naivete. As for Berowne, Rosaline admires his merry disposition and ready wit, his "sweet and voluble" discourse (II.i.76). The Princess suspects aloud that her ladies are "all in love" and, given Lord Boyet's remark about Aquitaine being a fit dowry for a queen, the prospect of marriages indeed seems redolent in the spring air.

King Ferdinand, however, dampens the mood when he arrives in the park, failing to extend his hospitality with an invitation to the castle, as per his decree to keep women at arm's length. He is all business. Having fought on France's side in the religious wars during his father's time, Ferdinand expects France to honor the agreement to pay the expenses Navarre incurred, half of which France still owes. In the meantime, Navarre holds part of Aquitaine as surety. The problem is that a letter from the French king intimates that the money has already been paid, and so Navarre should yield back the territory; yet Ferdinand has no record of the payment. At the same time, he is attracted to the princess. "Dear Princess, were not his requests so far / From reason's yielding, your fair self should make / A yielding 'gainst some reason in my breast, / And go well satisfied to France again" (II.i.149–53). He requests proof of payment, but Boyet has none, promising that the diplomatic pouch containing them will arrive tomorrow. Please then, Princess, "deem yourself lodg'd in my heart, / Though so denied fair harbor in my house" (II.i.173–74). He leaves, but Berowne stays behind to flirt with Rosaline, who rejects him; Dumaine and Longaville soon return to confess their interest in Katharine and Maria, respectively. Boyet answers them with courtesy laced with irony, then suggests to the princess that the King is in love with her.

It is easy for romantically inclined modern readers to overlook the stakes, although the courtly audience of Shakespeare's play would not. There is the potential for a serious diplomatic incident here. The French king does not likely send his daughter to head a mission to the bachelor King of Navarre without political intent. Does he hope to marry her off and cement the alliance? Or does he hope to evade a debt by sending such a charming delegation of ladies? What is love's labor? How might it be lost? What will be the consequences if it is lost? With no war against common enemies to unite them, will France and Navarre (now with a foothold on French soil) turn on each other? This comedy might or might not end happily.

In still another part of the forest, Armado grants Costard his liberty and money in exchange for carrying a letter to Jaquenetta, evidently trusting that these boons will overcome any feelings Costard may still entertain for the girl. On the way, Costard meets Berowne, who gives him a letter for delivery to Rosaline. One cannot expect these arrangements to end well, given Costard's mixed motives, to say nothing of his doltishness.

In her part of the park, the Princess expects to leave soon, after proof of payment arrives. Meanwhile, she prepares, Diana-like, to hunt a deer, conferring with the forester who directs her to "a stand where you may make the fairest shoot" (IV.i.11). Pretending that he praises her beauty with the word "fairest," she builds the exchange into a criticism of King. Ferdinand's policy. To accept praise for beauty would be vain; better to deserve praise for merit. Praise is a form of glory or fame, the ambition with which Ferdinand sought to fire the lords in support of his regime of austere pursuit of learning. But "Glory grows guilty of detested crimes, / When, for fame's sake, for praise, an outward part, / We bend to that the workings of the heart; / As I for praise alone now seek to spill / The poor deer's blood that my heart means no ill" (IV.i.31–35). The quest for honor interferes with more natural loves, great and small. As for the greater hunt she and her attendants evidently have undertaken, however, "praise we may afford / To any lady that subdues a lord" (IV.i.41–42). In that case, honor honors nature.

Speaking of which, Costard arrives, misdelivering Armado's letter to Jaquenetta while announcing that it's a letter from Berowne to Rosaline. Badinage about arrows and pricking ensues. The Princess, her attendants, and Boyet now know more about ongoing love aspirations than anyone in Navarre. They have achieved a substantial diplomatic advantage, thanks to superior intelligence-gathering. How will they exploit it?

The final pair of characters now enter the play. The schoolmaster Holofernes and his curate friend, Sir Nathaniel, are passing the time with Constable Dull, a man neither of great learning nor of conspicuous piety. Costard and Jaquenetta enter with the love-sonnet letter they believe to be from Arnaldo. They need someone to read it to them. Holofernes does so; in recognizing the real author, he tells them to deliver it "into the royal hand of the King," who will find in it evidence of Berowne's disobedience (IV.ii.134). Sir Nathaniel approves of this charge as a thing done "in the fear of God, very religiously," an act of deference to a ruler, as commanded by Paul the Apostle (IV.ii.138). But Holofernes cares more about the author's literary style, which he deems "very unlearned, neither savoring of poetry, wit, nor invention" (IV.ii.149–50). He promises a thorough critique at dinner.

Scholars have identified in 'Holofernes' a demi-anagram for the name 'John Florio,' the famous scholar who first translated Montaigne into English. They point to the contemporary debate over the question, 'Love or Learning?'—the theme of the play. The eminent Cambridge University scholar Gabriel Harvey was the leading polemicist among the defenders of learning, called the 'Artists.' Cambridge university graduate and satirist Thomas Nashe spoke for the 'Villainists,' who argued for love and for experience generally—contending, for example, that the debtors' prison from which he had also graduated offered more useful instruction than the university. A learned man who translated the learned Montaigne, Florio nonetheless commended experience, subtly praising Machiavelli rather than the Renaissance humanists, whose vast erudition both Montaigne and Machiavelli could be said to have matched. Shakespeare, well-acquainted with Florio's translation, would have noted the paradox. And he would have known Florio's stricture, "It were labor lost to speak of love," since there are so many books about it. Obviously, Shakespeare disagreed, and his Florio-figure is a figure of fun. But will Shakespeare side with Machiavelli's understanding of the lessons of experience, given the skein of geopolitical plotting in the story he tells?

It's now the Navarrians' turn to learn the truth about one another, about how they fought love with the law and love won. Berowne soliloquizes about his losing attempt to conquer his desires. "By heaven, I do love," he confesses to himself, "and it hath taught me to rhyme, and to be melancholy"—the melancholy of the lover who knows not whether he's loved in return, who must admit he cannot maintain his self-sufficiency, even in banding together with his peers in the study of books (IV.iii.11–12). Seeing the King approach, he hides, quickly learning that the King himself has turned sonneteer. In his poem to the Princess, which he recites, Ferdinand takes up the traditional imagery of his lady's eyes, which are something like the sun, making her lover's tears shine in "thy glory through my grief" (IV.iii.33). "O queen of queens! How far dost thou excel / No thought can think nor tongue of mortal tell" (IV.iii.36–37). The rhyme of love sets limits on the prose of reason.

The King himself now hides, as Longaville arrives, his own sonnet in hand, unwittingly to join the King's "sweet fellowship in shame" (IV.iii.45). Against courtly and scholarly rhetoric, "the heavenly rhetoric" of Maria's eye, "'gainst whom the world cannot hold argument," has "persuad[ed] my heart to this false perjury," this evasion of the king's law (IV.iii.56–58). If rhymes set limits on reason, they also set limits on love as "guards on wanton Cupid's hose," in attentive Berowne's words (IV.iii.53). To make rhyme requires the speaker to set his passion to music, to give it measure, to form unreason to a rule of reason. Set to rhyme, love's reason is not the King's 'rationalist' or book-learned reason; it is rather the kind of reason right for loving and for lovers. It is 'New Testament' love set against 'Old Testament' law. For Longaville, poetry enables him to justify his love as lawful: "A woman I forswore; but I will prove, / Thou being a goddess, I forswore not thee. My vow was earthly, thou a heavenly love; / Thy grace being gain'd cures all disgrace in me, / Vows are but breath and breath a vapor is; / Then thou, fair sun, which on my earth dost shine, / Exhal'st this vapor vow, in thee it is. / If broken, then it is no fault of mine; / If by me broke, what fool is not so wise / To lose an oath to win a paradise?" (IV.iii.61–69). Protestant Berowne immediately spots the fallacy, which consists of the argument's false premise, "which makes flesh a deity / A green goose a goddess—pure, pure idolatry"

(IV.iii.70–71). The argument will need a natural, not a theological premise, if it is to hold.

No time for that, as Longaville too hides and Dumaine walks by, soliloquizing (as he supposes) on Katharine. "Once more I'll mark how love can vary wit," Berowne observes, contentedly (IV.iii.96). Dumaine is a man of fewer words than the others. His imagery isn't sunlight or tear-water or the earth, nor does he attempt initially to reason either legalistically or theologically. For him, the ruling image is another element, air. "Love, whose month is ever May, / Spied a blossom passing fair / Playing in the wanton air" (IV.iii.98–100). Love "wish'd himself the heaven's breath," so that he could blow on the cheeks of his beloved: "Air, would I might triumph so!" (IV.iii.106). The theology comes not at the beginning but at the conclusion of Dumaine's sonnet, as he pleads, "Do not call it sin in me / That I am forsworn for thee," since Jove himself loved Juno, "turning mortal for her love" (IV.III.112–16). Like Dumaine, Jove loved one who resisted his advances. He won her heart by transforming himself into a helpless little bird, which the kindly goddess did love; he then transformed himself back into the shape of a god, and his lady's love kept on. Dumaine's sonnet is the intended bird, singing to his lady. He will send "something more plain," too, more prosaic, "express[ing] my true love's lasting pain" (IV.iii.117–18)— as pitiable, he hopes, as Jove in a form of helplessness.

In turn, each hidden man steps forward, Longaville to accuse Dumaine, Ferdinand to accuse Longaville, Berowne to accuse the King and the others. He justly rebukes their "inconstancy" with the rhetorical question, "When shall you see me write a thing in rhyme?" (IV.iii.177). Right away, as it happens, as Costard and Jaquenetta pop up, Berowne's love-sonnet to Rosaline in hand.

This calls for a conference to settle on a change of policy and to formulate a justification for the correction. Fortunately, Berowne already had argued against the King's new regime, and so has an argument ready, this time addressing an audience eager to give its consent.

"Sweet lords, sweet lovers, let us embrace: / As true as we are as flesh and blood can be," he begins (IV.iii.210). Since "young bloods doth not obey an old decree" (IV.iii.213); since beauty makes old age feel "new-born," giving "the crutch the cradle's infancy," being "the sun that maketh all things shine" (IV.iii.240–42); since all these things are true, Berowne is more than happy to fulfill the King's request to "prove our loving lawful, and our faith not torn" (IV.iii.280–81). It is really quite simple, Berown explains. For young men to swear "to fast, to study, and to see no women" in obedience to a king who rules by convention is nothing less than to commit "flat treason 'gainst the kingly state of youth" (IV.iii.288–89)—that is, against the rightful authority of nature, which ordains the seasons of life as the ruler of rulers. Philosophy seeks understanding of nature. But the bookish philosophic regime of the King does not teach nature in full. Berowne's companions have spoken of nature's light, earth, water, and air, but they have forgotten nature's other element, fire. "From women's eyes this doctrine I derive: / They are the ground, the books, the academes, / From whence doth spring the true Promethean fire" (IV.iii.298–300). "Where has any author in the world / Teaches such beauty as a woman's eye" (IV.iii.308–09). Where did you, who came so recently to sonneteering, find "such fiery numbers as the prompting eyes / Of beauty's tutors have enrich'd you with?" (IV.iii.318–19). Surely not in "leaden contemplation" (IV.iii.317). Love "first learned in a lady's eyes / Lives not alone immured in the brain, / But with the motion of all elements / Courses as swift as thought in every power, / And gives to every power a double power, / Above their functions and their offices" (IV.iii.323–27). Love is what sets the other elements of nature in motion, harmonizing and vivifying all the senses, and also every virtue, whether it be courage, wisdom, or moderation. Love civilizes the savage and, with respect to justice, "plant[s] in tyrants mild humility" (IV.iii.345) by teaching them the happiness of unfeigned reciprocity. Therefore, let us "lose our oaths to find ourselves" (IV.iii.357). As the Gospels teach, "charity itself fulfills the law, / And who can sever love from charity?" (IV.iii.360–61). If not quite the Gospel of *agape*, this speech is a sportive gospel of *eros*.

Having declared war on love, which he'd conceived as low, unworthy of the human mind, newly converted King Ferdinand now declares war on behalf of Saint Cupid: "Soldiers, to the field!" (IV.iii.362). Suddenly respectful of nature's time, less concerned with his own timetable, the King urges haste in preparing for the campaign. Preparations will include "some entertainment for them in their tents" (IV.iii.369), "for revels, dances, masks, and merry hours / Forerun fair Love, strewing her way with flowers" (IV.iii.375–76). He drafts none other than Quixote-Armado for the task, who in turn engages Latin-mangling pedant Holofernes and the English-bungling curate

Sir Nathaniel—men who "have been at a great feast of language and stol'n the scraps," as impish young Moth remarks, men who "have liv'd long on the alms-basket of words," as plain-speaker Costard puts it (V.i.35–38). Under Holofernes's direction, they will present a pageant of the Nine Worthies, famous conquerors from Joshua to Pompey the Great. As there are nine worthies but only four players to represent them, Holofernes will play several. Never will so many owe so little to so few.

With the gentlemen absent, the ladies are beginning to bicker amongst themselves, with Rosaline and Katharine exchanging barbs. Pronouncing the exchange "a set of wit well play'd," the Princess redirects their hostilities toward the suitors, asking them to compare the love-sonnets they've received (V.i.29). Rosaline deprecates Berowne's flattery: his "numbers" or meters are "true" but his "numbers" in the sense of his reckoning exaggerated; according to him, "I were the fairest goddess on the ground" (V.ii.36–37). With characteristically greater asperity, Katharine dismisses Dumain's effort as "a huge translation of hypocrisy, / Vilely compil'd, profound simplicity" (V.ii.52–53). As for Longaville, Maria confines herself to opining that she wishes his poem shorter, the accompanying chain of pearls longer. The Princess finds King Ferdinand's poetry equally verbose, although she has kinder words for the diamond necklace he enclosed with it. ("We shall be rich ere we depart" [V.ii.1], she had exulted, at the beginning of their conversation.) In all, "We are wise girls to mock our lovers so" (V.ii.59), and as for the young men, "none are so surely caught, when they are catch'd / As wit turn'd fool; folly, in wisdom hatch'd / Hath wisdom's warrant and the help of school, / And wit's own grace to grace a learned fool" (V.ii.69–72). As one scholar has observed, in *Love's Labor's Lost* "the word *wit* is used more often than in any of the other plays" of Shakespeare. [2] Among other things, the play is a witty meditation on wit. When learning outpaces prudence it acts as an accelerant to "fool'ry's" fire, providing false proofs of stupid thoughts (V.ii.76).

The lovers have arrived, Boyet announces, and they have disguised themselves as Russians. He overheard their planning session—quite by accident, or so he says. He advises the ladies to prepare their defenses, and the Princess is battle-ready: "Saint Dennis to Saint Cupid!" (V.ii.87). The Cupidians of Navarre will meet the forces of Saint Denis, the third-century martyr who brought Christianity to Gaul, was eventually named Bishop of Paris, then martyred by the Romans. One might have expected the Princess to invoke St. Louis, patron saint of the French monarchy, but instead she chooses the patron saint of the French people. A republican at heart? Perhaps rather a just sharer in monarchy. The real French king who preceded Henry of Navarre, Henry III, provoked a popular uprising after murdering his brothers; his criminal attempt to secure his authority undermined it. Under those circumstances, it is better to invoke the saint of the people instead of the so-recently betrayed saint of a monarchy turned unsaintly.

Be this as it may, the Princess tells her attendants to confuse the invaders by posing as one another, masking themselves and claiming each other's identities. (Rosaline will play the Princess.) Each man will woo the wrong woman. Crucially, based on Boyet's somewhat slanted account, the women assume that the men come only to mock them. Just as there's no fool like a learned man, so "there's no such sport as sport by sport o'erthrown" (V.ii.153).

The Navarrians walk into the trap and exit soon after, verbally cut and bruised. "The tongues of mocking wenches are as keen / As the razor's edge invisible," Boyet gloats (V.ii.256–57). The Romans beheaded Saint Denis; his devotees have beheaded the followers of Saint Cupid. The Princess pronounces it to have been an unequal battle: "Better wits have worn plain statute-caps," the headgear of commoners (V.ii.281). After his beheading, Saint Denis was said to have carried his head in his arm, continuing to preach sermons; Boyet predicts that the Cupidians will be equally resilient. When they do return, Rosaline advises the Princess, we should mock them for their silly disguises, and so they will.

Berowne has now understood Boyet, that "ape of form, Monsieur the Nice" (V.ii.325); he sees what the Princess has seen, that Boyet wears a mask of flattering words. When the King worries that the ladies saw through the men's disguises and now will "mock us downright," Dumaine recommends, "Let us confess, and turn it into a jest" (V.ii.389–90). Very well, but this will only reinforce the ladies' conviction that they are being toyed with. It is of course the ladies who are toying with the men, and they humble them in revealing their disguises. Upon this revelation, Berowne can only scold Boyet: "Might not you / Forestall our sport, to make us thus untrue?" (V.ii.472–73). Boyet smirks, "Full merrily / Hath this brave manage, this career, been run" (V.ii.483–84).

As the men prepare to retreat a second time, Costard arrives, announcing the approach of the Nine Worthies. When the King worries that the impending farce will only "shame us" further, Berowne cogently replies that that can scarcely happen, given the ignominy of their defeat. What is more, "'tis some policy / To have one show worse than the King's and his company" (V.ii.509–11). As for the Princess, her appetite for watching men make fools of themselves has yet to be sated: "That sport best pleases that dost least know how" (V.ii.514); and, most acutely, when "zeal strives to content, and the contents / Dies in the zeal of that which it presents," such "confounded" form "makes most form in mirth," as "great things laboring perish in their birth" (V.ii.515–18). "A right description of our sport, my lord," Berowne tells Ferdinand (V.ii.519), and indeed it is a fine assessment of the nature of incompetence in love and poetry, to say nothing of philosophy, piety, and play-writing. The Princess has explained how love's labor is lost, how any kind of labor can be lost.

As hapless Holofernes and his troupe essay their entertainment, the forces of saints Dennis and Cupid unite for the first time, heckling them. Eventually, the Princess takes pity on the poor players; she is less thoroughly merciless than she has seemed. Even Armado begins to see how silly he is. Player and audience alike have moved toward self-knowledge—the purpose of all true comedy, which holds up the mirror to human nature.

Human nature is political, and a messenger arrives to remind everyone of that. "Thou interruptest our merriment," the Princess complains, but the news is grave; her father, the king of France, is dead. Graciously excusing herself from Navarre, with both an apology for any offense given and a reminder that the men had earned it, she thanks King Ferdinand for granting her "great suit" for recovering Aquitaine (V.ii.727)—the first mention of it since the beginning of her embassy. She has successfully completed the diplomatic mission her father sent her to accomplish. The French ladies will leave in triumph, having sacrificed nothing to gain much, including much amusement.

Ferdinand now presses his own mission, the love-suits undertaken by himself and his attendants. Offering an apology in both senses of the word—a defense and an expression of regret—he argues that "your beauties, ladies, / Hath much deformed us, fashioning our humors / Even to the opposed end of our intents," making we lovers seem both ridiculous and cynical (V.ii.744–46). This being so, "ladies, our love being yours, the error that love makes / Is likewise yours. We to ourselves prove false, / By being once false for ever to be true / To those that make us both" (V.ii.760–62). Our falsehood, our Russian gambit, admittedly was "in itself a sin," but the true intent behind it purifies, "turns to grace," the foolish and sinful attempt at deception (V.ii.763–64). "Now, at the last minute of the hour, / Grant us your loves" (V.ii.775–76). Do not let the cormorant of time devour us.

The Princess repeats her own defense, that her party had interpreted the King and his court as mockers, pretenders in love. A most politic woman, she will not be pressured into a hasty decision, become an idolater of time. The last minute is "a time, methinks, too short / To make a world-without-end bargain in" (V.ii.777–78). She intends to observe the right form, to mourn her father's death for the next twelve months. If you, King, will yourself retreat "to some forlorn and naked hermitage," then I shall marry you at the end of that time (V.ii.782). Rosaline, Katharine, and Maria make the same guarantee—Katharine characteristically with more reserve ("then, if I have much love, I'll give you some," Lord Dumaine [V.ii.818]), and Rosaline characteristically with more vigor. Berowne is not merely to seclude himself but to reform himself, learn to bridle his sarcasm by visiting the sick and dying, to learn that "a jest's prosperity lies in the ear / Of him that hears it, never in the tongue / Of him that makes it" (V.ii.849–51). If Berowne finds his jesting ill-met by ill men, "throw away that spirit, / And I shall find you empty of that fault, / Right joyful of your reformation" (V.ii.855–57). Navarre is Protestant, a man of the Reformation; French Catholic Rosaline would reform the Reformer, who has too often deployed his wit to reform others, seldom turning it on himself. His love must become Christian, charitable. [3]

At this, Berowne reflects. "Our wooing doth not end like an old play: / Jack hath not Jill. These ladies' courtesy / Might well have made our sport a comedy," but it hasn't (V.ii.862–64). The men's foolish and conventional love-labors have been lost, new and more austere love-labors imposed. As one scholar puts it, the ladies' final commands, their final love-test, will discover whether the Navarrian aristocrats can love after they've endured for a year, outside courtly conventions. [4] The King is ready for the challenge; after all, a year is only one-third of the time his men had agreed to sacrifice for the sake of liberal-arts learning. Berowne remains as skeptical as ever in assessing such vows. "That's too long for a play," he concludes (V.ii.867). It is indeed too long for a theatrical play, a fiction, and too long to sustain a self-deceiving vow. This love-test will uncover the reality of the men's vows (and the women's), one way or the other.

The play isn't too long for a closing song. Newly sobered Armado returns, this time with a shorter, simpler, and much more pointed performance by his players. During the time of the love-test, and for the rest of their lives if they pass it, the men will know the anxiety love's exclusivity necessarily brings. The first song, sung by "Spring," reminds them that in that season "The cuckoo then on every tree / Mocks married men, for thus sings he: 'Cuckoo,'" cuckold (V.ii.885–86), "a word of fear, / Unpleasing to the married ear" (V.ii.897–98). The second song, sung by "Winter," "when icicles hang on the wall," reminds them that in that season every night "the staring owl" sings "Tu-who, Tu-whit, Tu-who"—"a merry note" heard indoors, out of the cold (V.ii.900–07). While the anxiety of unknowing, unsure love comes with summer, winter brings men indoors, where they know, can say, can name (to-wit) those to whom they can truly address their love. To say 'tu' is to say 'you' with intimacy. It bespeaks knowing love of one's own, one's own household—the persons there, the warming fire, the food cooking on the stove.

The song reprises Berowne's prosaic initial critique of King Ferdinand's planned regime—sets it to music. Nature imposes the cycle of seasons, over time. Both the not-knowing and the knowledge of love will occur and recur, throughout every human life. Contra Florio, there is always more to write about love because love is the fire that moves the elements of nature, and nature cannot forever by denied by philosophers, theologians, or rulers. For commoners like Armado, Holofernes, Sir Nathaniel, Jaquenetta, Costard, Moth, Dull, and the Forester, the outdoor nature of the summer meadow and singing birds and the indoor household amidst the winter now (where "birds sit brooding" [V.ii.910]) will limit the pretensions of those who would rise above their station with self-inflating talk. For aristocrats like the Navarrian gentlemen and the French ladies, each season will limit the pretensions of those who would rise above their station as rulers, to suppose themselves Platonic philosophers minus Socratic irony, pretensions both impolitic and unnatural, ruinous both to rule and to sound reasoning. For rulers, the harsh realities of war, territorial disputes, and succession crises jar them out of the pretensions peculiar to the prominent, the thought that their sayings must make things so.

"The words of Mercury are harsh after the songs of Apollo," Armado says, to both sides (V.ii.917). Mercury's words come from the gods; Apollo, god of music, makes reality seem sweeter than it is. And finally, Armado delivers himself justly of a thing he had longed to deliver unjustly and foolishly: a command. "You that way: we this way" (V.ii.918). You aristocrats, we commoners. You French devotees of Saint Denis, we Navarrian disciples of Saint Cupid. You Catholics, we Reformers. You women, we men. If unity comes, it will need to be an articulated unity, the hard-won unity of lovers who remain distinct from one another—not a rushed and thoughtless amalgamation but a unity founded on practical wit, not on the unsteady show-wit of learning for fame's sake.

Notes

1. There may also be a critical glance at the Protestant emphasis on book-learning in the form of Book-learning, Bible study.
2. C. L. Barber: *Shakespeare's Festive Comedy: A Study in Dramatic Form and Its Relation to Social Custom* (Cleveland: The World Publishing Company, 1963), p. 99.
3. In their excellent article on the play, Denise Schaeffer and Mary P. Nichols criticize the Princess's declaration of a one-year period of mourning as arbitrary—an expression of continued resistance to the suitors. But a one-year period of mourning is in no way arbitrary; Christian traditions have varied over the centuries, sometimes prescribing a period up to three years, that is, the length of time the King proposed for the courtly fast. Further, in this case, the Princess is quite sensible. She could hardly return home to bury her father and marry a suitor more or less at the same time. She must balance the Navarrian King's ardor against the need for propriety in her court and for fidelity in her marriage, and in the marriages of her attendants. The one-year love test is hardly unreasonable, given the King's own proposal of a three-year period of celibacy; she strikes a mean between the King's austerity and Berowne's impatience.
4. Barber, p. 112.

CHAPTER TEN
THE WISEST BEHOLDER

At the palace of Leontes, king of Sicilia, a Sicilian lord, Camillo, and a Bohemian lord, Archidamus, compare their countries. "If you chance,
Camillo, to visit Bohemia, on the like occasion whereon my services are
now on foot"—namely, an extended visit to Sicilia by the Bohemian king,
Polixenes—"you shall see, as I have said, great difference betwixt our Bohemia and your Sicilia" (I.i.1–3), namely, that Bohemia is far less wealthy.
At the planned reciprocal visit to Bohemia next summer by King Leontes,
you will never see such "magnificence" as we Bohemians have seen here
(I.i.12). Archidamus playfully suggests that we will need to give all of you
Sicilians "sleepy drinks, that your senses, unintelligent of our insufficience,
may, though they cannot praise us, as little accuse us" (I.i.13–14). Camillo
assures him that a stronger bond than expense in hospitality binds the two
kings. It is the natural bond of a friendship close to brotherhood. As boys,
they shared the same education and planted a seed of "affection which cannot choose but branch now" (I.i.22), separated even as they have been by
"their more mature dignities and royal necessities" (I.i.23). They are loving
brothers, and Archidamus agrees that "there is not in the world either malice or matter" to alter their love (I.i.31–32).

This amity in their foreign relations matches the amity King Leontes
enjoys at home. His young son, Prince Mamillius, "is a gentleman of the
greatest promise that ever came into my note," Archidamus says (I.i.33–
34). And the king's subjects love both father and son. Sicilia enjoys the
blessing of a sound regime and the civil peace it fosters.

Elsewhere in the palace, the two kings discuss King Polixenes' departure.
Unlike King Leontes, faction may be arising in Bohemia. He fears "sneaping
winds at home" (I.ii.13)—biting, rebuking criticism by his subjects for his
nine-months' absence. Nor does he wish "to tire our royalty" by prolonging
his visit (I.ii.14). "My affairs / Do drag me homeward" (I.ii.23–24). When

his liberal request to his friend to extend his stay still further fails, King Leontes turns to his queen, Hermione, to plead his case. Addressing her guest through her husband, she says to tell him that all in Bohemia is well, and that she grants Leontes permission to stay a month longer when he visits Bohemia. She good-humoredly threatens to take Polixenes prisoner.

He yields. Reminiscing to her of the childhood he shared with her husband, he tells her that each then supposed he were "the boy eternal" (I.ii.64). "We knew not / The doctrine of ill-doing, nor dream'd / That any did" (I.ii.69–71). Had the "stronger blood" of sexual maturity not overtaken them, the could have stood before God in complete innocence (I.ii.72).

This friendly dialogue, slightly suggestive of possessiveness and eroticism, causes what could only have been a deep reserve of jealousy in King Leontes' soul to erupt. "My heart dances," he tells himself in an aside, "But not for joy, not joy" (I.ii.110–11). Considering his son, he reassures himself that Mamillius looks "like me" (I.ii.135). No adultery went into his making. But his wife is pregnant, nearing childbirth, which corresponds agonizingly with the nine months his brother has been in his palace. Does he linger in Sicilia only to witness the birth of a child who is really his own? Is that why Hermione wants him to stay a month longer?

Leontes casually asks Polixenes if he's as fond of his own son as Leontes is of Mamillius. Indeed so: "If at home, sir, / He's all my exercise, my mirth, my matter; / Now my sworn friend, and then mine enemy; / My parasite, my statesman, my soldier, all" (I.ii.165–68). A true son. But Leontes has used his question only to set up his friend and his wife for surveillance; as he prepares for a walk with his own son, leaving them alone, he confides to the audience, "I am angling now" (I.ii.180). He watches as they converse, taking ordinary gestures of true friends talking as proofs of adultery, and even universalizing them: "It's a bawdy planet" (I.ii.201). This inverts the Christian theme that God created the universe in the spirit of agapic love; in the eyes of jealousy, the world consists instead of erotic anarchy. When Lord Camillo refuses to confirm his suspicions of the queen, even going so far as to defend her honor, Leontes puts him on the traitor list, too. To Leontes, slender evidence weighs heavily: "Is whispering nothing?" (I.ii.284). If their many gestures of affection are nothing, "then the world and all that's in't is nothing; / The covering sky is nothing; Bohemia is nothing; / My wife is nothing; nor nothing have these nothings, / If this be nothing" (I.ii.292–95). The answer is that yes, all these tokens are not-noth-ings, literally, but nothing much when it comes to grounds for reasonable suspicion. Small 'somethings' may or may not add up to a bigger one. Only prudence and moderation will tell the difference. But that isn't an answer Leontes would hear. In making something out of near-nothings, he apes God while throwing his kingdom into chaos. The king is a creative un-cre-ator, about to unmake his family and hazard the unmaking of his family's rule.

In Leontes' mind, Camillo can redeem himself from the charge of trea-son by passing a kind of love test or loyalty test. He must agree to poison Polixenes—a lethal version of the sleeping potion with which Archidamus playfully proposed to dope Camillo and the rest of next year's Sicilian vis-itors in Bohemia. This is the only way Leontes can eliminate his imagined rival while maintaining Hermione's reputation, which he needs to keep in-violate so as not to call the royal succession into question.

As befits his name, which means 'freeborn,' or 'noble,' Camillo will have nothing to do with the murder. To obey such a master would be to obey "one who, in rebellion to himself, will have / All that are his so too" (I.ii.354–55). He hints of the plot to Polixenes, who appeals to him to dis-close it fully: "I conjure thee, by all the parts of man; / Which honor does acknowledge, whereof the least / Is not this suit of mine, that thou declare / What incidency thou dost guess of harm / Is creeping toward me; how far off, how near; / Which way to be prevented, if to be; / If not, how best to bear it" (I.ii.401–06). That is, your obligation to human nature overrides your obligation to your master. Camillo does yield to the higher obligation, asking only that when Polixenes embarks for Bohemia he take Camillo with him. Polixenes rightly believes the lord's story, as he saw for himself a ma-lignant glance his friend cast at him when last he saw him. "This jealousy / Is for a precious creature; as she's rare / Must it be great; and, as his person's mighty, / Must be violent; and as he does conceive / He is dishonor'd by a man which ever / Profess'd to him, why his revenges must / In that be made more bitter" (I.ii.451–57). Love and honor rightly comport with one an-other, but here their combination has turned lethal.

The two men have been 'brothers' not in birth-nature but in the more refined natural relation of friendship. Yet they are also kings, and kings must concern themselves with conspiracies against their rule. They will hear rumors of such conspiracies, or even suspect conspiracy without hearing rumors but by observing the behavior of possible rivals. King Leontes invents a conspiracy against himself by 'over-reading' the behavior of his brother and his wife. When a trusted advisor disagrees with his misinterpretation, he not only rejects his testimony but commands him to murder the man he wrongly accuses. King Polixenes observes hostile behavior but only puzzles at it when told of a possible conspiracy by a man subordinate to the conspirator; he carefully tests this testimony, confirming it by comparing it to his prior observation. The clinching evidence is Camillo's willingness to exile himself, to join Polixenes in fleeing Sicilia. Living up to the meaning of his name, which means 'hospitable,' Polixenes tells the older man, "I will respect thee as a father, if / Thou bear'st me off hence" (I.ii.461–62). Given Leontes' jealousy-sparked, lethal madness, Polixenes is glad to 'adopt' a new father in place of his natural, deceased father. His brotherly friend has made himself unnatural both by rebelling against his own nature and his own rule, causing faction in his kingdom, where there had been unity in the ruling household and among the elders, and by sundering the alliance between Sicilia and Bohemia. Obsession with loyalty ruins the union the obsession demands, causing first of all a new and unusual reconfiguration of the Bohemian king's family, via the 'adoption' of a 'father' by a 'son.'

At the palace, Hermione temporarily hands off her son to the ladies in attendance: "He so troubles me, / 'Tis past enduring" (II.1–2). Judging from the boy's badinage with the lady, he is indeed something of an insolent little wiseacre, and a pregnant mother might well find him taxing. When Hermione returns, she tries to settle him down by asking him to tell her a tale. "A sad tale's best for winter," the boy replies, foreshadowing more than he knows; he proposes a winter's tale within *The Winter's Tale*, a story about "sprites and goblins" (II.i.26). Before he begins, Leontes enters the room, along with Lord Antigonus and several other courtiers. He will prove the greater goblin than any the boy may imagine.

Having heard the report that Polixenes and Camillo have fled, confirming his suspicions that they must have been plotting against him, he continues to believe that Hermione was a co-conspirator and is now pregnant with his brother's child. "She's an adultress," a "bed-swerver," and a traitor (II.i.78,93)—a royal home-wrecker who, because royal, has betrayed her country, as well. He orders her imprisoned. Hermione takes his decree stoically: "There's some ill-planet reigns. / I must be patient till the heavens look / With aspect more favorable" (II.i.105–07). She will not weep, and adjures the overlooking lords and ladies not to weep, either. Weep only if you "know your mistress / Has deserved prison" (II.i.119–20). As for Leontes, "Adieu, my lord. / I never wish'd you sorry; now / I trust I shall" (II.i.123–24).

Lord Antigonus remonstrates but Leontes rejects his criticisms as he had rejected those of Archimadus. "Why, what need we / Commune with you of this, but rather follow / Our forceful instigation? Our prerogative / Calls not your counsels; but our natural goodness / Imparts this…" (II.i.162–66). In the mind of the jealousy-addled tyrant, his will trumps his counselor's reason because his will speaks the mind of one by nature superior to his advisers. "We need no more your advice" because the whole matter "is all properly ours" (II.i.168–70). Jealousy registers love of one's own; overweening jealousy registers a love of one's own that spurns reason, including rational advice, for the solipsism of fury. The king recognizes only one authority above himself He's sent to Apollo's temple at Delphi for the word of the oracle, which he expects to confirm his charges not in his own mind but in the mind of his subjects.

Paulina, wife of Antigonus, attempts to visit Hermione in prison. She is allowed to see only the queen's attendant, Emilia. Hermione has given birth to a daughter. Paulina would bring the infant to King Leontes in the hope of softening his heart at the sight of the child. When the jailer worries that he might be punished for letting the child out of jail, Paulina appeals to nature: "You need not fear it, sir. / This child was prisoner to the womb, and is / By law and process of great Nature thence / Freed and enfranchis'd—not a party to / The anger of the King, nor guilty of, / If any be, the trespass of the Queen" (II.ii.48–53). What is more, "I will stand betwixt you and danger" (II.ii.66). That is, the child was imprisoned by natural necessity because her mother was, but now that she has been born, she cannot be justly imprisoned any longer, being as innocent of wrongdoing as any human being can be. To this argument in principle, this rational argument from natural right, Paulina prudently adds a promise of political protection, inasmuch as arguments from principle can have no purchase in the world as it is without political security.

With Polixenes the "harlot king" out of reach, King Leontus plans capital punishment for Hermione, the imagined accomplice and traitor (II.iii.4). Meanwhile, sleepless and without appetite since hearing of his mother's "dishonor," Mamillius has taken ill (II.iii.13). Completing the derangement of nature within the royal household, the king too has been unable to sleep. But that hasn't prevented him from strategizing. Calculating that King Polixenes' throne is too secure and his alliances too strong for a successful attack on Bohemia, King Leontes reserves revenge on him for another time. This speech provides two important insights into the king's mind: first, he isn't so thoroughly insane as to have lost his ability to reason altogether; second, his jealousy isn't a mere pretext for making war on Bohemia. His irrationality is limited to one dimension of his soul and his rule, albeit a dimension that threatens to ruin both his soul and his rule.

Paulina approaches the king's court with Hermione's baby in her arms. Delayed by one of the attending lords, she tells him not to fear the king's "tyrannous passion" more than "the Queen's life" (II.iii.27–28). Her "gracious, innocent soul" is "more free than he is jealous" (II.iii.28–29). When he persists in blocking her, she tells him, "I do come with words as medicinal as true, / Honest as either, to purge him of that humor / That presses him from sleep" (II.iii.37–39). Hearing the disputants, the king comes forth to command his men to remove her. A woman of spirit (in this not unlike the manly apostle for whom she is named), Paulina threatens to scratch their eyes out if they try, provoking the king to call her a masculine witch, to accuse his attendants of treason, and to charge "thou dotard" Antigonus with fearing his wife (II.iii.74). "This brat is none of mine" (II.iii.92). He commands that mother and daughter both be burned.

Knowing that the king can't commit this act of judicial murder without accomplices, Paulina turns to the attendants. Look at the evidence, she tells him: The infant's features are miniature copies of the king's. Appealing to "the good goddess Nature," she suggests that not only the shape of the body but "the ordering of the mind, too," is under Nature's rule, and that yellow, the color of jealousy, has no rightful part in the natural order. This only enrages Leontes, as he tells Antigonus he deserves to be hanged for failing to "stay her tongue"—to which the good lord coolly replies, "Hang all the husbands / That cannot do that feat, you'll leave yourself / Hardly one subject" (II.iii.109–11). Threatened by the king with burning, Paulina professes to "care not," since "it is an heretic that makes the fire, / Not she which burns in't" (II.iii.113–15). You, king, in an attempt to defend your honor, and therefore the crown that depends upon its maintenance, make yourself instead "scandalous in the world" (II.iii.120). Your rule has become the derangement of the honor upon which your authority depends.

Paulina catches the king in another contradiction. Having called his passion tyrannical, she stops short of calling him one: "I'll not call you tyrant," only cruel and daft, a ruler whose acts savor of tyranny which "will ignoble make you" (II.iii.115,119). Leontes sputters at his courtiers, "Were I a tyrant, / Where were her life? She durst not call me so, / If she did not know me one" (II.iii.121–24). But she did in fact not call him so, and therefore, by the logic of his own charge, she must know him one. She hands the infant to her husband and issues a parting insult to all the king's attendants: "You that are thus so tender" of the king's "follies will never do him good, not one of you" (II.iii.127–28). Obedience is not enough, when dealing with the anti-natural, the tyrannical. She effectively calls for civil disobedience by the king's men, and unknowingly prophesies the ruin of her own husband.

After accusing Antigonus of setting his wife to this action, King Leontes initially commands that he burn the child, or he will dash out her "bastard brains" with "these my proper hands" (II.iii.136–37). When his fellow lords attest to Antigonus' innocence, Leontes cries, "You're liars all" (II.iii.145). In his insane jealousy he has constructed an entirely fictional world around himself, all founded upon the initial fiction that his wife and friend have committed adultery against him.

King or rather Tyrant Leontes still hasn't lost every vestige of sanity, however. Evidently seeing that he faces a palace revolt, he tells Antigonus that he will pardon his wife in exchange for his vow to carry the child out of Sicilia and leave her exposed, "Where chance may nurse or end it" (II.iii.182). Thus the end of Act II echoes the beginning of Act I, when the Bohemian Lord Archidemus told his Sicilian counterpart, Camillo, that he would see the "great difference" between Bohemia and Sicilia if chance were to bring him to Bohemia. Chance has brought Camillo to Bohemia, fleeing in the company of the Bohemian king; the important difference between the two countries has turned out not to be an 'economic' difference, the difference in wealth, but the political difference between kingship and tyranny, between a just and reasonable natural ruler and an unjust, irrational, unnatural one.

Leontes now learns that Cleomenes and Dion, his messengers to the Delphic oracle, will arrive in an hour. Having failed to hear the voices of natural reason, even when Nature has been described as a goddess, what will the voice of the god tell him? And how will he respond to its divine judgment?

On the road to the Sicilian capital, the messengers discuss the beauties of Delphi—its delicate climate, its sweet air, its fertile soil, and its impressive temple. In describing the oracle, Cleomenes moves from the beautiful to the sublime: "The ear-deaf'ning voice o' th' oracle, / Kin to Jove's thunder, so surprised my sense / That I was nothing" (III.i.9–11). Dion affirms that when the sealed contents of the oracle's answer are revealed, "something rare even then will rush to knowledge" (III.i.20–21). In precise contrast to Leontes' attempt to make something out of nothings, something significant out of human, all too human trifles, the Delphic oracle's teachings make human beings feel insignificant in comparison to the wisdom and power of Jove's son, Apollo. What Leontes has deranged the oracle would set right, substituting divine knowledge for the king's baseless surmise.

Meanwhile, the tyrant Leontes wants to be "clear'd of being tyrannous" in Sicilia's law court (III.ii.4–5). Submitting to the rule of law gives the appearance of constitutionalism to his rule. Hermione stands charged with treason on three counts: as queen, she has committed adultery; she has conspired to murder the king; she has aided the flight of her co-conspirators. The murder charge is a new invention, derived from the first invention; it was of course Tyrant Leontes, and him alone, who conspired to have a king murdered.

At trial, Hermione points out the lawless character of Leontes' appeal to the law. "Mine integrity / Being counted falseness," she is being considered guilty until proven innocent (III.ii.24–25). She nonetheless makes her defense, appealing to three authorities: the "pow'rs divine" (III.ii.26); "my past life" (III.i.31); and the king's own conscience. With respect to her past life, she says she loved Polixenes "as in honor he requir'd" as a visiting king and as "yourself," Leontes, "commanded" (III.ii.62,65). In her central answer, the evidence of her good character, she cites her chaste and true previous conduct, her status as a royal wife, herself the daughter of "a great king," the emperor of Russia, and mother of a prince, and, finally, her integrity, the evidence for which she brings out by saying she prizes her honor, not her life (III.ii.31–43). "My life stands in the level"—the gunsight—"of your dreams, / Which I'll lay down" (III.ii.78–79). Now deprived of her husband's favor and of both her children, she is unafraid to die, but will continue to defend her honor. As for the king's conscience, he has replaced proofs with "surmise," exhibiting "rigor, and not law" (III.ii.110,112).

The only answer among these that might sway the tyrant—judge in his own case—is the appeal to powers divine. Accordingly, Hermione asks for the oracle of Apollo, which she expects will vindicate her honor. Leontes agrees to her request, confident of his own charges. When the messengers appear and are duly sworn, the court officer breaks the seal and reads a message from Delphi which not only exonerates Hermione but calls Leontes "a jealous tyrant" and prophesies that "he shall live without an heir" (III.ii.131–33). To this, Leontes proves his tyranny by denying the authority of the god: "This is mere falsehood"; let the trial continue (III.ii.139). He would make the oracle at Delphi a nothing.

But the god is not to be mocked. One of Leontes' servants reports that Mamillius has died of sickness brought on by worrying over his mother's peril. His father immediately understands that this is evidence of Apollo's anger at "my injustice" (III.ii.143). His line of succession has been destroyed. He was quite willing to deny the words of the god, but he cannot deny the action of the god. He confesses, "I have too much believ'd mine own suspicion" (III.ii.149). He speaks one of the very rare prayers in all of Shakespeare's writings, asking Apollo to pardon "my great profaneness 'gainst thy oracle" (III.ii.151) and promising to atone by reconciling himself with Polixenes, "new woo my queen," and recall "the good Camillo," a "man of truth, of mercy" (III.ii.151–53). He further confesses that his several jealousies led him "to bloody thoughts and to revenge" (III.ii.156) against persons who unfailingly acted with humanity, honor, self-sacrifice, and piety.

But Apollo has not done acting. The queen has collapsed, and Paulina pronounces her dead. She condemns Leontes, telling him that the gods will not forgive him, however contrite he may be, or seem to be. "Therefore betake thee / To nothing but despair" (III.ii.206–07). This would be the final "nothing" for him; nothing came of nothing.

Whatever Paulina may suspect, Leontes has truly humbled himself.

"Go on, go on," he tells her, "thou canst not speak too much," as I have deserved "all tongues to talk their bitt'rest" (III.ii.212–14). When Paulina herself repents and asks his forgiveness, he replies with humility, "Thou didst speak but well / When most the truth; which I receive much better / Than to be pitied of thee" (III.ii.229–31). After burying his queen and his son in one grave, he will continue to rule Sicilia "in shame perpetual," "so long as nature" will let him live (III.ii.235,237). "Once a day I'll visit / The chapel here they lie; and tears shed there / Shall be my recreation"—in both senses of the term (III.ii.235–37). Nature, the true 'something,' which he had spurned and deformed with his passion and the acts deriving from that passion, will have the last word.

On the seacoast of Bohemia, Antigonus, with the royal infant in his arms, hears the mariner who has escorted him say that the area is "famous" for its "creatures of prey" (III.iii.12). Antigonus fears rather the spirit of Hermione, who appeared to him in his sleep last night—"ne'er was dream / So much like waking" (III.iii.18–19). "Good Antigonus," the spirit told him, "Since fate against thy better disposition, / Hath made thy person for the thrower-out / Of my poor babe, according to thine oath," call her Perdita, meaning 'lost' (III.iii.27–30). As punishment, you will never see your wife Paulina again. Antigonus obeys the spirit, whom he takes as having been sent by Apollo. He places the infant on the ground, "either for life or death," ground ruled by the one he mistakenly supposes to be her father, King Polixenes (III.iii.45). He puts a bundle down beside her; if she is found, its contents will pay for her support. "Most accurs'd am I / To be by oath enjoin'd to this" (III.iii.52–59). He is indeed: As a storm blows up, one of the local creatures of prey, a bear, attacks him. "I am gone for ever" (III.iii.57), a victim of nature at its most violent, driven into it by a tyrant whose name means 'lion.'

Not so, Perdita. A shepherd finds her. Believing some "waiting-gentlewoman in the scape" has abandoned her, he determines to "take it up for pity" (III.iii.72–75). His son arrives to report that he has seen a ship capsized in the storm and found a man mortally wounded by a bear. Their mood brightens when they discover that the infant has come equipped with a sack of gold and jewels. The shepherd is suddenly rich.

Suddenness is a recurring motif in the play. Leontes veers from apparent contentment to raging jealousy to just and humble penitence. Paulina too goes from severe judge to pleader for forgiveness. Suddenness is a form of the intersection between thought, speech, and/or action with time; Act IV opens with Time himself speaking to the audience in the role of a chorus. I "please some, try all"; I bring "joy and terror," "good and bad"; perhaps above all, Time "makes and unfolds error" (IV.i.1–2) (as Viola sees in *Twelfth Night*). Therefore, Time continues, it is no crime in me if I violate the laws of the classical 'unities,' which decree that all actions in a play occur within a twenty-four-hour span After all, "it is in my pow'r / To o'erthrow law, and in one self-born hour / To plant and o'erwhelm custom" (IV.i.7– 9). And so I shall now "slide o'er sixteen years" (IV.i.6) and return you to Bohemia, where King Polixenes still lives with his son, Florizel, and Perdita has "now grown in grace / Equal with wond'ring" (IV.i.24–25).

At the palace, plots are being formed. Camillo laments the loss of his country, which he hasn't seen since he fled to Bohemia. A faithful lover of his own, he wants to be buried there. Now it is safe for him to return, as in the intervening time King Leontes has shown himself as penitent in action as he had been in speech. In contrast, King Polixenes still doubts the sincerity of his former friend's longstanding shows of remorse, having seen how quickly the man's mood can turn. He has another task for his trusted courtier; he wants him to accompany him to the house of the wealthy shepherd, whose daughter Florizel has been courting, according to reports the king has received from his spies. Even in childhood Florizel was changeable, Polixenes had told Leontes, back in Sicilia. So he has longstanding reasons to keep an eye on him. The king and Camillo will disguise themselves and investigate, as Polixenes remains a cautious man when it comes to his own suspicions. This mission is far more urgent than Camillo's natural but private longing, as the prince's alleged action implicates the royal succession in Bohemia.

Bohemia, land of predators, features at least one human specimen of the breed. A rogue named Autolycus (literally, 'wolf-self') ambles along a road near the shepherd's house singing of early spring, when "the red blood reigns in the winter's pale" (IV.iii.4). The sixteen years' shift in chronology accompanies a one-season shift in the natural cycle, from winter in Sicilia to spring in Bohemia. Red blood hints at both love and predation; while the prince walks in the spirit of the first, Wolf-Self walks in the spirit of the second. He was once a servant of Florizel but has been let go, from the Bohemian court to the Bohemian wilds, where a self-made wolf belongs.

He finds his next prey in the shepherd's son, who's been sent to purchase food, spices, and flowers for a feast Perdita is planning. Pretending to have been beaten and robbed, Autolycus picks the youth's pocket, relieving him of money he would have given the pretended victim, in pity. Enjoying his sport, Autolycus blames a man called 'Autolycus' for the beating. He is a true lord of misrule, but unfit for Twelfth Night celebrations, fit only for the Hobbesian 'state of nature' *avant la lettre*—shammer, liar, law-breaker.

At the shepherd's cottage, Florizel and Perdita also play with role reversal but for love, not profit. He's dressed as a shepherd swain, she as a queen. Perdita worries that the king, "by some accident," might discover them and object to their play (IV.iv.19). Florizel tells her that it's only done in "jollity," that the gods themselves condescend to take the form of beasts, for love (IV.iv.19,25). Apollo himself transformed himself into "a poor humble swain, / As I seem now" (IV.iv.30–31). Such an allusion to Ovid's tales, which suggest a rather bawdy planet indeed, might well unsettle a virtuous shepherdess, but Florizel assures her that unlike the gods, "my desires / Run not before mine honor, nor my lusts / Burn hotter than my faith" (IV.iv.33–35).

Yes, but what of the real difference in rank between the prince and the shepherdess? She remarks that "Your resolution cannot hold, when 'tis / Oppos'd, as it must be, by the pow'r of the King" (IV.iv.36–37). One of us must change, for real. Florizel brushes her worries aside; "prithee, darken not / The mirth of the feast" (IV.iv.41–42). If forced to choose, "I'll be thine" and "not my father's" because "I cannot be / Mine own, not anything to any, if / I be not thin" (IV.iv.42–44). He will be constant in this purpose, even if "destiny say no" (IV.iv.46). Think of today's feast as the precursor to the celebration of that nuptial which "We two have sworn shall come" (IV.iv.50–51). Perdita can only hope that Lady Fortune will "stand you auspicious" (IV.iv.52). Very well, he says; the guests approach, so "let's be red with mirth" (IV.iv.54), with the rising blood of the Bohemian springtime.

To whom does the prince belong? His father considers him his own, by nature. As ruler, and as future ruler, both belong to Bohemia, and it to them, as sovereign monarch and monarch-to-be. The prince considers himself more fundamentally his own, by an even more elemental nature; having vowed to marry his beloved, he anticipates becoming 'one flesh' with his bride, making this a matter of honor. Marriage is the natural foundation of the political community, but this marriage seems to challenge the natural foundation of the ruling family, the regime of that community. Perdita sees the tension, even contradiction, between the ruling intentions of father and son, king and prince. The prince, ardent for her, prefers not to think about it.

For his part, the shepherd wants to prepare his adopted daughter for rule, in his own more limited domain. You, Perdita, are "hostess of the meeting" (IV.iv.64). The guests include shepherds and shepherdesses but also King Polixenes and Camillo, in disguise. Welcome these "unknown friends" to the feast, the shepherd says; in the absence of your mother, whom Perdita assumes to be the shepherd's late wife, put away your girlish blushes "and present yourself / That which you are, Mistress o' th' Feast" (IV.iv.65–68). And she does so, greeting king and courtier with gifts of rosemary and rue, dried flowers that keep "all the winter long," representing "grace and remembrance" throughout hard times (IV.iv.75–76).

Needless to say, the king wants to get to know her better. He has every reason to suspect her motives regarding his son. Complimenting her beauty, he graciously remarks that her gifts of "the flowers of winter" fits the old age of her uninvited but welcomed guests (IV.iv.78). She tells him that the springtime flowers, carnations and gillyvors, are hybrids, "nature's bastards," and she will not grow them in "our rustic garden" (IV.iv.83–4)—unknowingly reprising the false suspicions about herself that lodged in the mind of her own natural father. Such flowers are products of art, not nature—Sicilian, as it were, not Bohemian. The king corrects her, however, arguing that "nature is made better by no mean / But nature makes that mean; so over that art / Which you say adds to nature, is an art / That nature makes" (IV.iv.89–92). Marrying "the gentlest scion to the wildest stock" "does mend nature—change it rather; but / The art itself is nature" (IV.iv.93–97). Given her own vows, she cannot but agree. The king seems to bless the union: "Make your garden rich in gillyvors, / And do not call them bastards" (IV.iv.98–99). Since bastardy had been exactly the issue respecting her own birth, unbeknownst to her, unbeknownst to himself the king is teaching the girl he was falsely accused of siring. Both understand nature; neither knows the other.

She distributes more flowers, always in accordance with the nature of the flowers and the age of her guests, matching nature with time. She flirts with Florizel, whose name means 'flower.' In turn, he calls her royal by na-ture. Polixenes agrees, confiding with amazement to Camillo that Perdita is "the prettiest low-born lass that ever / Ran on the green-sward; nothing she does or seems / But smacks of something greater than herself, / Too noble for this place" (IV.ib.156–59). Camillo too can only agree "She is / The queen of curds and cream," queen of the natural (IV.iv.160–61). The lovers dance.

Autolycus prowls in, now disguised as a piper, avoiding recognition by any of the three men who know him from the king's court. Ever ready to separate others from their money, he sings of the trinkets he would like to sell. The lovers have other goods in mind. Florizel professes his love for Perdita in front of his disguised father, saying he loves her more than any other of his gifts: beauty, force, or knowledge. The shepherd happily gives his daughter to the man he takes for another shepherd.

The king, however, has a few questions for his unsuspecting son. "Soft swain," he begins, "Have you a father?" (IV.iv.383). *Yes*, "but what of him?" Florizel replies (IV.iv.384). Not an auspicious beginning. Does he know of your plans to wed? "He neither does nor shall" (IV.iv.385). "Methinks" (Polixenes ventures to say) "a father / Is at the nuptial of his son a guest / That best becomes the table. Pray you once more, / Is not your father grown incapable / Of reasonable affairs?" (IV.iv.386–90). Not at all, he is quite healthy. But then surely there is something "wrong" and "unfilial" about your conduct; a man should use reason to choose his wife, "but as good reason / The father—all whose joy is nothing else / But fair posterity—should hold some counsel / In such a business" (IV.iv.398–402). Florizel agrees but insists that "for some other reasons…I do not acquaint / My fa-ther of this business" (IV.iv.403–04). He has already pledged himself to Perdita, and there is the matter of the difference in social rank that she has warned about.

It is indeed both understandable yet astonishing that Florizel and Perdita have formed no plan, conceived of no plot, beyond marriage. What exactly do they intend to do after the ceremony and the wedding night? This is understandable in view of their ardor, but comical in view of the re-markable circumstance which they both see so clearly, the incongruity of a prince marrying a shepherdess—however rich the bride's father may (again incongruously) be. Father Time cannot be on their side. In this, the dilemma of springtime in Bohemia, the season of red blood in the land of natural riches and civil-social poverty, parallels comically the tragic dilemma of winter in Sicilia, land of civil-social riches and natural poverty. In Sicilia, the king's love of his own ruins itself with marital jealousy; in Bohemia, the king's love of his own threatens to ruin itself with filial and patriotic jealousy. This Bohemian comedy veers toward tragedy.

The enraged king rips off his disguise, excoriating first his son, "whom son I dare not call," as "too base to acknowledge"; then the shepherd, an "old traitor" whose hanging, unfortunately, would only shorten his feeble life for a week; and finally Perdita, "thou fresh piece / Of excellent witch-craft" who has taken advantage of his fool of an unworthy son (IV.iv.410–15). The woman he'd praised as nature's epitome suddenly has changed—in his mind—into a practitioner of the black arts. Polixenes now behaves ex-actly as his brother had done in his succession crisis, although in this case he has command of the facts. Disowning his son, barring him from suc-ceeding to the throne, he threatens Perdita with death if she ever contrives to see his son again. (It must be said that his commands are incoherent, if understandable, inasmuch as if he disowns his son why should it matter if she continues to see him, indeed marry him?) With that he stalks out, leav-ing not only the lovers but Camillo behind. In his rage, he has forgotten his own teaching on nature, which he had delivered to Perdita—that purity of breeding is no more, and perhaps somewhat less natural than intermixing of breeds by the art that is itself natural, including the natural arts of family formation and even politics, the founding and maintenance of cities, in-cluding the governance of monarchic succession.

"Even here undone!" Perdita laments (IV.iv.433)—here in the coun-tryside, in nature, far from the court. With noble spiritedness, she says she would have liked to tell the king that the same sun which shines on his court shines on this cottage. And she doesn't forget to remind her beloved that "I told you what would come of this" (IV.iv.439). For his part, the shepherd blames both Florizel and Perdita for bringing ruin upon him.

The ever-sanguine prince remains happy to relinquish his future throne for her: "I am heir to my affection" (IV.iv.477), heir to his truest nature, the nature that aims at ardent yet reasonable and artful "hybridization." Camillo objects: "This is desperate, sir" (IV.iv.477). You may call it so, Florizel replies, "but it does fulfill my vow," uphold my honor (IV.iv.478).

"Not for Bohemia, nor the pomp that may / Be thereat glean'd, for all the sun sees or / The close earth wombs, or the profound seas hide / In unknown fathoms, will I break my oath / To this my fair belov'd" (IV.iv.480–85). He intends to put to sea with her; he does not say where, as he doesn't know. He announces that he and his future bride will be "slaves to chance" (IV.iv.532). And so they must be, the lad having failed to respect old Father Time any more than he respected his father the king, conceiving no serious plan for the future, for the days after the wedding.

Full of noble sentiments, Florizel decidedly lacks prudence. In this he is unlike his betrothed, and (fortunately, as it happens) old Camillo. Old Father Time knows him, but he doesn't know Old Father Time. But Camillo sees how his own intention, to return to Sicilia, and Florizel's intention, to escape Bohemia with Perdita, may unite for the benefit of all. Citing his loyal services to his father, he suggests that he can be equally devoted to his son, the one "nearest to him" (IV.iv.514). If you will but "embrace my direction," I can contrive a better plot than whatever Fortune will likely impose. "You know / Prosperity's the very bond of love, / Whose fresh complexion and whose heart together / Affliction alters" (IV.iv.564–65). Perdita objects, saying that "affliction may subdue the cheek / But not take in the mind" (IV.iv.568–69)—another worthy sentiment (to which Camillo gives due praise) but not one that addresses the problem at hand.

Camillo proposes that they embark for Sicilia, where King Leontes will treat you, Florizel, as a son, having lost his own son as one consequence of his jealous rage, sixteen years ago. Once again, the couple will disguise themselves. Florizel will wear the clothes of Autolycus, which he obtains in exchange for his fine court-garments. For his part, Camillo will return to King Polixenes, report the escape, then accompany the king on his chase after them, to Sicilia—effectively hitching a free ride on the royal train.

As for Autolycus, he never lacks a scheme of his own, never lacks a way to exploit time. He has just returned from picking the pockets of a crowd gathered to hear the shepherd's son sing to his two favorite shepherdesses, which is "the time that the unjust man doth thrive" (IV.iv.662). He doesn't so much plan ahead as he seizes immediate opportunities, "smell[ing] out work for th' other senses" (IV.iv.364). Just as Leontes defined the world in terms of bawdry, Autolycus defines it in terms of theft. The young prince is stealing himself from his father. The gods themselves are thieves, and

Mercury, the god-chief, is Autolycus' model. Although he could disclose Camillo's plot to the king, he won't. "I hold it the more knavery to conceal it, and therein am I constant to my profession" (IV.iv.672). A person whose wit is all in his senses, his knowledge is the cunning of the 'con' artist, his morality the honor among thieves.

The times provide him with another ripe opportunity for gain. The shepherd's son advises his father to tell King Polixenes that Perdita isn't his daughter but a foundling. He can prove this by showing the king the "secret things" he found in the bag next to the infant (IV.iv.684). Now dressed in the finery he acquired from the prince, Autolycus overawes the rubes, frightens them into giving him some of their gold as protection money, then accompanies them on their mission to catch up with the king before he leaves for Sicilia. Autolycus pauses to praise himself: Fortune is courting him now "with a double occasion and a means to do the prince my master good, which who knows how that may turn back to my advancement?" (IV.iv.816–18).

By far the longest scene in the play, Scene IV of Act IV takes more time because in it Shakespeare portrays the intricate patterns human beings can weave into time, the equally intricate patterns events over time weave into human beings; at the same time, he shows the work of nature, which weaves its own patterns, in time. Human beings can improve nature by their art, especially by prudent 'breeding' of flowers and of themselves, through marriage. Good marriages can perpetuate a good regime, through time. Human beings can also corrupt nature by their art, by thinking of nature and the gods as their partners in crime. Human beings, and especially their rulers, can corrupt nature by letting their natural passions, especially their love of their own, override their natural reason. What King Leontes did to himself, his family, and to Sicilia in letting his love for his wife run beyond any reasonable limits, King Polixenes has begun to do in his love for his son, and his son has begun to do in his love for Perdita. Camillo, who also loves his own, his own native country and king, is the only one who has the prudence to plot a good end to the badly plotted plans of the others.

At the palace in Sicilia, Cleomenes would persuade King Leontes that he has done his penitence, performing it with "saint-like sorrow" for many years, more than repaying his trespass (V.i.2). "Do as the heavens have done: forget your evil; / With them forgive yourself" (V.i.5–6). Cleomenes speaks rather like a twenty-first-century therapist or New Age 'Christian' pastor. The king will not forgive himself for making his kingdom "heirless" and for causing the death of his wife, "the sweet'st companion that e'er man / Bred his hopes out of" (V.i.10–12).

Concurring with the king, not the counselor, Paulina speaks like her namesake, the Apostle Paul, one who never overlooked human guilt. *You killed your wife*, she reminds him—a woman superior to the amalgamation of all the virtues of all the other women in the world. Leontes can only ask Paulina for mercy, if in the kingly manner of commanding: "Say so but seldom" (V.i.19).

Cleomenes persists. You, Paulina, "might have spoken a thousand things that would / have done the time more benefit, and grac'd / Your kindness better" (V.i.21–23). Here, time means circumstances, the conditions prevailing at this time—more specifically, the political circumstances. Cleomenes would have Paulina consider them in accordance with nature (kindness) and grace, which might be a human enhancement of nature or a gift of God. Dion then unfolds the political consideration more fully, saying that the king should marry again. In refusing to consider such an act, Paulina shows no pity "for the state" of Sicilia, and no "remembrance of [the king's] most sovereign name" (V.i.25–26). You "consider little / What dangers, by his Highness' fail of issue, / May drop upon his kingdom and devour / Incertain lookers-on" (V.i.27–29). Given this time, what could be more holy than a new marriage for the king, a new heir to his throne for his kingdom?

Paulina has a ready answer to this politic consideration: God disagrees. Apollo's oracle decreed that Leontes shall not have an heir until his lost child has been found. This, she adds, is as unlikely as the chance that her husband, Antigonus, long missing and rightly presumed dead, will rise from the grave. And she reminds the king that even Alexander the Great left his crown not to an heir (his wife was pregnant with his only son) but to "th' worthiest" man in his empire, "so his successor / Was like to be the best" (V.i.98–99); she refers to one version of Alexander's last words, "I bequeath my kingdom *tôi kratikô*"—to the strongest. Stopping short of imitating Alexander, whom Paulina has presented as a man of honor and goodness, the king agrees that there are "no more such wives" as Hermione, and "therefore no wife" for him (V.i.56). If I were to take another wife,

Hermione's spirit, he says, would arise to rebuke him, and he swears never to marry without Paulina's permission, which she tells him she will not grant unless another "as like Hermione as her picture" appears (V.i.74), or rather "when your first queen's again in breath" (V.i.83).

As in so much here, such a one will appear suddenly, accompanying the son of the king's childhood friend. Leontes himself so remarks: Florizel's arrival is "out of circumstance"—untimely—"and sudden," which suggests to the experienced king that "'Tis not a visitation framed, but forced / By need and accident," especially in view of the few attendants accompanying the couple (V.i.91–92). For her part, Paulina is skeptical in another way. To the servant who announces their approach, praising Perdita as "the most peerless piece of earth, I think, / That e'er the sun shone bright on," she laments, "O Hermione / As every present time doth boast itself / Above a better gone, so must thy grave / Give way to what's seen now" (V.i.93–98). True enough, but the servant insists, that *this* woman—well, "Women will love her that she is a woman / More worth than any man; men that she is / The rarest of all women" (V.i.110–11). When the couple does arrive, Leontes sides with the servant, calling Perdita a goddess, while expressing his regret, misery, and remorse for "mine own folly" in ruining his family and his friendship with Florizel's father.

Florizel has prepared his covering lies. His father commanded him to come to Sicilia with the message that he remains Leontes' friend, that only infirmity prevents him from making the trip himself, and that Florizel's 'wife' is from Libya. Their retinue is modest because he has ordered several of his attendants to return home to assure his father of his safe arrival. Again suddenly, news arrives that the supposedly home-ridden king has arrived with Camillo, whom Florizel assumes has betrayed him.

Having caught the young man in his lies, King Leontes at first gravely admonishes him: "I am sorry / Most sorry, you have broken from his liking / Where you were tied in duty; and as sorry / Your choice is not so rich in worth as beauty, / That you may enjoy her" (V.i.210–14). Florizel can only plead his faithful love as his defense. Fortune may have proved his enemy, bringing the king of Bohemia so soon behind his own arrival, but Fortune has the power "to change our loves" (V.i.218). This being so, he tells King Leontes, remember when "you ow'd no more to time / Than I do now," when you were young, with few years behind you (V.i.219–20). Be "mine advocate" with my father; he will listen to his old friend (V.i.221). Quite reasonably, Leontes doubts that he will do so, and relentless Paulina chimes in to chide the king for looking too intently at the beauteous Perdita, and to tell him to remember something else, namely, that Hermione "was more worth such gazes / Than what you look on now" (V.i.226–27). After excusing himself to his own accuser by remarking the astonishing resemblance of Perdita to his wife, he tells Florizel that, in light of her beauty, he will defend him to his father on the grounds that "Your honor [was] not o'erthrown by your desires" in choosing her (V.i.230).

Shakespeare does not present the discovery of Perdita's true identity. He leaves the description of that scene to an observer. In front of the palace, Autolycus—who very much wants to know what has happened—asks for an account of what happened from a gentleman who witnessed the event from a distance, having been ordered out of the room along with all who were not principals in the matter. When shown the contents of the bag the shepherd found with the infant, the gentleman reports, Leontes and Camillo "look'd as they had heard of a world ransom'd, or one destroyed. A notable passion of wonder appeared in them; but the wisest beholder that knew no more but seeing could not say if th'importance were joy or sorrow—but in the extremity of the one it must needs be" (V.ii.14–18). The wisest beholder cannot know the human things only by seeing. He must hear human speech, as Socrates taught by going to the marketplace instead of gazing at the stars (then supposed to be the rulers of human destinies); as Plato taught in the dialogues he wrote after following his teacher into the marketplace and listening silently to his conversations with the persons he met there; and as Shakespeare teaches in every play.

A second gentleman arrives; he has heard them speak. "The oracle is fulfill'd: the king's daughter is found" (V.ii.23–24). This satisfied the men's wonder at what's been seen; the first gentleman saw joyful not sorrowful men. But who is the king's daughter? A third gentleman, the king's steward, emerges to tell them that it is Perdita, and that the royal families have reconciled. Paulina's sorrow at hearing the suspected death of her husband, many years earlier, has its countervailing joy in the fulfillment of the oracle, the return of Hermione's daughter.

The third gentleman concludes his report by saying that Perdita and her newfound families have gone to see a statue of her mother, "which is in

the keeping of Paulina—a piece many years in doing and now newly performed by that rare Italian master, Julio Romano, who, had he himself eternity and could put breath into his work"—as God had, and God
did—"would beguile Nature of her custom, so perfectly is her ape" (V.ii.90–
94). A pupil of Raphael, a contemporary of Shakespeare's grandparents,
Romano was an extraordinarily versatile artist—painter, architect, sculptor
and, perhaps dearest to the playwright's heart, a costume and scenery de-
signer for comedies. And like his master, Romano combined Christian and
classical motifs in his works, furthering the same dialogue between the 'ancients' and the (Christian) 'moderns' Shakespeare himself engaged.

The gentlemen go to witness the viewing, leaving Autolycus, the shepherd, and the shepherd's son (newly ennobled by the prince for services to
himself and the royal families) to perform their own parody of reconciliation,
which depends not on true speech but empty words, when the son promises
to pronounce Autolycus "as honest a true fellow as any in Bohemia" when
presented to the royals (V.ii.150–51). Although some may detect a hint of
irony, intended or not, in that formula, the main point concerns speech.
After all, the shepherd's son may have deduced, if shepherds can become
nobles by being pronounced to be such by a prince, surely a rogue may be
pronounced honorable by the newly ennobled. Wiser beholders of the scene
will consider that while words are indispensable supplements to sights, when
it comes to insight, their mere incantation has no power at all, independent
of consent or obedience. The exception to this may be seen in the Book of
Genesis, when words pronounced by a supremely powerful god themselves
constitute the power of action. Both kings have learned this distinction between all too human kings and gods. Leontes learned that thinking and calling his wife an adulteress didn't make her one; Polixenes learned that
commanding his son to obey didn't make him obedient.

At the chapel on Paulina's property, the two kings, their children, along
with Camillo and Paulina wonder at the statue of Hermione. Before the
unveiling, Leontes and Paulina exchange graceful blessings; Paulina especially, knowing the harshness with which she has treated the king for so
long, welcomes his presence: "It is a surplus of your grace, which never /
My life may last to answer" (V.iii.7–8).

When she unveils the statue, all wonder at its lifelikeness, its likeness
to nature, even to the detail of new wrinkles on her skin, wrinkles Romano

is said to have added, revising her face in accordance with time—in Paulina's words, "mak[ing] her as she liv'd now" (V.iii.31). Leontes marvels at the statue's appearance of "warm life," shamed once more "for being more stone than it" (V.iii.35,38). The statue is "royal," magical in its "majesty" because it has "my evils conjured to remembrance" and has caused Hermione's living daughter to stand still, like a statue, transfixed (V.iii.38–42). Her father's words reawaken Perdita's power of speech and action. "Do not say 'tis superstition that I kneel" before this statue (V.iii.43); *it is so life-like, I do not commit idolatry.* She addresses a prayer to her mother, asking, "Give me that hand of yours to kiss" (V.iii.46).

Paulina interrupts to warn that the statue is newly painted, not yet dry; do not touch it. She would like to re-veil it, lest Leontes think it really moves, and indeed Leontes does so think, saying that its eyes seem to move, its veins pulse blood. When he moves forward to kiss the statue, Paulina again warns against staining oneself "with oily painting" (V.iii.83). Obeying the command not to touch, Leontes and Perdita nonetheless refuse to leave off gazing. This forces Paulina to make a crucial choice.

"If you can behold it"—if you are strong enough to bear it—"I'll make the statue move indeed, descend, / And take you by the hand" (V.iii.88–90). But then you will think not that I am an idolater but a witch—the accusation Polixenes had leveled against Perdita, perhaps unbeknownst to Paulina. To do so, therefore, I require you to "awake your faith" or, if you refuse, to leave (V.iii.95). No one leaves; each passes the test set by Paulina.

"Music, awake her," she commands (V.iii.98). Music, which had enlivened and given harmony to the dancing shepherds in Bohemia—music, the sound which keeps time, and to which human beings keep time—accompanies Paulina's command to the statue. "'Tis time; descend; be stone no more; approach; / Strike all that look upon with marvel... Bequeath to death your numbness, for from him / Dear life redeems you." (V.iii.99–103). It is time: words and actions now fit the circumstance not only of the king's contrition but of the daughter's return, the redemption of the mother's hope. And to the living witnesses, Paulina commands, "Start not; her actions shall be holy as / You may hear my spell is lawful" (V.iii.104–05). Hermione is no less good than when she was falsely accused, but from 'standing accused,' statue-like, she now moves, living, among the living. "O, she's warm!" Leontes exclaims (V.iii.110)—alive as she had seemed to him when looking but disallowed from touching, from feeling that warmth, that life. "If this be magic, let it be an art / Lawful as eating" (V.iii.111–12). He had obeyed Paulina's command not to touch the 'statue' as a king respecting the property of a citizen. He now issues a royal command to legalize good magic, confirming Paulina's suggestion that her "spell" may be pronounced lawful.

If it is magic. The king may well doubt it. The funeral of wife and son which he attended but Shakespeare did not describe; the claim that an Italian artist had painted wrinkles on a statue to make the figure appear to have aged; his own perception of life and movement in the figure when he stood beholding it; Paulina's caution in speaking truth (*I am not a witch*) even as she maintained a pious lie: all this has pointed to the truth, that Hermione has been living in seclusion at her friend's house all along. And Hermione's words confirm this. To her daughter she says, "Thou shalt hear that I, / Knowing by Paulina that the oracle / Gave hope thou wast in being, have preserv'd / Myself to see the issue" (V.iii.125–28). If she had been a statue, she could have known nothing, heard nothing; if she had been a statue, she did not preserve herself. Statues don't make themselves, although some of Shakespeare's Romans might be said to aspire to make themselves into statues. [1]

"There's time enough for that" hearing of the story, Paulina interrupts—again discreetly, knowing that the elaborate ruse she and Hermione have now brought to completion in the fullness of time ought to be disclosed opportunely, at the right time (V.iii.128). But first she laments, all of you are "precious winners" in this plot, but "I, an old turtle[dove] / Will wing me to some wither'd bough," with no loving mate (V.iii.131–33). Good-humored King Leontes puts an immediate stop to her understandable self-pity. "O peace, Paulina! Thou shouldst a husband take by my consent / As I by thine a wife" (V.iii.135–37). Camillo shall be your "honorable husband" (V.iii.143). The honor of every member of the royal party has been vindicated.

Calling Polixenes again his brother, asking his pardon, and Hermione's, "that e'er I put between your holy looks / My ill suspicion" (V.iii.148–49), King Leontes concludes, "Good Paulina, / Lead us from hence where we may leisurely / Each one demand and answer to his part / Perform'd in this wide gap of time since first / We were dissevr'd. Hastily lead away"

(V.iii.152–55). The king has learned to use his time well: slowness for discussion, haste for executive action. Seeing is the knowledge reason brings, insight; hearing is the knowledge faith brings by taking someone at his word; touch is the knowledge action brings, the only knowledge that affects both human knower and the human known at the same time. Leonine Leontes has learned how to rule rightly by coordinating all these senses, and all the ways of knowing they represent.

The royal succession of both regimes has been secured, along with the alliance of Sicilia and Bohemia, founded upon the renewed brotherly friendship of the kings. Paulina's rapid action in leading the royal part—in her leading, her Pauline character is acknowledged by the king—will lead to leisured discussion, the prerequisite of learning. Each person will learn of the parts performed by the others. By fusing the fiction of the characters' many plots with the reality of actors playing roles on a stage, Shakespeare returns his audience to reality, having invited them better to understand nature and convention, truth-telling and lies, seeing, hearing, and touching—the portals of understanding—better than they had before.

Love, especially the love of one's own, and honor stand at the core of the play. Each can be perverted into jealous passion that dismisses any evidence contrary to the suspicions of the lover. The remedy for restoring the lover to reason, to bringing the honor-lover back from the dishonor incurred by his passion cannot be philosophy if the lover is no philosopher and has no prospect of becoming one. The remedy must be another form of love. This is where Christian humility and *agape* come in. Paulina's love for King Leontes is Pauline—harsh and exacting on the sinner but for his own good, and open to mercy and forgiveness when repentance has been demonstrated. This partly explains her patience, another distinctively Christian virtue, seen in the long endurance of her plot to conceal the queen's survival, seen among Christians in their waiting for the *Parousia*. Paulina understands that 'only time will tell.'

Paulina's plot also bespeaks her patient faith in the oracle of Apollo. The mixture of classical-pagan and Christian themes in the play has led to disputes over when the action occurs. Clearly, given the specific reference to Guilio Romano, it must be set in Christian-modern times, at the height of the Renaissance. Renaissance Italy extended the familiar practice of typology—of seeing Old Testament figures as 'types' or precursors of Christ—

to figures in classical antiquity. Apollo was often represented as one such; Michelangelo gives the Christ in his painting "The Last Judgment" the face of the Apollo Belvedere. In this play, Apollo is described as the son of Jove, and in English the pun on 'son' and 'sun' can be deployed in allusion to the pagan god's association with the sun, carried daily in a chariot across the sky. In Italian Renaissance literature, in Dante and Ficino, this association was well-established; more, Apollo was understood to be the enemy of Aphrodite, to be a god of reason not of passion. Jesus, who commands his followers to be as prudent as serpents and as harmless as doves, who is described in John's Gospel as the *Logos*, who firmly opposes eroticism in favor of agape, can thus be considered as having been foreshadowed by the pagan god, now considered as entirely mythical. Both natural sun and the Son of God do indeed shine on courts and cottages alike, as Perdita once remarked.

Christianity also enters into Shakespeare's treatment of time. In the New Testament, time does not always march steadily, as old Chronos does. Time is not only *chronos* but *Kairos*. It can overthrow laws and either plant or overwhelm customs, not only by wearing them down over the years but suddenly, in an hour as it were, in the moment of God's creation or in the resurrection of Christ. The suddenness of so many events in the play— and especially the long-prepared 'return to life' of Hermione, an *imitatio Christi*— registers this dimension of time. Hence also the importance of memory, necessary in a world in which time brings changes, slow or instantaneous; without remembrance, timeless nature and timeless divinity cannot be respected.

It is the Christian aspect of the play that confuses playgoers and readers accustomed to Shakespeare's other comedies and tragedies. In his comedies, Shakespeare often presents an incipiently tragic circumstance, happily resolved. In his tragedies, Shakespeare brings in fools, clowns, and loveable rogues, often to show the tragic folly of his heroes. Nonetheless, the genres are clear-cut. *The Winter's Tale* points to Christ, Christian love—to the tragic death of the Man of Sorrow which nonetheless has a supremely happy ending in His Resurrection, and looks ahead, with patience, to the final happy ending prophesied in the Book of Revelation. In this play, Shakespeare first separates tragic Sicilia from comic Bohemia, then marries them. In this, he is quite Christian.

It is also true that to represent Apollo as a 'type' of Christ can go in the other direction. Many atheists conclude that Apollo isn't a type of Christ but the prototype, that Christianity merely takes up Jewish and pagan motifs. Such ambiguity may be seen in the play. Is Hermione first a woman, then a statue magically or miraculously transformed not a woman again? Or is she rather the natural Hermione, all along? In the first case, the wonder of the royal party is religious; in the second, it is philosophic or more precisely proto-philosophic. Yet even if Paulina's device is a natural ruse, a noble lie, it may be understood as one that points to Christian revelation.

When Shakespeare leaves his stage, he always leaves such wonder behind. He sees his characters and he sees his audience, hears them and speaks to them, and acts out of knowing them and loving what is best for them. He is the wisest beholder.

Note

1. See Michael Platt: *Rome and Romans According to Shakespeare* (Lanham: The University Press of America, 1983), 186. As Dr. Platt has observed, the apparent transformation of Hermione from a living woman to a statue to a living woman reverses the Caesarian aspiration.

CONCLUSION
SHAKESPEARE'S POLITIC MERRIMENT

Such words as 'politic' and 'prudent' have a chilly tone to them. If blended with comedy, they can lend themselves to cynicism. How to make them attractive to ardent and generous souls? Shakespeare shows the way.

'Merry' is one of the oldest English words, meaning not only pleasant, delightful, cheery but measured, as in a 'merry mean,' a happy medium. It can be said of a country, and especially of England, of weather (although not often of England and of weather at the same time), of times, especially seasons, when the merriness of England and its weather may come together, after all. It can be said of persons—of their looks when they are comely, of their words when they are witty, of their sounds when they are musical. Who but Shakespeare could take the *Nicomachean Ethics* and make of it a cheerful tune? Yet Aristotle himself hints at this, when he criticizes Platonic austerity when it comes to thinking about the just regime, saying that it reduces a theme to a single beat.

The regimes in Shakespeare's comedies are the rule of the few and the rule of the one. In England, where the warrior-aristocrats have given way to commercial oligarchs, the aristocrats are Falstaffian, laughable, and chivalry is dead. Oligarch-husbands mimic the angry and honor-loving aristocrats of old, but foolishly; they are no heroes. Their wives, merry and honest, restore them to the happy medium in accordance with the maxim of the Fairy Queen, "Evil be to him that evil thinks." The wives uphold the right use of the English language, against Sir John's ignoble lies and their husbands' sputterings; they stand for the right use of social conventions and for just, reciprocal love—marital love as Aristotle understands it. They do these things against the commercial tendency toward the sharp, deceptive, Machiavellian inclination toward the useful and usurious, a tendency which undermines even commerce itself, which depends upon trust. They play merry tricks on their husbands to restore their men to the center of loving, away from their jealousy, and to punish Falstaff for having fallen into the other extreme, fecklessness. There is, however, one good husband, Mr. Page, the mean between jealous Page and feckless Falstaff.

On the Continent, the aristocrats remain, inclining to make war not love, or to making love into a sort of war—the "merry war" of words between Beatrice and Signor Benedick (a name that could mean both 'well-spoken' and 'good sex' in Shakespeare's lexicon of naughty puns). Aristocratic comedy almost but never quite loses its balance, nearly falling into tragedy, as the prince of Aragon, a victorious warrior, faces a real threat in his envious and resentful bastard brother. Here, Shakespeare averts tragedy only by plotting the fortunate arrival of English-like clowns and introducing a good Friar who turns out to be harmless as a dove but prudent as a serpent. In *Much Ado About Nothing*, as in *The Merry Wives of Windsor*, the wit of deception stands in debt to the wit of perception, lest its practitioner deceive himself.

The Two Gentlemen of Verona brings commerce and war, aristocracy and oligarchy, together with the additional and complicating new aristocracy of the Christian Church, 'the elect.' The aristocratic gentlemen in question leave their city, which is ruled by commercial-oligarchic Venice, looking for wives in Milan, the seat of the Holy Roman Empire. There, they find servants who are smarter than their masters and mistresses—a comic reversal Christianity makes plausible. In view of that reversal, aristocrats need to become genuinely worthy of rule, again, but not in the Machiavellian way by mastering the arts of acquisition, whether warrior-high or oligarch-low. They need to become aristocrats by nature not convention. They find that love can bring out the natural virtues and that Christian love enables both the innocence of doves and the prudence of serpents, as seen in the loving patience of Valentine in contrast with the changeling Proteus, a man of ever-shifting appetites. Proteus comes to admit that inconstancy is the original sin; broadly considered, inconstancy would mean that nature has no nature, no fidelity to itself. Here, in Milan, natural right and Christian grace can be made to cohere.

In each of these comedies of 'the few,' comedy is aristocracy gone right, tragedy aristocracy gone wrong; oligarchy comic if moderated by wit, never tragic but melodramatic if not. Monarchy, by contrast, is comic mostly in our dreams. Like aristocrats, monarchs depend upon hereditary succession to sustain their rule, and therefore upon prudent marriage. Love can ruin such orderly regime perpetuation, as the one who rules may love not wisely but too well. Erotic love and war share the intention to acquire, but before entering into either one, one must first think. According to convention, fathers do the thinking for the ardent young. As Theseus tells Hermione in *A Midsummer Night's Dream*, "your eyes with his [father's] judgment must look." But nature is the higher source of judgment, which is why the young lovers flee the city when a father's judgment falters.

Here, the prudence of the Fairy King, who rules the forest, nature, at night, attempts to set the standard rightly upheld by the touchstone of Windsor's merry wives, the Fairy Queen. His own Fairy Queen, Titania, needs her jealousy corrected, but in Oberon's attempt at comic deception leading to such justice, his servant's potion causes imprudent, misdirected love, bringing out the darker side of human and fairy nature alike. These misadventures show that erotic or desiring love depends on selecting the right object. This holds true above all for marriage, the legal foundation of the political community, and in a monarchic regime above all for the monarch and his heirs. Just and prudent statesmanship applies all the law according to the standard of natural right, avoiding the extreme passion of a Demetrius and the extreme legalism of Egeus by emulating the moderate judgment of Theseus and Hippolyta.

Shakespeare provides a fuller consideration of the laws regimes rule by in *The Comedy of Errors* and *Twelfth Night*. In the *Comedy*, Ephesus and Syracuse engage in a trade war, with an aristocrat, the Duke of Ephesus, and a merchant, Aegeon, as the principals. Here, law is in tension with natural right and Christian mercy. Errors are easy to make in law courts and indeed in life, generally; hence the need for both equity and mercy. What counts as true evidence? And how can one reason from such evidence? Christianity lends itself to error because much of what seems supernatural is only natural; supernatural explanations are often hasty generalizations resulting from failure to inquire fully, to investigate thoroughly. Taking the role of the good Friar in *Much Ado About Nothing*, a wise abbess consults nature in making her judgements, showing the assembled judges, lawyers, and law students at the play's first performance that law, natural inquiry and equity, and Christian mercy need to be coordinated if a right outcome is to be reached.

Also first performed for legal professionals on Epiphany Eve, when men of wisdom met the Child who embodied agapic love, *Twelfth Night* considers not so much law as the pre-conditions of law, particularly the right way of understanding the rule of law. Duke Orsino of Illyria loves the wealthy countess Olivia, who does not love him, and whose servant, Malvolio or 'Ill-Will,' loves no one. Shipwrecked on Illyria's coast, Viola is the one who falls in love with the Duke while searching for her twin brother, who was also lost at sea. Both love and exile-by-nature pushes men and women to the boundaries of love. On its right track, human nature issues in virtue; on the wrong track it issues in *virtù* or mere capacity to acquire 'what you will'—the play's subtitle and Malvolio's constant aim. Rulers, including those who rule by the law, might be tempted to bend the law toward that wrong track, toward hypocrisy and deception, double-mindedness, and away from marriages and friendships of true—that is, faithful—minds. The principle of non-contradiction, which animates the human power of reasoning, provides a beacon to the right track but for it to be effective (especially when it comes to matters of love), it needs the measured assistance of music. Rulers must learn the limits of their power, especially in love; Duke Orsino cannot 'make' his beloved love him. Such men and women therefore need the self-knowledge that alone can ensure that they who wield the power of law will not abuse it. They must learn not only the kind of rule that commands but the kind of rule that is also ruled in turn, that rules reciprocally—the political rule of husband with wife, citizen with citizen.

If, as the adage goes, 'power shows the man,' then *ethos* or character comes to sight most clearly in rulers. Rulers conspicuously exhibit *thumos* or spiritedness, the part of the soul that gets angry, loves honor if good, domination if bad. Shakespeare's comedies consistently identify anger, not appetites, as the central ethical problem. In *The Taming of the Shrew* an unnamed "Lord" undertakes to transform a drunken, swinish man by presenting to him a play designed to cure him of his shrewishness—the anger underlying drunkenness. The theme of the play is conversion. Christopher Sly, the drunk in question, needs civilizing. His counterpart in the play, shrewish Katherine, needs 'naturalizing,' needs to be made into a fit wife for a good man. In her case, conversion occurs not by gentle suasion but by sharply contradicting every expression of her bad temperament; the rational part of her soul becomes reasonable after her suitor breaks her spiritedness by opposing her at every turn. In Biblical terms, she is a Saul, knocked off her high horse not directly by God but by 'Petruchio' or 'Peter,' a servant of God. In Platonic terms, she has a wrongly ordered soul, in which spiritedness rules her *logos*, her capacity to reason; Petruchio exercises a vigorous cure by means of contradiction, compelling her reasoning capacity to take charge in her soul. She is now ready to join with him in forming a family.

In *As You Like It*, Orlando's tyrannical older brother, animated by *libido dominandi*, plots murder against the young man whom he unwarrantedly regards as a threat to his rule. This suggests that beneath anger fear may palpitate, driving it. Cain-and-Abel conflict mirrors the circumstance faced by Duke Senior, exiled since his brother usurped his throne, living in the Forest of Arden—a decidedly un-Hobbesian 'state of nature' whose name combines 'ardor' with 'Eden,' love with nature untainted by sin. True, uncorrupted nature teaches that love and fidelity form the foundation of both marriage and the political community which depends upon families. Here, conversion comes outside the corrupted political community, and so does not entail spirited contradiction of a tyrannical spirit but a return to true nature, which eventually moderates the tyrants. Contradiction brings maddish Katherine to her 'right mind'; in Arden, loving fidelity defeats fearful-angry tyranny by proving the more reliable bond in both families and cities.

All of Shakespeare's comedies are 'politic,' invitations to practical wisdom. His plays that most directly address political life point to the relation of politics, of regimes, to philosophy, the love of wisdom that strives to rise above the opinions and the conventions all regimes must enforce.

All's Well That Ends Well asks whether a commoner is beneath an aristocrat by nature, not only by convention. Helena believes so, initially. But elevation to nobility is not by nature but by kingly prerogative. Kingly prerogative can be sudden, arbitrary. Nature works in its own time, seldom in haste. Kings elevate commoners to nobility by pronouncing them noble. But words can be duplicitous, as the comic villain, Parolles ('Speeches'), shows in by his words and his actions. Helena's husband, the Count, proves his foil because he doesn't understand the nature of speech and therefore lacks self-knowledge as a human being, the being that speaks and reasons.

Duplicity in speech confuses human beings when it comes to the duality of virtue and vice—specifically, the contradiction between courage and cowardice, prudence and folly, justice and injustice, moderation and immoderation. Because human beings can both confuse themselves with speech and guide themselves by it, political communities will always feature discord. A good regime will imitate nature, the overarching *concordia discors*, in balancing discordant elements. But the discord perennially threatens to overturn the concord, leading to tyranny if uncorrected by wise rulers who understand speech and know sophistry when they hear it.

Philosophers distinguish their speech, and especially their thought, from sophistry. A ruler who sees that he must learn to do that might immerse himself in philosophy. But a monarchic or aristocratic ruler must also think of the line of succession, the perpetuation of his line—love of women not of wisdom. *Love's Labor's Lost* opposes such love to merely 'bookish' thought. The prudential reason needed by rulers, especially in love, shows up in Berowne, who teaches his fellow aristocrats not to attempt to override their passions with an impossibly austere life of abstinence and study but to govern the passions by seeking good wives. The play is a witty meditation on wit, as 'learning' alone makes a man more foolish, a writer of clanky love-sonnets in the case of Berowne's fellow lords. In terms of nature's *concordia discors*, the object of philosophic (as distinguished from scholarly/bookish) investigation, inquiry shows that love is what hold the discordant elements together. Nature's elements, being distinct and inclined to collision with one another, need love's attractive force to bind them, uniting men and women (to take the politically pertinent example) into mated pairs that generate by nature what no ruling human edict or law can produce—more human beings. Given the witty nature of the aristocratic women who accept the reformed men as husbands, love can bind without ruining the individual characters of those it binds. The reformed or refounded regime that follows will live in accordance with the rightful law of nature.

Set initially in a season unseasonable for comedy, *The Winter's Tale* examines another dimension of *thumos*: how its derangement abuses time. Jealousy issues from a too-prickly sense of honor, an inordinate love of one's own. King Leontes' jealousy of his wife's imagined flirtation with his boyhood friend and fellow king makes him impatient, hasty in judgment, precipitous in action—so much so that he would kill his wife and newborn daughter. Defying Apollo or reason, he suffers the death of his son. His 'commoner' counterpart, the thief Autolycus, also abuses time by seizing immediate opportunities; he moves as fast to acquire as the king moves to lose.

Against Leontes' rash actions, time takes its own course. His wife and daughter survive, unbeknownst to him for two decades. That they live becomes known to the king only after he has long repented at leisure what he attempted to do in haste. In comedy, nature takes its time and rules in the end. Human beings need to learn to coordinate nature and time; that is the work of prudence. The remedy for tyrannical love of one's own cannot be philosophy, love of wisdom, if one isn't a philosopher. For a king, it cannot even be prudence, if one isn't a statesman. As the character of Paulina suggests, it is rather patience, which lets time tell. Patience is a feature of Christian love, *agape*.